Studies in the Acts of the Apostles

Studies in the Acts of the Apostles

Collected Essays

Rick Strelan

☙PICKWICK *Publications* • Eugene, Oregon

STUDIES IN THE ACTS OF THE APOSTLES
Collected Essays

Copyright © 2020 Rick Strelan. All rights reserved. Except for brief quotations in critical publications or reviews, no part of this book may be reproduced in any manner without prior written permission from the publisher. Write: Permissions, Wipf and Stock Publishers, 199 W. 8th Ave., Suite 3, Eugene, OR 97401.

Pickwick Publications
An Imprint of Wipf and Stock Publishers
199 W. 8th Ave., Suite 3
Eugene, OR 97401

www.wipfandstock.com

PAPERBACK ISBN: 978-1-5326-7627-7
HARDCOVER ISBN: 978-1-5326-7628-4
EBOOK ISBN: 978-1-5326-7629-1

Cataloguing-in-Publication data:

Names: Strelan, Rick, author.

Title: Studies in the acts of the apostles : collected essays / by Rick Strelan.

Description: Eugene, OR: Pickwick Publications, 2020. | Includes bibliographical references and index.

Identifiers: ISBN 978-1-5326-7627-7 (paperback) | ISBN 978-1-5326-7628-4 (hardcover) | ISBN 978-1-5326-7629-1 (ebook)

Subjects: LCSH: Bible. Acts—Criticism, interpretation, etc.

Classification: BS2625.2 S77 2020 (print) | BS2625.2 (ebook)

Manufactured in the U.S.A.　　　　　　　　　　　　　　　　03/10/20

Permissions

This book is a collection of previously published articles with one exception. The following indicates the journals and books in which they have been published.

"We Hear Them Telling in Our Own Tongues the Mighty Works of God." *Neotestamentica* 40.2 (2006) 295–319. Republished with permission.

"The Keys to the Gate Beautiful." *Journal of Biblical Studies* 1.3 (2001). Online. Republished with permission.

"Gamaliel's Hunch." *Australian Biblical Review* 47 (1999) 53–69. Republished with permission.

"The Running Prophet." *Novum Testamentum* 43.1 (2001) 31–38. Republished with permission.

"Tabitha: The Gazelle of Joppa (Acts 9:36–41)." *Biblical Theology Bulletin: Journal of Bible and Culture* 39.2 (2009) 77–86. Republished with permission.

"Who Was Bar Jesus? (Acts 13:6–12)." *Biblica* 85.1 (2004) 65–81. Republished with permission.

"Strange Stares: Atenizein in Acts." *Novum Testamentum* 41.3 (1999) 235–55. Republished with permission.

"Recognizing the Gods (Acts 14:8–10)." *New Testament Studies* 46 (2000) 488–503. Republished with permission.

"Midday and Midnight in the Acts of the Apostles." In *"I Sowed Fruits into Hearts": Festschrift for Professor Michael Lattke*, edited by Pauline Allen, et al., 189–202. Strathfield: St Pauls, 2007. Republished with permission.

"Acts 19:12: Paul's 'Aprons' Again." *The Journal of Theological Studies* 54.1 (2003) 154–57. Republished with permission.

The article "Luke's Use of Isaiah LXX in Acts" was presented to the Septuaginta Seminar of the Conference for Studiorum Novi Testamenti Societas, Bonn, July 2003.

Contents

Preface | ix
Abbreviations | xi

"We Hear Them Telling in Our Own Tongues
the Mighty Works of God" (Acts 2:11) | 1
The Keys to the Gate Beautiful (Acts 3:1–10) | 22
Gamaliel's Hunch | 37
The Running Prophet (Acts 8:30) | 54
Tabitha: The Gazelle of Joppa (Acts 9:36–41) | 61
Who Was Bar Jesus? (Acts 13:6–12) | 78
Strange Stares: Atenizein in Acts | 94
Recognizing the Gods (Acts 14:8–10) | 113
Acts 19:12: Paul's "Aprons" Again | 129
Going In and Out: Israel's Leaders in Acts | 133
Midday and Midnight in the Acts of the Apostles | 140
Luke's Use of Isaiah LXX in Acts | 153

Bibliography | 181
Author Index | 193

Preface

This collection of essays in the Acts of the Apostles represents the bulk of my research in that New Testament book while I was Lecturer in New Testament and Early Christianity at the University of Queensland. In my undergraduate years, I completed a double major in Anthropology and that is indicative of my interest in other cultures and how they view the world. Some of that interest comes across in these essays. When reading the Bible in general, but especially when reading The Acts of the Apostles, I begin with the assumption that I can never really understand the culture which soaks the literature it produced. In my research and in these articles, I was always trying to understand the joke and to interpret the wink, as Clifford Geertz used to say. In order to understand, I saw myself trying to avoid the main roads and streets and instead to sneak down the side streets and the back roads. One of the things that bothered me was the awareness of how dependent I was on the literature available from that period and those cultures. It still bothers me because I realise that this literature reflects views and opinions of an elite and that I cannot assume those views were shared by the vast majority of peoples at that time.

The reason for re-publishing these essays is to give some cohesion to my research and to make the results of my research accessible to a wider audience than those who have access to academic journals. I also offer them in the hope that it will encourage others to explore and so to throw light on a text that still retains some mysteries.

There are people to thank. Mainly, thanks are due to those scholars past and present who have stimulated my imagination (some might rightly claim it has been excessively stimulated). It is always a privilege to sit on their shoulders and to see what they saw or at least to look at what they were looking at and to hope that from that vantage point I might see even further and more. There are also my colleagues and students at the University of Queensland who in their way encouraged me and let me bounce ideas around with them. Thanks are also due to my wife, Joy, who justifiably wonders why I do this and to my daughter, Chelle, who assisted with the editing and formatting.

Finally, thanks to Chris Spinks and Daniel Lanning of Pickwick Publications who have decided to accept this for publication and have generously given their editorial direction and other suggestions along the way.

Abbreviations

ANRW	Aufstieg und Niedergang der römischen Welt
BegChr	The Beginnings of Christianity
BDAG	Greek-English Lexicon of the New Testament
BGU	Berliner Griechische Urkunden
Bib	Biblica
BSOAS	Bulletin of the School of Oriental and African Studies
HUCA	Hebrew Union College Annual
HzNT	Handbuch zum Neuen Testament
JBL	Journal of Biblical Literature
JRel	Journal of Religion
JSJ	Journal for the Study of Judaism
LAB	Liber antiquitatum biblicarum (Pseudo-Philo)
LCL	Loeb Classical Library
NovT	Novum Testamentum
NTS	New Testament Studies
PGM	K. Preisendanz and others (eds.), Papyri Graecae Magicae: Die griechischen Zauberpapyri, 2 volumess. 2nd edn. (1973–4)
P. Lond.	Greek Papyri in the British Museum.
P. Mag. Leid. W.	Leiden Magical Papyrus W.
TDNT	Theological Dictionary of the New Testament
TDOT	Theological Dictionary of the Old Testament
ThKNT	Theologischer Kommentar zum Neuen Testament
TLNT	Theological Lexicon of the New Testament
VigChr	Vigiliae Christianae
ZAW	Zeitschrift für die alttestamentliche Wissenschaft
ZNW	Zeitschrift für die neutestamentliche Wissenschaft

Talmud/Mishnah

Ar.	Arukh
Bekh.	Bekhorot
Ber.	Berakhot
Hag.	Hagigah
Hul.	Hullin
Ketub.	Ketubbot
M. Kat	Mo'ed Katon
Meg.	Megillah
Ned.	Nedarim
Shabb.	Shabbat

Greek and Latin Works

Aen.	Aeneid
Aeth.	Aethiopica
A.H.	Against Heresies
Alex.	Alexander (Pseudomantis) Alexander the False Prophet
Ant.	The Antiquities of the Jews
Apol.	Apologia
1 Apol.	Apologia
Ant. rom.	Antiquitates romanae
Bell. civ.	Bella civilia
Bis acc.	Bis accusatus
Brut.	Brutus
Caes.	Caesar
Cat.	Cataplus
Cat. Maj.	Cato Major
Cels.	Contra Celsum
Char.	Charon
Cor.	Marcius Coriolanus
Dial.	Dialogus cum Tryphone

Def. orac.	De defectu oraculorum
Descr.	Graeciae description
Ep.	Epistulae
Fab.	Fabius Maximus
Fast.	Fasti
Geogr.	Geographica
H.E.	Historia ecclesiastica
Hist. rom.	Historia romana
Icar.	Icaromenippus
Il.	Ilias
Inst.	Institutio oratoria
Sat.	Satirae
Math.	Adversus mathematicos Against the Mathematicians
Memorab.	Memorabilia
Men.	Menippus (Necyomantia) Menippus
Metam.	Metamorphoses
Migr.	De migratione Abrahami
Mor.	Moralia
Mos. 1, 2	De vita Mosis I, II
Nat.	Naturalis historia
Noct. att.	Noctes atticae
Od.	Odyssea
Philops.	Philopseudes
Pomp.	Pompeius
Pyr.	Pyrrhoniae hypotyposes
Quaest. conv.	Quaestionum convivialium libri IX
Quaest. rom.	Quaestiones romanae et graecae
Sobr.	De sobrietate
Strom.	Stromata
Theoph.	Theophania
Vit. Apoll.	Vita Apollonii
Vit. soph.	Vitae sophistarum
Wars	The Wars of the Jews

"We Hear Them Telling in Our Own Tongues the Mighty Works of God" (Acts 2:11)

IT IS CURIOUS THAT studies in the cultural world of the early Christians rarely mention the matter of languages, and when it is raised, two aspects dominate: Koine Greek and the languages of first-century Palestine. Other Greek dialects and local languages receive, at the very best, a passing comment.[1] This might be due, in part, to what Horsley calls "our wholesale ignorance about the majority of provincial languages in the Roman world."[2] The neglect of the language situation is particularly evident in recent publications. For example, *The Early Christian World* (2000) gives, at best, a little over one page to the language world of Jews, but it says nothing about native, local languages; *The Biblical World* (2002) has articles on Hebrew, Aramaic, and Greek, but is quiet on other languages; neither Raymond Brown's *Introduction* (1997) nor Ehrman's *The New Testament* (2000) mention the languages. *The Dictionary of the New Testament Background* (2000) has no entry under "languages," but refers the reader to the "Greek language" entry which deals largely with Koine.[3]

This article has three objectives: to nuance the use of Koine Greek in the first Christian centuries; to draw attention to the survival of local languages; and to emphasize that a variety of languages was spoken in most early Christian communities. The situation in Palestine will be left aside, since it has been thoroughly discussed elsewhere.[4] The multilingual nature of that region, however, is typical of the linguistic map elsewhere. Nor am I concerned with Egypt and North Africa, or with regions to the west and north of Rome. In most of those regions too, the evidence is clear that indigenous vernaculars were very strong and remained so for centuries into the Common Era. The evidence from Egypt itself is that, despite the large finds of Greek papyri,

---

1. Koester devotes some pages to the topic, but he makes almost no mention of local vernacular languages. See Koester, *History, Culture, and Religion*, 101–13.

2. Horsley, *New Documents*, 11.

3. See Esler, *Early Christian World*; Barton, *Biblical World*; Brown, *Introduction*; Ehrman, *New Testament*; Evans and Porter, *Dictionary of the New Testament*.

4. See, for example, Schwartz, "Language."

many Egyptians were illiterate in Greek. As Koester observes, "The native Egyptians did not even learn Greek, although all the official documents had to be written in the Greek language. Egyptian remained the country's spoken vernacular, which was soon to reappear as a literary language in the 'Coptic' documents of the early Christian church."[5]

According to Moulton, similar language conditions applied in other parts of the hellenized world as well: Demotic papyri in abundance survive to show that they (Egyptians) did not forget their native language. All over the east, as far as Alexander's arms penetrated, Greek inscriptions attest to this same condition.[6]

Brock has shown that in the eastern Roman Empire, Greek functioned as the language of political power, but major dialects of Aramaic (Nabataean, Palmyrene, Emesan Hatran, and Syriac) were very much alive and well around the beginning of the Common Era.[7] He also demonstrates the strength and durability of Syriac among literate Christians and its complex interrelation with Greek in the first half millennium of the Era.

Along with Syriac texts, Old Latin Christian writings also appeared in the second century; Punic psalms were known to Augustine in North Africa; Gothic Christian literature stemmed from the fourth-century Ulfilas; Armenian and Georgian scripture translations appeared by the fifth century. In fact, in Armenia, not only were the Scriptures translated, but by the fifth century so were some of the church fathers. As Bardy notes: "The speed which the leaders of the Armenian Church displayed in appropriating all the works of the Fathers in their national language is perhaps without parallel in the history of Christianity."[8]

If language death had occurred, it is impossible to explain this phenomenon. Local language survival can also be traced in regions of Asia, Greece, and Italy. In sum, I wish to emphasize that many of the local languages did not simply roll over and die, swamped by the wave of hellenization. The fact that the New Testament was (probably) first written in Greek often obscures the living and vibrant presence of these languages in Christian communities.

As a reading of Strabo, Diodorus Siculus, Pliny the Elder, and Pausanius will quickly indicate,[9] in the very early centuries of the Common Era

---

5. Koester, *History, Culture, and Religion*, 42.
6. Moulton in Porter, *Language*, 82–83.
7. See Brock, *From Ephrem to Romanos*.
8. Bardy, *La question des langues*, 36.
9. Translations of all pagan Greek and Latin texts in this book are from editions of the Loeb Classical Library.

there were hundreds and hundreds of tribal groups. Diodorus Siculus speaks of "the present existence of every conceivable kind of language" (παντοίους τε ὑπάρξαι χαραχτῆρας διαλέκτων) (1.8.4), and Pliny, a contemporary of the early Christian movement, writes, "A small matter to tell of but one of measureless extent if pondered on is the number of national languages and dialects and varieties of speech" (*tot gentium sermones, tot linguae, tanta loquendi varietas*) (*Nat.* 7.1.7).

It would seem that the majority of illiterate, oral cultures maintained their identity in spite of the powerful cultural influences around them. In the region of Asia Minor and thereabouts, tribal identity had already survived other powerful cultural influences from Persia and Egypt over the centuries. Of course, not every single tribal grouping had its own language—most, probably, spoke a dialect—and many tribes were associated with other, mostly neighboring, tribes through religious ceremonies or festivals, marriage and trade; and they were held together by a common language.

Christian communities mirrored the language complexities of their society and so consisted of members who spoke many and varied languages. Kaimio's general comments are true also of Christian groups:

> We must assume that most language communities of the Roman Empire were diglot or even polyglot and quite a few of their members in one way or another bilingual or multilingual. Even if they were unilingual, they had a certain language choice: for the purposes of communication, they could use the only language they knew, they could refer to an interpreter, or they could choose to say nothing. But for the others, there was a real choice between languages.[10]

It is well-known that the literate Greeks divided the world into two groups, Greeks and barbarians.[11] This division was largely language-based, and mastery of the Greek language was perhaps the most important component in the process of Hellenization.[12] But there were noticeable limits. As Jones notes, "The culture which the cities fostered, though geographically spread over a wide area, as limited to the urban upper class. The great mass

---

10. Kaimio, *Romans*, 14.

11. The word "barbarian" is commonly said to reflect the language of non-Greeks. Strabo observes that barbarian speech is not due to a vocal defect because the same thing happens when they learn to speak Greek; and in fact Greeks do the same when trying to speak other languages (14.2.28).

12. Momigliano, *Alien Wisdom*, 8–9.

of the population, the proletariat of the towns, and still more the peasants of the country, remained barbarians."[13]

Hellenization was not an inevitable process to which local cultures, including their languages, simply succumbed. In the Maccabean literature, faithful Jews mark their identity by speaking "the language of their fathers" (2 Macc 7:8, 21; 4 Macc 12:7; 16:15).

While many educated elite Latins were greatly attracted to Greek language, there are also signs of a stubborn refusal to bow to its superiority.[14] The first-century CE Latin writer, Valerius Maximus, himself familiar with Greek, shows his obvious bias towards Latin. He claims that the magistrates of old made it the rule to always reply to Greeks in Latin. And they made the Greeks discard their volubility,[15] which is their greatest asset, and to speak through an interpreter, not only in Rome but in Greece and Asia also, intending no doubt that the dignity of Latin speech be the more widely venerated throughout all nations they held that in all matters whatsoever the Greek cloak should be subordinate to the Roman gown, thinking it unmeet that the weight and authority of empire be sacrificed to the seductive charm of letters (*Memorab.* 2.2.2).

Koine in the Imperial Period

Wallace writes, "Koine Greek became the lingua Franca of the whole Roman Empire by the first century AD. . . . Even after Rome became the world power in the first century BC, Greek continued to penetrate distant lands. . . . Greek continued to be a universal language until at least the end of the first century AD."[16] While as a general statement this is an accurate picture of affairs, where it is misleading is in its very generality. It leaves open the questions: For whom was Koine the "common" language? Was it common for them in all language contexts—religious, social, political, legal, economic, conversational and others? Or was Koine only one of the available dialects that one could select for use, depending on the speaker's context? And important is the complex question: Since there are so many variants of Koine, just whose Koine is to be considered "standard"?

---

13. Jones, *Greek City*, vii.

14. For a detailed study of the relation between Greek and Latin speakers and writers, see Kaimio, *Romans and the Greek Language*.

15. Pliny Jr. also complains about the Greeks for mistaking "volubility for fullness of expression; they all pour out a torrent of long monotonous periods without taking breath" (*Ep.* 5.20.4).

16. Wallace, *Greek Grammar*, 17.

THE MIGHTY WORKS OF GOD (ACTS 2:11)

New Testament scholarship often gives the impression that Koine dominated the language scene. Greek and Roman scholars tend to be more circumspect and see Koine as a second language for the majority of people. Thomson, for example, says, "Koine was spoken as a second language. It is uncertain how widely it was known in the countryside, but except in some of the cities it did not replace the native language."[17]

It has to be seriously considered, then, that many—if not indeed the majority—in early Christian communities spoke or understood Greek as a second language. When they heard the Gospels or the letters of Paul being read to them, they heard them either through whatever competency they had in Greek or through a translator. It cannot simply be assumed that Greek was understood by all.

So, the notion that Koine Greek was a "universal language" needs balance. This is not an easy task, given that there are ample data to support the claims made of that dialect. The Egyptian papyri, the New Testament, other Greek literature, inscriptions and epitaphs, all give the impression that the Koine dialect of Greek was "common" across cultural borders. More careful scholarship will admit that much of this evidence comes from artifacts of the elite—the educated, literate, and wealthy—rather than of the great majority of the population. As Deissmann, who championed the papyri and ostraca of Egypt as illustrative of the language of the lower-classes, admits: "Of course among the inscriptions and papyri of that time there are very many (a majority in fact of the inscriptions) that do not come from the lower classes, but owe their origin to Caesars, generals, statesmen, municipalities and rich people. But side by side with these texts, particularly in the papyri and ostraca, lies evidence of the middle and lower classes."[18]

Most literates in the Mediterranean world probably could communicate in a dialect of Greek. In some cases, there could well have been a touch of wanting to appear "trendy." As Russell says, "In a number of cities the local dialect or language would still be spoken by some, but just as it was fashionable to "dress with the times" and keep up with cultural trends, so it was essential for all educated men, and indeed for any who had even a modicum of interest in culture, to speak the Greek tongue."[19]

When a second language is used as a communication code, that language inevitably is spoken and used with the accent, grammatical structures, vocabulary, and most important of all, the constructed worldview of the speaker's first language. Given that among the elite oratory was held in high

---

17. Thomson, *Greek Language*, 35.
18. Deissmann, *Light*, 9.
19. Russell, *Jews*, 86.

regard, the matter of accent and pronunciation is not insignificant. How one sounded was important. It might have been something that Paul felt, since his Corinthian audience saw his letters as "weighty and strong," but his speech (λόγος) as "something to be disdained" (2 Cor 10:10). He might have been less comfortable speaking Greek than he was writing it.

Strabo was aware that language variations and abilities were more than a simple matter of accent. Speaking of barbarian speakers, he astutely observed:

> When all who pronounced words thickly were being called barbarians onomatopoetically, it appeared that the pronunciations of all alien races were likewise thick, I mean of those that were not Greek. Those therefore they called barbarians, in the special sense of the term, at first derisively, meaning that they pronounced words thickly or harshly; and then we misused the word as a all other races. The fact is, however, that through our long acquaintance and intercourse with the barbarians this effect was at last seen to be the result, not of a thick pronunciation or any natural defect in the vocal organs, but of the peculiarities of their several languages (κατὰ τὰς τῶν διαλέκτων ἰδιότητας). (14.2.28 [italics mine])

Initially, there were many and various Greek dialects, and the ancients themselves were aware of these dialect differences, as indicated by the existence of verbs such as αἰολίζειν, ἀττικίζειν, δορίζειν, ἰωνίζειν, all of which could be contrasted with ἑλληνίζειν, a term initially limited to those who were "Hellenes." While the idea of being "Greek" and of a "Greek language" existed in people's minds, the various dialects remained. Quintilian says the Greeks have many dialects.[20] Carl Darling Buck identified some twenty-two Greek dialects, based largely on the inscriptional evidence.[21]

The language situation was very complex. Morpurgo Davies summarizes:

> There is no evidence before the Hellenistic period for a standard language used in Greece for either the purposes of literature or those of communication. There is on the other hand some evidence for a complicated pattern of dialect switching . . . and for an extensive passive knowledge of different dialects. The linguistic forms used differ extensively from region to region but the patterns of use and understanding create links between

---

20. "Plura . . . loquendi genera" (Quintilian, *Inst.* 1.5.29).
21. Buck, *Greek Dialects*.

the different dialects and contribute to mark them off as a unit which can be contrasted with non-Greek languages.[22]

Dialects of a language are often indicators of prestige and status. Attic, for example, was regarded as the dialect of the orator, of the "classy" writer and speaker, and so of the educated and elite. Many dialects were undoubtedly regional and local. While *poleis* might have been deliberately constructed on a Greek model, and a "common" Greek dialect was part of that structure, the further one moved outside of those structures and into the villages and rural communities, the less "common" was the Greek and the more were vernaculars used. Given that Christian communities were also to be found in κῶμαι and χῶραι (cf. Matt 10:11; Acts 8:25; Pliny, *Ep.* 10.96.9; Justin, *1 Apol.* 67), this is not an insignificant matter when trying to determine language usage among Christians.

I wish to emphasize for New Testament scholarship that even if Koine became "the standard language" in the Hellenistic period, dialect switching and dialect register remained, as did also many of the vernacular languages. To make matters more complex, the Koine dialect itself was not static. It had its roots in Attic, but like all living languages in constant interaction with other languages, it absorbed vocabulary and grammatical features from the environment in which it was used. In fact, according to Moulton, Kretschmer argued that oral Koine contained elements from the Boeotian, Ionic and North-West dialects more than it did from Attic. While he probably overstated the case, the influence of the other dialects is noticeable.[23] There was fluidity in Koine as it developed and changed, and it certainly did not instantly become the standard or common Greek dialect. It was a long process. And, as Moulton says, "In this process naturally those features which were peculiar to a single dialect would have the smallest chance of surviving, and those which most successfully combined the characteristics of many dialects would be surest of a place in the resultant "common speech.""[24]

The interaction with and influence of barbarian languages was true for all the Greek dialects, not just the Koine. The more one lives in communication with others, the more one's language is influenced. The language can be so "adulterated" that a language-elitist like Dionysios of Halicarnassus could complain: "By living among barbarians many others have soon forgotten [ἀπέμαθον] all their Greek heritage, so that they neither speak the Greek language nor observe Greek customs. . . . Those Achaeans who are settled near the Euxine sea prove my point; for, though originally Eleans,

22. Morpurgo Davies, *Greek Notion*, 161.
23. Moulton, "Characteristics," 313-14.
24. Moulton, "Characteristics," 311.

descendants of the most Greek people [ἐκ τοῦ ἑλλενικοτάτου γενομένοι], they are now the most savage of all barbarians" (*Ant. rom.* 1.89.4).

The various Greek dialects survived the rise of Koine. Valerius Maximus says that when P. Crassus went to Asia Minor (ca. 130 BCE) "he was careful to master the Greek language that divided as it was into five branches he learned each of them thoroughly in all its parts and aspects . . . in whatever dialect one of them applied at his tribunal, he gave his ruling in the same" (*Memorab.* 8.7). This might suggest that the dialects were not necessarily mutually understandable; it clearly implies that there was not always one dialect that was used in the courts of Asia Minor. It is also noteworthy that "the scholia are unanimous in including the Koine among the five dialects."[25] This common listing of Koine as just one of the five dialects of Greek calls into some question the standardization of Greek and the "common" nature of Koine.

While the written, elite form of Greek tended towards standardization, the evidence that the same thing happened with the spoken language is far less certain. Tatian, who was somewhat sensitive to charges of barbarisms in Christian writings, was aware of the living dialect variations within oral Greek and of the influences from barbarian languages:

> The way of speaking among the Dorians is not the same as that of the inhabitants of Attica, nor do the Aeolians speak like the Ionians. And, since such a discrepancy exists where it ought not to be, I am at a loss whom to call a Greek. And, what is strangest of all, you hold in honour expressions not of native growth, and by the intermixture of barbaric words (βαρβαρικαῖς φωναῖς) have made your language (διάλεκτον) a medley. (*Address to the Greeks* 1)

At the beginning of the third century, Clement of Alexandria still divided the Greek language into its five dialects, and he too was conscious of the many barbarian languages still in existence:

> A dialect is a mode of speech which exhibits a character peculiar to a locality, or a mode of speech which exhibits a character peculiar or common to a race. The Greeks say that among them are five dialects (διαλέκτους)—the Attic, Ionic, Doric, Aeolic, and the fifth the Common; and that the languages of the barbarians (τὰς βαρβάρας φωνάς), which are innumerable, are not called dialects, but tongues (γλώσσας). (*Strom.* 1.21.142)

---

25. Morpurgo Davies, *Greek Notion*, 163.

In any case, Greek speakers did not all shift into Koine. There is clear evidence that North-West Koine Greek persisted into the Common Era in Boeotia, in the Peloponnese, and in Crete; and that the Doric dialect "showed the greatest resistance to Koine Greek."[26] Pausanius knows that, in his time (ca. 170 CE), Doric was used in the Peloponnese (*Descrip.* 4.27.11; 5.15.12). Pliny knows of contemporary Dorians, Ionians and Aeolians living in Paphlagonia along side of barbari (*Nat.* 6.2.7). And besides the maintenance of regional Greek dialects, there were also elite Greeks advocating Attic, a move that began with Dionysios of Halicarnassus near the turn of the Era and continued through to the third century, as is indicated by Sextus Empiricus, and beyond. Swain notes an intensification of the "polarization between the language of the educated and the non-educated."[27] He believes there was an obsession with language "due to the elite's need to give itself a clearer and more readily definable identity."[28] The prestige language in oratory and writing was, for some, Attic; but "it never supplanted the educated Hellenistic standard in general communication."[29] On the other hand, there are indications that Attic was not only the domain of the orators and writers longing for some past golden age of language. Aulus Gellius reports an incident when he was dining at Athens and an eight-year old slave boy of Attic birth was ordered to do something. The boy replied "in Greek and excellent Attic Greek at that" (17.8.7). In other words, native Attic Greek speakers were still to be found in Athens in the middle of the second century, and they still taught their children to speak Attic, at least in certain language contexts.

The matter of register deserves further comment. Sextus Empiricus noted that no one speaks in common practice like orators do in the law-courts, because they would be ridiculed if they did. Even orators themselves spoke differently in court than they did with their friends (*Adv. Math.* 2.58). He also argues that the different sorts of speech should preserve their integrity (*Adv. Math.* 1.176). When one speaks with the philologoi, a more sophisticated, scholarly language should be used (1.235); but when one is speaking to slaves, appropriate vocabulary should be used. So, for example, instead of using the Greek word ἀρτοφόριον (bread-basket), masters should ask slaves for the πανάριον (from the Latin, *panarium*), "even if it is barbarian" (1.234). On that principle, I suggest that the Semitisms and Latinisms in Mark could say more about the social class of the audience than they do about the Greek language competency of the author. And can some of the

---

26. Palmer, *Greek Language*, 190.
27. Swain, *Hellenism and Empire*, 409.
28. Swain, *Hellenism and Empire*, 409.
29. Swain, *Hellenism and Empire*, 410.

variations that are apparent in the Koine of other New Testament writers also be attributed to language register? A rather delightful example of language register is given by Sozomen. The fourth-century bishop Triphyllius had occasion, in his discourse at a synod, to quote the text, "Take up thy bed and walk," and he substituted the more-refined word "couch" (σκίμπους) for the word "bed" (κράββατον). Another bishop, Spyridon, reacted indignantly, "Are you greater than he who uttered the word "bed," that you are ashamed to use his words?" and walked out (H.E. 1.11.9).

In summary, the status and use of the Greek language, in the first century CE at least, was complex and fluid. Various Greek dialects were maintained, and the gradual rise of Koine did not replace them by simply fusing or merging them all. Nor did Greek of any kind simply overwhelm other languages.

Traditional Languages in the Imperial Period

Clearly, the language terrain of the Greek and Roman world was not smooth. A considerable amount of language-mixing took place as local tribal groups intermingled with other foreign groups as a result of military rewards, recognition for civic patronage, forced settlement, or the placement of slaves and of prisoners of war. Marriages, in particular, led to a mixing of languages or to bilingualism. As Martial and Juvenal testify, the attraction to the bigger cities also saw mixed language populations in places like Rome, Athens, Corinth, Ephesus, and Smyrna. In these places, people formed guilds and associations partly on the basis of their common kinship and language. It is plausible to suppose that some Christian communities in these cities were divided into—and even by—various and different language groups.

In Asia Minor, Lydian, Carian and Lycian were the major known local language groups, especially along the western seaboard. They were ancient Anatolian languages which had been influenced by association with Assyrians, Persians, Egyptians and others, through military, political and commercial contact. Greek, however, was the dominant language in the Ionian cities like Priene, Miletus, Ephesus and Colophon. But even there, Ionian Greek itself was spoken in various dialects. Valerius Maximus says that Mithridates (ca. 60 BCE) learned the languages of the twenty-two nations in Asia that were under his rule so that he could speak to his subjects without using an interpreter (8.7.16).[30] Aulus Gellius says it was twenty-five languages (17.17.1). While these authors probably exaggerate and flatter

---

30. Interpreters were commonly used in courts, and especially in the army and in military and political communications.

Mithridates' linguistic ability, they reflect with some accuracy the diversity of languages and dialects in Asia Minor.

There are also signs that language-mixing had taken place in some areas of Asia Minor. Carian provides a good case in point. Strabo knows it as a living language and says that it "has extremely many Greek words mixed up with it" (*Geog.* 14.2.28). Nor was the language confined to Asia Minor. Strabo knows that the Caunians (near Rhodes) "speak the same language as the Carians" (14.2.3) and he notices the mobility of the Carian language-speakers and the impact it had on their use of Greek:

> The Carians roamed throughout the whole of Greece, serving on expeditions for pay. Already, therefore, the barbarous element in their Greek was strong, as a result of their expeditions in Greece; and after this it spread much more, from the time they took up their abode with the Greeks in the islands; and when they were driven thence into Asia, even here they were unable to live apart from the Greeks, I mean when the Ionians and Dorians later crossed over to Asia (14.2.28).

Things do not appear to have changed much in Asia Minor by the turn of the Era. True, Strabo claims that the annexation by the Romans meant that by his time, "most of the peoples had already lost both their languages and their names" (12.4.6). But he also says that "Lydians, Carians and Greeks" inhabited the region between Ephesus and Antiocheia in his own time (14.1.38), and that Lydians, Carians and Ionians, "both Milesians and Myesians" and Aeolians inhabited the region between Magnesia and Tralles (14.1.42).

These are areas of early Christian communities, and it can be validly assumed that the language mix was present among them too. Where local languages appear to have survived most strongly is in Phrygia (a strong Christian region in later centuries) and in areas to the north-west around the Black Sea and in the north of Greece itself. In these regions, the language terrain again is difficult to map. Tribal groups had moved in and out of these regions for centuries. Typical, in this region, was the resettlement practice, as noted by Diodorus of Sicily: "Many conquered peoples were removed to other homes, and two of these became very great colonies: the one was composed of Assyrians and was removed to the land between Paphlagonia and Pontus, and the other was drawn from Media and planted along the Tanais" (2.43). The resettled peoples brought their languages with them. In these areas, the number of languages known to the Romans and Greeks is staggering, even if the figures are exaggerations. Strabo knows the area as belonging to the Caucasii, of which, he says, there are seventy tribes all speaking different languages (11.4.6).

In Cybira in the Lycian region, Lydian, Solymian, Pisidian and Greek were all spoken.[31] The Phrygian tongue, which has survived mainly in epitaphs, remained in use until the fifth or sixth century CE.[32] Socrates (H.E. 5.23) tells of an early fourth-century bishop who preached in Gothic and Phrygian: "Selenas, bishop of the Goths . . . [was] a man of mixed descent; he was a Goth by his father's side, but by his mother's a Phrygian, by which means he taught in the church with great readiness in both these languages." Obviously, then, Phrygian and Gothic were both living languages in some churches of the fourth century.

Strabo knows of various languages in use among the Cappodocians (12.1.1), and of the Galatian tribes having a common language (12.5.1). These regions later had large Christian populations. He was also aware that the Bithynians further north had close links with the Thracians and Mysians (12.3.3; 12.4.8). Mysian was originally an ancient western Anatolian language that survived well into the Common Era and was spoken in a number of regions, especially on the north eastern coast of Asia Minor. It later merged with both the Thracian and Dacian languages.

The Celts settled in Galatia around 300 BCE from the west and northwest. There were three major and distinct tribal groupings in the area. According to Strabo, the Galatians all spoke the same language (4.1.1). He says they were still speaking Celtic in his time (although they were also very familiar with Greek). Jerome wrote in the fourth century that the Galatians of Ancyra and the Treveri of Treves spoke the same language.[33]

The Thracians were a very populous people, inhabiting the region largely in northern Greece, around the Black Sea and northern parts of Asia Minor. Strabo is aware that their language was alive and well in Mysia, Scythia and among the Getae and the Daci (7.3.10; 7.3.13). Sextus Empiricus knew that Thracian was still being spoken in his day (*Adv. Math.* 1.218). It was a language closely related to the Phrygian language group, and was one of the languages spoken in Thessalonika. It was still a living language, especially among the Bessi, in the fourth century CE.[34] It was into that region that Ovid was exiled in the first decades of the Common Era. In his opinion, Greek had been so barbarized there as to make it sound like a foreign language. It is yet another example of language mixing. Ovid also

---

31. Ramsay, *Cities and Bishoprics*, 265.
32. See Anderson, "Exploration."
33. Jerome, "Preface."
34. Iordanes, *Origin and Deeds of the Goths* 12.75.

worried that his Latin had become mingled with "the language of the Pontus" (*Tristia* 3.14.43–52). He complains that "the barbarian tongue knows not a Latin voice, and Greek is mastered by the sound of Getic" (nesciaque est uocis quod barbara lingua Latinae, Graecaque quod Getico uicta loquela sono est, 5.2.67–68). Though the region was "a mixture of Greeks and Getae," the latter were dominant (5.7.11–12); "a few retain traces of the Greek tongue, but even this is rendered barbarous by a Getic twang (in paucis remanent Graecae uestigia linguae, haec quoque iam Getico barbara facta sono). There is not a single man among these people who perchance might express in Latin any common words whatsoever" (5.7.51–56).

In the region of Italy, along its south-eastern coast, for example, the Messapians, Apali, Daunii and Peucetii all maintained their language into the Common Era (Strabo 6.3.6, 11). More important, from the perspective of constructing early Christian communities, is the language context in Rome. Late in the first century CE, there were people from many parts of the empire who brought their languages with them, as Martial observes, "What race is so distant from us, what race is so barbarous, O Caesar, that from it no spectator is present in your city! The cultivator of Rhodope is here.... The Scythian ... is here; he, too, who quaffs the waters of the Nile nearest their springing.... The Arabian ... the Sabaeans ... the Cilicians ... the Sicambrians ... the frizzled Ethiopians. Yet though their speech is all so different, they all speak together hailing you, O Emperor, as the true father of your country" (*Epigrams* 10.3).

Juvenal disliked the influence of Greek in Rome, but he also detested other eastern influences and their languages:

> I cannot, citizens, stomach
>
> A Greek-struck Rome.
>
> Yet what fraction of these sweepings
>
> Derives, in fact, from Greece?
>
> For years now Syrian Orontes has poured
> its sewerage into our native Tiber—
>
> Its lingo and manners. (*Sat.* 3.51–55)

A melting-pot of languages in Rome is also implied by Suetonius, who says that emperors like Julius Caesar presented "stage-plays in every ward all over the city, performed too by actors of all languages" (*Julius* 39). Obviously, then, not everyone in Rome understood Greek, as Philostratus makes clear: "When he [Favorinus] delivered discourses in Rome, the interest in them was universal, so much so that even those in his audience who did not understand the Greek language shared in the pleasure that he gave; for he fascinated even them by the tones of his voice, by his expressive glance and the rhythm of his speech" (*Vit. Soph.* 491).

If the Christians in Rome addressed by Paul mirrored the mixed language groups of wider Rome, then one might assume that Paul, who felt an obligation to Greeks and barbarians there (Rom 1:14), needed someone to translate his Greek for the benefit of "the barbarians" in the audience.

Later, around 200 CE, Sextus Empiricus, who lived in Alexandria and in Athens, was well aware that not everyone understood Greek: "All men do not understand the speech of all—Greeks that of barbarians and barbarians that of Greeks, or Greeks that of Greeks or barbarians that of barbarians" (*Adv. Math.* 1.37). Even dialectical differences were numerous: "Both the Dorian and the Attic dialects are numerous" (1.89) with variations in pitch and tone. Sextus says in his day there were basically "two kinds of Hellenism [ἤδη δὲ τοῦ ἑλληνισμοῦ δύο εἰσι διαφοραί]. . . . One stands apart from our common usage and seems to proceed in accordance with grammatical analogy; the other conforms to the common usage of each of the Greeks and is derived from framing words and from observation in ordinary converse" (1.176). He is referring to the Attic and Koine dialects of Greek, and he clearly believes the latter to be "good Greek," mainly arguing along today's common line that usage is what matters.

The survival of vernacular languages understandably is to be found commonly in religious rituals and practices. Quintilian refers to the "language of the Salian hymns now scarcely understood by its own priests." This is because "religion forbids us to alter the words of these hymns and we must treat them as sacred things" (*Instit.* 1.6.40-41). This also could be the case with the Greek-speaking Christians, who preserved some Hebrew/Aramaic in their worship. It certainly was the case with many others. The Eleans sang traditional hymns in Doric (Pausanius 5.15.12). Near Coroneia in Boeotia, a woman daily offered a ritual prayer for Iodama "in the Boeotian dialect" (Pausanius 9.34.2).

Diodorus Siculus notes that on Samothrace an ancient language had once been used "of which many words are preserved to this day in the ritual of their sacrifices" (5.47.3). Cumont refers to Phrygian rituals performed "in a foreign language" in the confines of the Palatine in Rome.[35] Harnack notes that in Lydia, in the temples of Anahita, the priests sang "hymns which were barbaric and quite unintelligible to Greeks."[36] And among the Greeks, there is some evidence that the vocabulary—and even larger parts of the

---

35. Cumont, *Oriental Religions*, 53.
36. Harnack, *Mission and Expansion*, 314.

language—of a ritual foreign in origin was incorporated into the language of its new cultural context. For example, according to Strabo, Thracian ritual and music was heavily influenced by its Asiatic contact, and some of the musical instruments used in Dionysian rituals were still called by their "barbarian names, nablas, sambycê, barbitos, magadis and several others" (10.3.17). He also notes that some Athenians in the time of Demosthenes used the language of the Phrygians in a Phrygian ritual: "êvoe saboe," and "hyês attês, attês hyês." It appears that Strabo himself knows this language because he adds, "for these words are in the ritual of Sabazius and the Mother" (10.3.18). Pausanius also knows from personal experience some Lydians in Hierocaesarea and Hypaepa who use a magos, who "sings to some god or other an invocation in a foreign tongue unintelligible to Greeks, reciting the invocation from a book" (5.27.6). The language might well have been either Lydian or Persian.

Clearly, the language map was complex, fluid and dense. It is a very reasonable assumption that Christian communities reflected that complexity.

Language Evidence from the New Testament

The New Testament itself reveals glimpses of the language environment of its writers and audiences. Of course, it was written in Koine Greek, albeit with differences in style and "correctness." Obviously, the New Testament authors assumed either that their audiences could understand Greek or that someone would translate for those who could not. It needs also to be said that the language choice the writers had was very limited indeed. In a culture where honor and reputation and status were high in one's aspirations, the ability to communicate in written Greek gave prestige, status, and importantly, authority to the very text being heard and to its author. The New Testament authors were probably aware of this factor when they wrote in Greek to their mainly illiterate audiences. The use of the prestige language bolstered their authority.

There is an occasional hint that some Christian communities did have some non-Greek speakers. As mentioned, Paul's use of the phrase "both to Greeks and to barbarians" (Rom 1:14) might reflect the standard two-fold division of peoples, a division largely made along language lines. Paul, then, felt that he had an obligation to Greek speakers and to non-Greek speakers in Rome. And in Col 3:11, the writer implies that among his Christian audience there are "Greek and Jew . . . barbarian, Scythian." "Barbarians" indicates those in the community who, at best, spoke Greek only poorly, if at all; "Scythians" was a general term used by the Greeks as a single designation for many and various peoples who came from the north around the Black Sea.[37] In Colossians, the term probably refers to any non-Jewish and non-Greek language speakers in Asia Minor and its eastern and northern surrounds.

Further, there is evidence that some Christians prayed in the vernacular. John Chrysostom even thought that tongue-speaking meant speaking in another known language, such as Thracian, Scythian, Latin, and Persian—an indication he knew Christians who prayed in those languages.[38] Clement of Alexandria says, "men confess that prayers uttered in a barbarian tongue are more powerful" (*Strom.* 1.21). The language of the heart comes out in religious expression.

The Pentecost narrative in Acts 2 suggests that Jews in the places mentioned spoke native languages. It might be noted that many of the regions listed were on the fringes of the hellenized world and so were less likely to have been influenced by Greek and Latin. It is quite possible that Luke was aware that there were Christians in these areas by his time and that they had "heard in [their] own tongues the mighty works of God" (Acts 2:11). There is also the well-known narrative in Acts, where the locals of Lystra are said to cry out in their own Lycaonian language (Λυκαονιστί) (Acts 14:11). Finally, the "barbarians" of Malta (Acts 28:2) presumably did not speak Greek as their first language. Archaeological evidence suggests they spoke some form of Punic.[39]

Languages in Worship

Presumably, the Christian communities of the first century predominantly used Greek as their language of worship. That assumption is made on the basis of Jewish practice; on the assumption that Koine Greek was commonly enough understood; on the premise that if there were a multilingual Christian community, a single language is likely to have been adopted to hold them together, and Greek is the most likely language to have served that purpose—in other words, Greek became the "church language"; and on the basis that all the New Testament writings were written in Greek.

But there are signs that other languages were also used in worship. It is well-known that Christians retained some Aramaic loan-words in their vocabulary, words such as maranatha, amen, hosanna, abba, and arrabon. These loan words were nearly all used in times of prayer and thanksgiving. In fact, it is especially in prayer that languages other than Greek appear to have

---

37. See Strabo 1.2.27; Pliny *Nat.* 4.12.81.
38. Chrysostom, "Homily XXXV," 491–92.
39. See Hemer, *Book of Acts*, 152.

been used. It is also possible that many Christians initially used Hebrew and Aramaic, especially in the fixed "liturgical" elements of their worship, such as readings and psalms. This might be especially true of those in the more eastern parts of the Roman empire such as Cappodocia, Cilicia, Phrygia, Galatia, eastern Ionia, where the Persian and other eastern influences had been very strong and where Aramaic had been the lingua franca. We might note Josephus's letter from Antiochos to Zeuxis (209 BCE) concerning the forced transfer of two thousand Jewish families to Phrygia and Lydia from Mesopotamia and Babylonia (*Ant.* 12.148–53). Presumably, these Jews brought their Hebrew and Aramaic with them, and their contact and communication with Jerusalem would have probably helped to maintain their identity through their language. It is feasible that many Jews in that eastern region of Asia Minor in the first century of the Era still used Aramaic in their synagogues, if not as their first language of communication. Choice of an ancient language like Hebrew might have been encouraged by the idea that such languages are changeless, unlike a contemporary vernacular which changes and in which words can take on different meanings. So, in some areas and at some times, Hebrew remained, even though everyone spoke Aramaic; in others, Greek remained even though most spoke Latin; in others again, Latin remained even though most spoke German or English or some other vernacular.

The Aramaic Targumim are an indication that translation was an acceptable—and probably a common—practice. The Scriptures were read in one language and then translated into the vernacular. The role and function of the meturgeman in the rabbinic period indicates too that translation was the norm in the synagogue. Given the acceptability of the practice, and given that in some Christian communities there were some non-Greek speakers, and given the evidence of such a practice in later churches, it is reasonable to assume that it also took place in the very early Christian churches.

Later Centuries

The language picture becomes clearer in later centuries. Christian apologists commonly claim that Christians "are not distinguished from the rest of mankind in country, speech or customs" and "live in Greek and barbarian cities."[40] The implication is that they spoke the dominant local language. There is also ample evidence that many Christians were uneducated, illiterate, rural, and "barbarian" in their language; that is, they did not speak Greek, or if they did, they spoke it very poorly. Justin, for instance, says some Christians are "uneducated and barbarous in speech" (*1Apol.* 60).

---

40. *Address to Diognetus* 5.1–5, is a good example.

Justin also claims, with hyperbole, "there is not one single race of men, whether barbarians or Greeks, or whatever they may be called, nomads, or vagrants, or herdsmen living in tents, among whom prayers and thanksgiving are not offered through the name of the crucified Jesus" (*Dial. Tryph.* 117). He infers that such "prayers and thanksgiving" were offered by both Greek and barbarian language speakers. Justin uses the expression "prayer and thanksgiving" elsewhere to include invocations and hymns (πομπὰς καὶ ὕμνους, *1Apol.* 13). Given the nature of prayer, it would not be surprising to find Christians praying and singing hymns in their own vernacular, and Justin suggests that this was the case.

Irenaeus implies that Christians used various languages in the transmission of the tradition when he says, "although the languages of the world are varied, the meaning of the Christian tradition (ἡ δύναμις τῆς παραδόσεως) is one and the same" (*A.H.* 1.10.2). He also explicitly speaks of Christians who were both illiterate and barbarian speakers, who did not understand Greek. Importantly, he also implies that other native languages were used orally to preserve the tradition:

> To which course many nations of those barbarians who believe in Christ do assent, having salvation written in their hearts by the Spirit, without paper or ink, and, carefully preserving the ancient tradition, believing in one God. . . . Those who, in the absence of written documents, have believed this faith, are barbarians, so far as regards our language. . . . If any one were to preach to these men the inventions of the heretics, speaking to them in their own language, they would at once stop their ears. (*A.H.* 3.4.2–4)

It is plausible that in earlier generations of Christians, those who were illiterate—and we would have to assume that they were many—orally "preserved the ancient tradition" in their own languages. To do that implies, of course, that translation took place in the process. The Hebrew or Greek "texts" were probably the starting points, but for many the tradition was passed on orally in the local vernacular. For example, in the *Recognitions*, Clement has heard Barnabas teaching in Rome and was attracted by "the word of truth" and so he requests of Barnabas: "Only expound to me the doctrine of that man who you say has appeared, and I will arrange your sayings in my language, and will preach the kingdom" (1.11). It is difficult to overestimate the significance of the oral transmission of stories and teachings in the early Christian movement.

Origen also provides evidence for the use of local languages, again in the matter of prayer. Answering Celsus's charge that Christians seek for divine help by calling upon barbarous names, Origen writes:

> Any one will be convinced that this is a false charge ... when he considers that Christians in prayer do not even use the precise names which divine Scripture applies to God; but the Greeks use Greek names, the Romans Latin names, and every one prays and sings praises to God as he best can, in his mother tongue. For the Lord of all the languages of the earth hears those who pray to Him in each different tongue, hearing, if I may so say, but one voice, expressing itself in different dialects. For the Most High is not as one of those who select one language, barbarian or Greek, knowing nothing of any other, and caring nothing for those who speak in other tongues. (*Cels.* 8.37)

There is no suggestion that this is an innovation in Christian practice. Origen echoes Justin's observation that people commonly prayed and sang in their mother tongue. Again, it is reasonable to assume that this was also a common and accepted practice in even earlier generations among Christians who were "barbarian."

In the early fourth century, there are indications that the Christian scriptures had been translated into different languages. Eusebius says, "He [God] gave them [the apostles] moreover, all this excellency and power, that they should compose and complete Books; and . . . that they should be received throughout the whole creation, in the languages of both the Greeks and barbarians, and, that in all nations they should be taught, and believed, as containing the written words of God" (*Theophania* 3.28). He seems to be aware, possibly, of both written and oral translations of the Gospel of John, "whose words have, through the Gospel which was delivered by him, also enlightened the souls of men—which has been translated into all languages, both of the Greeks and barbarians, and is daily preached in the ears of all nations" (*Theophania* 4.7; cf. 4.9).

Chrysostom makes similar claims of John's Gospel, "Are not these things [Greek philosophies] with good cause extinct, and vanished utterly? . . . But not so the words of him [John] who was ignorant and unlettered; for Syrians, and Egyptians, and Indians, and Persians, and Ethiopians, and ten thousand other nations, translating into their own tongues the doctrines introduced by him, barbarians though they be, have learned to philosophize."[41]

Theodoret, a fifth-century bishop of Cyrrhus, writes similarly, "Every country that is under the sun is full of these words and the Hebrew tongue

---

41. Chrysostom, *Homilies on the Gospel of John* 2.5.

is turned not only into the language of the Grecians, but also of the Romans, and Egyptians, and Persians, and Indians, and Armenians, and Scythians, and Sauromatians, and briefly into all the languages that any nation uses" (*Therapeutike* 5.66). In his *Church History*, Theodoret writes of fourth-century monks at Zeugma, some of whom sang hymns in Greek, others sang them "in their native tongue" (presumably, Syriac; *H.E.* 5).

There is also evidence that translators were used in Christian worship in Jerusalem in the fourth century. The pilgrim Egeria, who witnessed the Easter services at Jerusalem about the year 385, makes this interesting observation:

> In that province some of the people know both Greek and Syriac, while some know Greek alone and others only Syriac; and because the bishop, although he knows Syriac, yet always speaks Greek, and never Syriac, there is always a priest standing by who, when the bishop speaks Greek, interprets into Syriac, that all may understand what is being taught. And because all the lessons that are read in the church must be read in Greek, he always stands by and interprets them into Syriac, for the people's sake, that they may always be edified. Moreover, the Latins here, who understand neither Syriac nor Greek, in order that they be not disappointed, have (all things) explained to them, for there are other brothers and sisters knowing both Greek and Latin, who translate into Latin for them.[42]

The practice of reading or preaching in one language while another translated was not limited to Jerusalem. Procopius, born in Jerusalem, reared in Syriac, acted as an interpreter for the church in Scythopolis.[43] And Theodoret, speaking of John Chrysostom, says, "Appointing presbyters and deacons and readers of the divine oracles who spoke the Scythian tongue, he assigned a church to them, and by their means won many from their error. He used frequently himself to visit it and preach there, using an interpreter who was skilled in both languages and he got other good speakers to do the same. This was his constant practice in the city" (*H.E.* 30).

It would seem that Chrysostom was practicing something that others had done before him, in the synagogues and presumably also in the churches. He himself preached in correct Attic, and the entire worship at Antioch was in Greek. But he also had non-Greek, native Syrian language speakers in his congregations. At Constantinople, the lections were read in Gothic, but Chrysostom "preached to them in Greek, while an interpreter

---

42. McClure and Feltoe, *Pilgrimage*, 94.
43. *PG* 20:1459.

repeated his words to them in their own language."[44] At Antioch, Christians from the rural regions, "a people foreign to us in language," joined in with city Christians for a martyr festival (*On Statues* 19.2).

As mentioned earlier, Socrates knew of Selenas, a bishop of the Goths, "a man of mixed descent; he was a Goth by his father's side, but by his mother's a Phrygian, by which means he taught in the church with great readiness in both these languages" (*H.E.* 5.23). This clearly indicates what I believe to have been a common situation. Many Christians lived in multilingual communities and were taught the faith in languages other than the formal, official language of the region or of the church itself. While the evidence is clearer from later centuries, the situation is most likely to have been the same in earlier Christian communities.

Conclusion

The Hellenistic world was a multilingual one; a fact that is too easily ignored in studies of the context of early Christian communities. While much of the very earliest Christian literature was in Greek, it is a questionable assumption that all Christian audiences knew and understood Greek—the evidence suggests that at least some did not, and needed, probably, to have "texts" translated for them. Some, if not many, were illiterate in their vernacular, and used Greek as, at best, a second language, and only in certain social contexts. The oral traditions of the Gospel were communicated in many different languages, probably from the very beginning.

While evidence of vernacular usage in Christian worship practices is stronger from the later centuries, there is nothing in that evidence to suggest that this was an introduced phenomenon. The reasonable inference is that such was the case from the very earliest days of the Christian movement. Certainly, the evidence is strong that in the fourth century, some Christians in the empire heard the gospel and the Christian scriptures in their own languages. They also sang hymns and prayed in those languages. There is also good evidence that in the earlier centuries, local languages were used in prayer and in songs to the praise of God. There is also some evidence that illiterate Christians of the early generations of the movement maintained and passed on the tradition in an oral form in their vernacular. It is highly likely that such communication of the gospel, especially in story form, was common. Finally, there are hints within the New Testament itself that prayers, particularly, were offered also in languages other than Greek, and that Luke was himself aware of Christians in many parts of the empire who had heard in their own local languages "the mighty works of God."

44. Robertson, *Sketches*, 100.

The Keys to the Gate Beautiful
(Acts 3:1–10)

In Acts 3:2, it is said that a crippled man used to be placed every day πρὸς τὴν θύραν τοῦ ἱεροῦ τὴν λεγομένην Ὡραίαν, which is commonly translated, "at the gate of the Temple called Beautiful." The same location is mentioned again later in the episode (3:10) when the healed man is identified as the one who used to sit ἐπὶ τῇ Ὡραίᾳ Πύλῃ, translated, again commonly, "at the Gate Beautiful." This name is striking, but attempts by scholars to locate this gate have met with little success or agreement.[1] Scholars have suggested both the upper inner gate, the Nicanor, and the lower outer gate, the Shushan, as candidates for the Beautiful Gate.

There are at least three obstacles in satisfactorily identifying this gate: (1) Extant primary sources do not mention the Beautiful Gate (the Mishnaic tractate *Middoth*; Josephus, *Ant.* 15.410–25; *Wars* 5.190–221). (2) The manuscript traditions at Acts 3:11 are confused. One tradition implies that the Beautiful Gate is in the outer walls of the Temple precincts, thus favoring the Shushan identification. The Western text, however, has the disciples and the healed man pass out through the gate into Solomon's Porch, indicating that the gate is further inside the Temple, and thus supports the Nicanor theory. In addition, it is not clear when Luke understands τὸ ἱερόν to refer only to the sanctuary itself and when to the whole Temple precincts—if he intends any distinction at all. Also, the gate entering Solomon's Porch (3:11) had no door (Josephus, *Wars* 5.5; *Middoth* 2) and yet Acts 3:2 says the crippled used to be placed at a Temple "door" (θύρα). (3) Luke's knowledge of the Temple is problematic. As Haenchen says: "It is by no means certain that we may assume in Luke our own knowledge of the Temple, let alone a better."[2]

---

1. For the issues and theories, see Morgenstern, "Gates of Righteousness," 1–37; Lake and Foakes-Jackson, *Beginnings*, 5:479–86; Haenchen, *Acts*, 198n12; Hengel, "Luke the Historian," 102–4.

2. Haenchen, *Acts*, 198n12. Lüdemann understands the reference as a traditional element in the story (*Early Christianity*, 51, 53). Hengel is undecided: "It is impossible to conclude . . . either that he (sc. Luke) was generally ignorant or that he had exact knowledge" ("Luke the Historian," 104).

For my purposes, it is not necessary to repeat the arguments in favor of identifying the gate with either Nicanor or Shushan.[3] Suffice it to say with Hengel: "It is hardly possible to arrive at a really satisfying conclusion."[4] I do not propose to solve the problem, but rather to offer three very similar keys in an effort to unlock the mysteries of this Temple gate. The first key is to read the adjective ὡραῖος not in its aesthetic sense of "beauty," but according to its common meaning, "ripe"; the second, to locate Acts 3:1–10 as taking place during the Feast of Tabernacles (Sukkoth); and the third key is to use the Hallel psalms, recited during Tabernacles, as a text through which to read the passage.

The "Ripe Gate"?

It is clear that the gates of the Temple were known by different names not only in their history but also in their function. This makes sense of the fact that numerous names are given to the Temple gates and doors in the literary sources. For example, in the Mishnah, the eastern gate—often identified as the gate of Acts 3—is known by seven different names.[5] Mowinckel claims that Temple and processional gates were given symbolic names, noting as an example the "Gate of Righteousness," referred to in Ps 118:19–20, and claiming that this was so called because it was the gate through which the righteous entered in festive procession.[6] Whether Mowinckel is correct about that particular gate or not, there is no doubt that some gates were named according to what was brought through them: The Gate of the Firstborn, The Gate of Burning, the Water Gate, The Gate of the Offering, to name a few (*Middoth* 1–2).

In addition, it seems that some Temple gates were only used for activities that related to Temple ritual. For example, in Ezek 46:1 the Lord commands that "the gate of the inner court that faces east shall be shut on the six working days, but on the sabbath day it shall be opened and on the day of the new moon it shall be opened." The passage goes on to command the prince to take a special role and place at the gate and for the priests and people to worship at the gate's entrance on those holy days (Ezek 46:2–8).

---

3. The Mishna speaks of four gates that faced the east and led into the Temple proper: the Gate of the Porch and the Gate of the Sanctuary; Shushan and Nicanor (Morgenstern, "Gates of Righteousness," 26n45).

4. Hengel, "Luke the Historian," 102.

5. See Morgenstern, "Gates of Righteousness," 19n42.

6. Mowinckel, *Psalms*, 171, 180.

It seems reasonable to suggest, therefore, that the gate through which Peter and John entered on their way into the Temple, and at which the cripple was placed "each day" (Acts 3:2), was given the particular name, "ripe" (ὡραία), for a particular occasion. I suggest the occasion was a festive one, probably that of Tabernacles. Pentecost appears to have passed (2:43–47) and the next major festival in the Jewish calendar for which it was expected that all male Jews should go to the Temple was Tabernacles.

The adjective ὡραῖος then becomes a key to understanding the function of this gate, if not its location. It is a word that, as Hamm notes, indicates "beauty," and is used in the Septuagint (and elsewhere) of trees, fruit, speech, vessels, apparel, the messianic king, and other persons.[7] But, as Hamm also notes, it is used very commonly to indicate "ripeness." Josephus uses it regularly of ripe fruit (e.g., *Ant.* 2.83; 8.153) including the ripe fruit that grew from Aaron's rod (*Ant.* 4.65). And in wider Greek literature, in addition to indicating ripeness of fruit, it is used to express "the bloom of youth" (Aeschines, *Speeches* 1.42), a "beautiful" woman (Aristophanes, *Frogs*, 293), a woman "of marriageable age" (Herodotus, *Hist.* 6.122.2), "the summer season" (Demosthenes, *Speeches* 9.48), and "harvest" (Pausanias, *Descr.* 4.10.7).

The word ὡραῖος is also used of first-fruit festivals, not only in Jewish literature in relation to festivals like Castullus and Tabernacles, but also in Greek festivals. At the Jewish Castullus festival, people brought "vessels filled with every different species of fruit borne by fruit-bearing trees" into the Temple, as required by Deut 26:1–2. These pointed-bottom vessels were called "castulli," and were used to carry "the fruits of the season" (τὰ ὡραῖα) (*Spec. Laws* 2.220). Josephus also knows of the command to bring "the ripe fruits" (τὰ ὡραῖα) to the Temple in thanksgiving to God for his rescue of Israel from Egypt (*Ant.* 4.241–43). As for wider Greek usage, Plato, for example, writes of the legendary people of Atlantis who used to bring "year by year, their seasonable offerings to do sacrifice" (ὡραῖα . . . ἀπετέλουν ἱερά) (*Critias*, 116c).

The most detailed alternative reading of this adjective in Acts 3 is that by Hamm who believes that 3:1–10 contains "six signals of symbolic intent" and that the "beautiful gate" is one such signal.[8] He interprets ὡραῖος as "the beauty that comes from being ripe, seasonable," and then links it with ἐλεημοσύνη (3:3) which he reads as "mercy."[9] He suggests then that it is "not unreasonable to ask whether Luke—either using a rare gate-name

---

7. Hamm, "Acts 3:1–10," 317. See Hamm, "Acts 3:1–10," 305–19.
8. Hamm, "Acts 3:1–10," 307.
9. Hamm, "Acts 3:1–10," 317.

not otherwise attested or providing the name himself—chose the name precisely for its connotations of ripeness."[10] The gate, and the healing itself, says Hamm, is a symbol that the time is ripe for the mercy of God.

Hamm's symbolic interpretation of the adjective—and, indeed, of the whole episode—is helpful and avoids some seemingly unanswerable questions about the gate. However, I suggest another possible key. The gate is called "ripe" because it is linked with a festival closely linked with the Temple, possibly Tabernacles, in which people brought the ripened fruit to the Temple, an institution and building of great interest to Luke.[11] Both Temple and festival were in turn linked with high expectations of God establishing a new order of things under a new authority. The healing of the lame man is symbolic of a new order with a new Temple that has Jesus Christ as "the head of the corner" (Acts 4:11).

Sukkoth, or The Feast of Tabernacles, was celebrated on the 15th of Tishri, the seventh month, as a "feast of the Lord" to give thanks for the produce of the land. On the first day of this eight-day festival, pilgrims brought the ripened tree fruit to the Temple. Lev 23:40 commands: "You shall take on the first day the fruit of goodly trees [καρπὸν ξύλου ὡραῖον] [LXX], branches of palm trees, and boughs of leafy trees, and willows of the brook; and you shall rejoice before the Lord your God seven days."

I suggest that the gate or door through which they entered for that festival "is called Ripe" (τὴν λεγομένην Ὡραίαν) (Acts 3:2). In other words, the gate is so-named because ripe fruit was carried through it. At the feast, booths, which people erected, were adorned with fruit such as peaches, almonds, pomegranates, and grape clusters suspended from the roofs (*Shabb.* 22a; see also *Sukkah* 10a). *M. Kat.*13b allows a shopkeeper on the day before the last day of the feast to "bring out fruit and decorate the markets all round the town in honor of the last day of the feast."

Acts 3:1–10 and the Feast of Tabernacles

Given that the "ripe-Tabernacles" keys at least fit the lock of the Gate, are there any indications in the narrative that might allow the keys to be turned a little, if not to actually open the Gate? I suggest that there are a number, which, when taken cumulatively, support this possibility.

According to Deut 16:16, "three times a year all your males shall appear before the Lord your God," the three occasions being the three major feasts of Passover (Luke 22:1), Pentecost (Acts 2:1), and Tabernacles.

---

10. Hamm, "Acts 3:1–10," 317.
11. See, for example, Walker, *Jesus and the Holy City*, 57–68.

Tabernacles was the major festival in the Temple era following Pentecost and was often known simply as "the Feast" (e.g., 1 Kgs 8:2; Ezek 45:25; Neh 8:14; and commonly in the Talmud). Josephus calls it "the holiest and greatest feast" (*Ant.* 8.100).

According to Acts 3:1, Peter and John "were going up into the Temple" (ἀνέβαινον εἰς τὸ ἱερόν) at the ninth hour of prayer. The verb is a "standing formula" for going to Jerusalem and to the Temple especially, but not only, for a feast (cf. John 7:8, 10, 14; 11:55; 12:20).[12] The ninth hour probably refers to the daily afternoon sacrifice (*tamid*) offered in the Temple, as commanded in Exod 29:38–41. Such sacrifices were maintained also throughout the Festivals and, in fact, "the supplies of the sacrifices are more numerous" at Tabernacles (Philo, *Spec. Laws* 1.189). It might refer explicitly to the prayers that preceded the actual afternoon sacrifice (*Sukkah* 53a). The Talmud indicates that statutory prayers were to be recited during Tabernacles (*Sukkah* 41b), and the performance of such prayers was more obligatory during a festival such as Sukkoth.[13]

A crippled man is being carried to the Temple to beg alms from those entering (3:2). The text emphasizes the fact that he has been unable to walk from his birth.[14] He is being carried or lifted (ἐβαστάζετο) to the Temple late in the afternoon, presumably because it was the high time of festivities when the whole-offering was sacrificed and the crowd was at its peak. If it were festival time, then a beggar had better chances of receiving generous alms at the daily high point of that festival.[15] It is also likely that he was placed there "every day" (καθ' ἡμέραν) of the festival (there were eight days for Tabernacles), and possibly at the same time each day. In any case, the Talmud indicates that the celebrations of Tabernacles went on into the night since they made wicks and kindled lamps "and there was not a courtyard in Jerusalem that was not illumined by the light of the place of the water-drawing" (*Sukkah* 51a).

The point of the passage obviously is that the man is lame, cannot walk, and so must be carried. The Talmud lists the lame among those who were not "bound to appear" at the Temple during the major festivals (*Hag.* 2a; cf. *Sukkah* 26a; *Ar* 2b). The Mishnah specifically states that those "unable to go up by foot" were exempt from temple attendance (*Hag.* 2a), and it argues from Exod 23:14 that "the pilgrim must have use of both feet" (*Hag.*

---

12. Schneider, "ἀναβαίνω," *TDNT* 1:519.

13. For those exempt from the prayers, see *Suk* 25b–26a.

14. Some rabbis understood that lameness at birth was due to parents "overturning the table" (*Ned* 20a), a reference to their copulating position.

15. Hamm, following Foakes-Jackson, thinks this is a late, and therefore curious, time of the day to be taking a cripple there to beg (Hamm, "Acts 3:1–10," 307–8).

3a). Thus "going by foot" or "walking" was a significant aspect of pilgrimage to the festivals. In order to participate in a feast, a man had to be able to walk—something the lame man of Acts cannot do.

More broadly, it is known that the lame were banned from performing or participating in certain cult actions. Lev 21:18 bans a lame priest from approaching the sanctuary, and 2 Sam 5:8 repeats a saying that the "blind and the lame shall not come into the house." 1QSa 2.5-7 bans the lame among other unclean men from entrance into the assembly. They are also banned from participating in the final battle (1QM 7.4).

In Acts 3:5, the cripple asks for something from Peter and John. Acts of charity (ἐλεημοσύνη) were expected of pious Jews, especially at festivals (see, for example, John 13:29). At festivals, thank-offerings were obligatory: Those attending "shall not appear before the Lord empty-handed" (Deut 16:16). And further, "every man shall give as he is able, according to the blessing of the Lord your God which he has given you" (16:17). In addition, the "sojourners, the fatherless, and the widows" were to be included in the festival (16:14). Therefore, a beggar could especially expect alms from those going to the Temple during a festival such as Tabernacles.

Peter and John are expected to have thank-offerings with them and they are expected to give alms. But they claim to have no "silver or gold." Dunn thinks that this "representation of apostolic poverty is partly at least a story-telling device."[16] Others relate the reference to silver and gold to idol-worship, or think it must be understood on the background of 2:44-45, or, as evidence that the apostles' power has nothing to do with money, a common motif in Acts.[17] However, it is also possible that Peter is saying that he does not have the offering that festival pilgrims were expected to make. Beth Shammai held that the pilgrimage offering must be worth at least two pieces of silver and the festal offering at least one ma"ah of silver. Beth Hillel said that the pilgrimage offering must be worth one ma"ah of silver and the offering two pieces of silver (*Hag.* 2a). If Peter is referring to this offering, then why does he not have the obligatory "silver and gold" as he goes into the Temple?

At the anticipated ideal Feast of Tabernacles, everything in Jerusalem will be holy and there will be no more traders in the Temple (Zech 14:20-21). Significantly, Zechariah 14, was the *hafterah* read on the first day of Tabernacles (*Meg.* 31a), Does the Peter of Acts 3 believe such a time and such a celebration of the Feast have arrived? That this might be the case is implied in what he offers the man and in what follows.

---

16. Dunn, *Acts*, 41.
17. See Jervell, *Die Apostelgeschichte*, 160, 160n319.

Instead of giving him silver and gold, Peter says: "In the name of Jesus Christ the Nazaraios,[18] walk!" (ἐν τῷ ὀνόματι Ἰησοῦ Χριστοῦ τοῦ Ναζωραίου περιπάτει) (3:6).[19] It is tempting to suggest that Luke is playing with the word Ναζαραῖος as a pun on the "ripe" (ὡραῖος) gate. Be that as it may, this exact combination of words is found again in Acts only in this same context (4:10). Otherwise, the term "Jesus the Nazaraios" (Ἰησοῦς ὁ Ναζωραῖος) is used at 2:22; 6:14; 22:8; 26:9; and "Jesus Christ" (Ἰησοῦς Χριστός) is found commonly, e.g., 2:38; 3:20; 5:42; 8:12. Given the context and combination of Temple and healing, the identification of Jesus as "Christ" cannot be insignificant. The significance increases if the situation is festal since messianic expectations were often very high at festivals and especially at the Feast of Tabernacles.[20] The Tabernacles *haftorah* again provides a hint of this as he sees nations coming to Jerusalem to celebrate Tabernacles and to worship "the King, the Lord of Hosts" (Zech 14:16–17).

Peter raises the cripple by grabbing him forcibly (πιάσας) with the right hand (τῆς δεξιᾶς χειρός) (3:7). Tabernacles was the time for all males to appear before the Lord "according to the power of your hands (κατὰ δύναμιν τῶν χειρῶν ὑμῶν), according to the blessing of the Lord your God, which he has given you" (Deut 16:17 LXX). Peter has been given the promised power (δύναμις) (Acts 1:8) and this is what he has to give to the lame man. The right hand in particular was a symbol of power, of victory, and of protection, all of which are important elements in Tabernacles celebration.[21] According to *Sukkah* 55a, Pss 29; 50; 94; 81; 82; 92 were recited on consecutive days during the festival, and in these Psalms the strength, might and glory of God are a common motif.

The man's feet (βάσεις) and ankles (σφύδρα) are strengthened (3:7). The use of βάσεις to indicate "the feet" is unusual and is commonly explained as a technical, medical term, even though it is "not confined to medical books."[22] Is it coincidental that βάσεις very commonly—with only one exception—is used in the Septuagint to refer to the bases of the tabernacle and temple, especially the base of the altar? An altar with a damaged base is not valid for service (*Suk* 49a). If the lame man symbolizes the temple, then the

---

18. For a brief comment on the term, see Barrett, *Acts*, 1:140.

19. Following B, A, and D against UBS4 and NA27. The Majority Text inserts ἔγειρε καί before περιπάτει. UBS4 rates the confidence level in this reading with a 'C': "The editorial Committee had difficulty in deciding which variant to place in the text" (UBS4, 2). Resolution of this variant does not affect my argument.

20. See Smith, "Tabernacles," 130–46, esp. 143; Bergler, "Jesus, Bar Kochba," 143–91.

21. See Rubenstein, *Symbolism*, 371–87.

22. Barrett, *Acts*, 1:184.

reader might well understand that the Temple has not been fully fit for the service of God.

The man leaps up, stands, and walks (3:8). Bruce sees this as a progressive testing of strength on the part of the cripple.[23] I propose an alternative interpretation. The ability to walk now means the man has the right to enter the Temple (and to participate in any festival), which he duly does. Significantly, he goes into the Temple with Peter and John, "walking and leaping and praising God" (περιπατῶν καὶ ἁλλόμενος καὶ αἰνῶν τὸν θεόν) (3:8). Haenchen thinks such actions performed in the Temple exhibit "the un-Jewish use of ἱερόν and must be attributed to Luke."[24] Bruce calls the man's reaction "indecorous behavior."[25] Barrett thinks "it was hardly necessary, or indeed desirable, to add περιπατῶν καὶ ἁλλόμενος."[26] Most scholars understand it as the natural exuberance of one who is healed. But, again, much more can be read from "the curiously repeated descriptions"[27] of the man's behavior. When each action is examined more closely, it becomes possible to understand how Luke "came to write such a clumsy sentence."[28]

"Walking" (περιπατεῖν) is particularly significant in the narrative, since it is mentioned four times in 3:6–9 and again in 3:12, and takes place inside the Temple. I have already noted the significance of walking in pilgrimage to Jerusalem for the festivals, and that the lame were excused simply because they were not able to "trample the courts." More importantly, Tabernacles was the feast at which "all the people"—and not only the priests—"walked around the altar" once every day and seven times on the seventh day of the Feast (*Suk* 43b). As they walked, they would recite from Ps 118:25: "We beseech You, O Lord, save now; we beseech You, O Lord, make us now to prosper" (*Sukkah* 45a).

The man's second action is "leaping" (ἁλλόμενος) (3:8). Leaping, in the context of the Temple and its festivals, is synonymous with dancing. The Feast of Tabernacles was marked by joyous celebration that followed the afternoon prayer, the evening sacrifice, and the rejoicing at the place of water-drawing (*Sukkah* 53a), and central to that celebration was dancing.[29] The Talmud says that at Tabernacles "men of piety and good deeds used to dance before them with lighted torches in their hands, and sing songs and

---

23. Bruce, *Acts*, 78.
24. Haenchen, *Acts*, 200.
25. Bruce, *Acts*, 78.
26. Barrett, *Acts*, 1:184.
27. Barrett, *Acts*, 1:177.
28. Barrett, *Acts*, 1:184.
29. Safrai, "Temple," 895.

praises," and Levites "without number" accompanied the songs with many instruments, including the trumpet (*Sukkah* 51b). Ginzberg also refers to the people "jumping and skipping like goats" at Tabernacles.[30]

In Acts 3, the healed man joins in the dance. That he should do so is a sign of the messianic age. Isa 35:6 speaks of the lame "at that time" jumping like the deer (τότε ἁλεῖται ὡς ἔλαφος ὁ χωλός). In fact, the very healing of the lame man by Peter in the Temple, and possibly at a festival, would have been interpreted by some as a sign of the age-to-come, and this would partly explain the ecstatic reaction of the people (3:10). According to Jesus, the lame walking (χωλοὶ περιπατοῦσιν) is a sign that the expected Coming One is present (Matt 11:2-6). It is also evident from Matt 21:14 that the healing of the lame that took place in the Temple, approaching Passover, was a messianic sign.

It is also consistent with festival celebrations that the healed man should "praise God" (αἰνῶν τὸν θεόν). The Hallel Psalms 113-118 were sung on each day of the Feast of Tabernacles, and the call to praise God heads them Αἰνεῖτε, παῖδες, κύριον, αἰνεῖτε τὸ ὄνομα κυρίου (Ps 112:1 LXX). Luke uses precisely the same verb (αἰνεῖν) in 3:8-9 to describe the action of the healed man.

The Codex Bezae adds that the man went into the Temple "rejoicing" (χειρόμενος). According to Safrai, the distinguishing feature of Sukkoth was its spirit of rejoicing.[31] This element of joy is highlighted in Jub 16:20-31, a passage claiming that the Feast was first celebrated "on earth" by Abraham. It is called a "festival of joy" (16:20). For seven days, Abraham was "rejoicing with all his heart and with all his soul" (16:24). He named the festival "the festival of the Lord, a joy acceptable to the Most High God" (16:27). Israel is to celebrate the seven days "with joy" (16:29). And the passage concludes: "Abraham took branches of palm trees and the fruit of goodly trees and every day going round the altar with the branches seven times a day in the morning, he praised and gave thanks to his God for all things in joy" (16:31).

For Israel, joy at Tabernacles was an obligation since "the Lord will bless you . . . so that you will be altogether joyful" (Deut 16:15). It is the great feast of joy, and the actions of the healed man reflect that joyous and celebratory aspect of that feast. His movements indicate not only that he is healed and that he is happy with the new strength and abilities he has, but that he is now able to "walk," to celebrate the feast as a true and full Israelite.

The man's actions of walking, leaping, and praising God were standard behavior at Tabernacles (*Sukkah* 51a-b) and are consistent with the festival

---

30. Ginzberg, *Legends*, 4:405.
31. Safrai, "Temple," 894.

celebrations that took place in the Temple after the afternoon daily whole-offering sacrifice (*Sukkah* 4:5).

The Hillel Psalms as a Key to Acts 3–4

If the gate was known as the "Ripe Gate," and if that was so because of its use at Tabernacles, then the Psalms recited at Tabernacles might provide us with extra leverage to turn the key a little further. As already intimated, it is possible to interpret many of the actions in Acts 3–4 in the light of the Hallel Psalms[32] which were sung on all eight days of Tabernacles (*Ta'anith* 28b; *Arukh.* 10a). A reading of Acts 3–4 through the lens of these Hallel Psalms is quite revealing, and I intend to draw attention to some of the possible parallels, some being more significant than others.

In the first place, Peter and John go up into the Temple via a gate (3:2), as do all pilgrims going to the temple for a festival. In Ps 118:19-20, it is the "gate of the righteous" and the "gate of the Lord" by which the pilgrims enter. The possibility that the Psalm is itself referring to the festival of Tabernacles cannot be ruled out.[33]

The expressions, "the Name" (τὸ ὄνομα), "raises" (forms of ἐγείρω), and "the right hand" (δεξιά) occur in both the Hallel Psalms and Acts 3:1–4:10. The opening Hallel Psalm calls on Israel to "praise the name of the Lord" and sings: "Blessed be the name of the Lord . . . the name of the Lord is to be praised (113:1-3). The "name" is the source of strength, blessing, and salvation in Ps 113:9; 114:4; 115:4; 117:10-12, 26 LXX as it is also in Acts 3:6, 16; 4:7, 10, 12, 17–18, 30. In Acts 3, Peter, in the name of Jesus, raised (ἤγειρεν) the lame man from his crippled state. The Hallel Psalm 112 praises God who is "the one who raises" (ὁ ἐγείρων) (LXX) the poor from the ground (v. 7). Peter raises with "the right hand" (3:7), and the Psalms praise "the right hand of the Lord" which "has lifted me up" (δεξιὰ κυρίου ὕψωσέν με) (Ps 117:16 LXX).

On being healed or saved from his forty-year lameness, the man in Acts is seen leaping as he goes into the temple. It is an action paralleled in the Hallel where "the mountains skipped like rams and the hills like lambs" at the salvation of Israel from Egypt (Ps 113:4, 6 LXX). The healed man enters the Temple because he has been enabled to do so "in the name (ἐν ὀνόματι)

---

32. There is some debate as to whether the Hallel consisted of all these Psalms in NT times or only Psalms 113–14.

33. Morgenstern, "Gates of Righteousness," attempts to show that the gate of Ps 118 and that of Acts 3 are identical.

of Jesus Christ of Nazareth." Ps 117:26 LXX pronounces "blessed" the one who enters "in the name of the Lord (ἐν ὀνόματι κυρίου)." The people in Acts respond to the healing with wonder and ecstasy (ἐπλήσθησαν θάμβους καὶ ἐκστάσεως) (3:10), a reaction echoed in the Hallel: The Lord has done something which "is wondrous in our eyes" (ἔστιν θαυμαστὴ ἐν ὀφθαλμοῖς ἡμῶν (Ps 117:23 LXX).

In addition, there are a number of expressions in Ps 116:12–19 which are echoed in Acts 3:1–10: "What shall I render . . . loosed my bonds . . . call on the name of the Lord . . . presence of all his people . . . in the courts of the house of the Lord."

Peter's justification for the healing given in Acts 4:8–12 adds legitimacy to reading the healing episode in Acts 3 through the filter of the Hallel Psalms. It would appear that this short speech reveals Luke's own understanding of the event. In that speech, Peter explicitly quotes from one of the Hallel Psalms, 118:22: "The stone that the builder rejected has become the head of the corner." Peter interprets that stone to be Jesus. He then goes on to claim that there is "salvation (σωτηρία) in no one else" (4:12), a thought that clearly echoes the previous verse of the Psalm: "You have become my salvation" (Ps 117:21 LXX), and is a theme prominent in the Hallel.

These same Psalms were recited on every day of Tabernacles, the feast at which ripe fruit was brought to the Temple by pilgrims, and at which those pilgrims entered the Temple *via* the Ripe Gate. For this reason, the Hallel Psalms are one possible key for interpreting the healing of the cripple.

Further Signs of a Feast

That the healing episode can be read as occurring during a Feast is also indicated in Acts 3:9, 11 which refers to "all the people" (πᾶς ὁ λαός), and in 3:12 where Peter speaks to "the people" (πρὸς τὸν λαόν; see also 4:1). In 4:2, the leaders are anxious that Peter and John are teaching "the people" (τὸν λαόν). Jervell suggests that πᾶς ὁ λαός refers to "all of Israel" ("ganz Israel")[34] and I would agree. It might be remembered that "all of Israel" was expected to attend the feasts (Deut 16:16). In Deut 27:15–26 LXX; Ps 105:48 LXX, the phrase πᾶς ὁ λαός is used in a solemn cult setting as Israel commits itself to the covenant with God. Affirmation of the covenant between God and Israel was an essential purpose of the major feasts. Dunn misses the point of "all the people" and thinks it is "a typical story-teller's hyperbole."[35] Barrett also misses the point by suggesting, with others, that it refers to Christians since

---

34. Jervell, *Die Apostelgeschichte*, 160, 163.
35. Dunn, *Acts*, 44.

"the Christians frequented Solomon's Portico," and "Luke represents Christians as gathering somewhere within the perimeter of the Temple."[36] But "the people"[37] are in the Temple because it was the Feast, and in that context, the phrase would refer to Israel. The use of "all the people" and "the people" adds weight to the argument that this was a time of festival.

A significant aspect of Tabernacles is that "most of the special ceremonies are connected with the people's presence in the Temple."[38] Safrai says: "The people participated in all the rites of the feast of Tabernacles, and with the exception of the water-libation which was performed by a priest or the high priest, their role in the Temple rites and customs were equal to that of the priests." As part of the ritual, "all the people participated in the procession around the altar."[39] The priests and Temple authorities took a back seat at Tabernacles and it was "the people's festival." Josephus records an episode illustrative of the "power of the people" at the feast. Alexander, an Hasmonean high priest, was about to offer the sacrifice when "the nation rose upon him and pelted him with citrons . . . they reviled him . . . as . . . unworthy of his dignity and of sacrificing" (*Ant.* 13.372). On feast days, it seems that authority over the Temple shifted from the Sadducees and priests to the people.[40] In Acts 3, the dominance of "the people" and the freedom Peter has in speaking suggest that the normal authorities were in the background, and this is the impression given by 4:1-3.

There are further indications of a Feast, probably Tabernacles, detectable from what immediately follows the healing (3:12-26). Peter speaks in Solomon's Porch, a prominent location in the Temple grounds near a Temple gate. Prophets were known to speak "the word of the Lord" at festivals and in gate areas of the Temple. It was often a word calling for repentance. So, for example, Jeremiah is told: "stand in the gate of the Lord's house, and proclaim there this word. . . . Amend your ways and your doings" (Jer 7:2-3). Ezra reads the law to Israel at the Water Gate (Neh 8:1-8; cf. 1 Esd 5:47-51; Josephus, *Ant.* 11.154-55). According to Neh 8:18, Ezra read the law on every day of the festival of Tabernacles. In the Fourth Gospel, Jesus teaches at the Festival of Tabernacles in the Temple (John 7:14, 37). Peter's address to "the people" in Solomon's porch is consistent with the behavior of

---

36. Barrett, "Attitudes," 348.

37. While one gets the impression of "crowds," that word is absent in the whole episode.

38. Safrai, "Religion in Everyday Life," 812-13.

39. Safrai, "Temple," 894-95.

40. Safrai, "Temple," 891.

Ezra at Tabernacles, and of Jesus at the same feast since in 4:2 he is accused of "teaching the people."

So, then, is Solomon's Porch mentioned (3:11) simply to indicate location? As already noted, the word "temple" is used too often in this episode for it to go unnoticed, and Peter's citing of Ps 118 also indicates its importance in the narrative. I suggest that the reference to Solomon's Porch is another pointer to a Tabernacles context since it was commonly thought that the Temple of Solomon was dedicated during that feast. In addition, among the readings set for Tabernacles was 1 Kgs 8, a chapter telling of the Temple's dedication by Solomon. According to the Talmud (*Meg.* 31a), on the second day of Tabernacles, for *haftarah* 1 Kgs 8:2 was read: "and all the men of Israel assembled unto King Solomon." On the last day, "and it was so that when Solomon had made an end" (1 Kgs 8:54); and on the next day was read, "And Solomon stood" (1 Kgs 8:22). It seems reasonable, then, to suggest that the reference to Solomon's Porch in Acts 3:11 is a pointer to Tabernacles.

In the Porch, Peter addresses the people as "men of Israel" (Ἄνδρες Ἰσραηλῖται) (3:12). Such a form of address is consistent with the use of "the people" (ὁ λαός). All Israel is meant and probably in a covenantal sense. In addition, according to Acts 3:19, Peter calls on Israel to "repent and turn again, so that your sins may be blotted out." The Feast of Tabernacles included a renewal ritual that took place on the steps leading to the inner court in the eastern section of the Temple (in which the "Beautiful" Gate is believed to have been located). In that ritual, the priests confessed that Israel's ancestors had turned their back on the Lord but the present generation would not: "We are the Lord's and our eyes are turned towards the Lord" (*Sukkah* 51b).

When all of these factors are taken cumulatively, the suggestion that Acts 3:1–10 can be understood to be set within the context of a Feast like Tabernacles has substance. If Tabernacles is below the surface of the narrative, then it seems reasonable to see that festival as a key to unlocking the Gate of 3:2 and 10.

Summary and Conclusions

The adjective ὡραία used in Acts 3:2 and 10 as a designation for a gate of the Temple can be understood as "ripe." The Ripe Gate, then, was the gate through which pilgrims entered the Temple bringing ripe fruit with them, probably during the Feast of Tabernacles, as required by Lev 23. The healing of the cripple and his subsequent actions fit well in the context of such a Feast.

The Hallel Psalms are an important element in the second key to interpreting this episode. These were the psalms sung on each day of the Tabernacles festival. Some central motifs in these psalms appear to be echoed in the Acts narrative. In particular, Ps 118:22 and its reference to the rejected stone is taken up by Peter in his explanation for the healing.

Hamm thinks the healing episode symbolizes the restoration of Israel through the apostles' ministry.[41] He is probably right to read the story as symbolic; Luke does have his characters identify the healing as a sign (σημεῖον) (4:16, 22). But rather than interpreting it as symbolic of the restoration of Israel in general, I suggest it has to do with the Temple. Two important indicators are given within the text for this view. The one is the six-fold use of τὸ ἱερόν in the ten verses of the episode; the other is Peter's citing of Ps 118, which, I think, is a key offered by the author himself for an interpretation of the healing.

The Ripe Gate was used for the entrance of pilgrims as they came to the Temple to celebrate Tabernacles. In Acts 3:1–10, it can be understood to symbolize that the time is ripe for the Temple. While the Gospels of Matthew and Mark understand the cursed fig tree to symbolize the end of the Temple (Mark 11:12–14; Matt 21:18–19), in Acts the "Ripe Gate" symbolizes that the Temple has reached its ripeness in the person of Jesus Christ.

The lame man also can be read as a symbol of the Temple. As he had been carried for forty years from birth because of his lameness, so the Temple has never been fully fit for its service and for the celebrations of its feasts. As the man is raised and his "bases" strengthened in the name of Jesus Christ to enable him to "walk and leap and praise God," so the Temple now has been restored but in the person of Jesus Christ whom God raised from the dead. This Jesus has become God's temple, the sign of God's presence, protection, love, and mercy—those very blessings joyously celebrated and symbolized by the Feast of Tabernacles.

The Feast of Tabernacles was a time when it was anticipated that God might act in a very dramatic and public way, as John 7:2–4 implies: "Now the Jews' feast of Tabernacles was at hand. So his brothers said to him, 'Leave here and go to Judea that your disciples may see the works you are doing. For no man works in secret if he seeks to be known openly. If you do these things, show yourself to the world.'" But all three major feasts were not only times pregnant with the hopes of some "theophanic" activity, but they were also times of sociological and political opportunity, as is well illustrated by Jesus" action against the Temple at Passover. As Weitzman puts it, the festivals were used as times to "temporarily reshape the present order

---

41. See Hamm, "Acts 3:1–10."

of things—to promote new modes of authority, to push outsiders in, to force insiders out, to overturn established hierarchies and values."[42] The healing of the lame man symbolizes this new order. The adjective "ripe," used to describe a Temple gate, brackets the narrative (3:2, 10) and is used as a sign that the time is ripe for this new order.

---

42. Weitzman, "From Feasts," 545–59.

Gamaliel's Hunch

ACCORDING TO LUKE, GAMALIEL had a hunch that the followers of Jesus might be doing "the will and work of God" (ἡ βουλὴ . . . τὸ ἔργον . . . ἐκ θεοῦ). He knew that if that were the case, the council could do nothing to stop them and in fact, might be found to be opposing God (Acts 5:39). Luke writes Acts to prove Gamaliel's hunch correct. Peter and Paul, in particular, are "of God" and that is shown by the divine power that is at work in them. Anyone who opposes them is made to feel the full force of that power, as if they are found to be opposing God.

This portrayal of Peter and Paul as men of divine power stands in marked contrast with Paul's own version of his person and work which were not only marked by ignominy and weakness, but which were even identified by him as being "of God" precisely in their weakness and suffering (1 Cor 4:10-13; 2 Cor 4:7-12). Haenchen says it well: "It is not the power of Christ in the weakness of Paul that he [Luke] portrays, but the power of the Lord in the power of his disciple."[1] Luke's agenda is to show his readers, whether Jew or gentile, that the power of God defeats any rival claims to power.

So Peter and Paul are set apart to do the work of God. "The work" (τὸ ἔργον) is a technical term in Acts for the creative, salvific, eschatological activity of God.[2] Barnabas and Paul are set apart "for the work" (εἰς τὸ ἔργον) (13:2); Paul has problems taking Mark along with him "for the work" (εἰς τὸ ἔργον) (15:38); and in 14:26, Paul reports to Antioch from whence he had been commissioned "for the work" (εἰς τὸ ἔργον). That this work is "of God" is made clear in 14:27 as the apostles report to Antioch "all that God had done (ἐποίησεν) with them." A similar expression appears in 15:4, and again in 15:12, as the apostles report to the council the signs and wonders that God had done (ἐποίησεν) among the nations. "To do a work" (ἔργον ποιεῖν) is a common phrase in the Septuagint[3] and often refers to the marvellous acts of God (θαυμάσια τὰ ἔργα).[4] Luke sees the words and deeds of the apostles as a

---

1. Haenchen, *Acts*, 433.

2. There are parallels in the Fourth Gospel (cf. John 6:29; 9:3; 10:37-38).

3. For example, see Judg 2:7, 10. More often with the plural, ἔργα (e.g., Deut 11:7; Isa 28:21; 64:4).

4. Ps 138:14, for example.

37

work which God was doing; and it is a work on a par with the great works of God that are found in the heart of Israel's confession (Deut 6:22; 26:8). The apostles can rightly claim that the word of Habakkuk has been fulfilled because God has "done a work which you will never believe" (13:41).[5]

This is confirmed by Luke's use of the verb ἀναγγέλλειν as Paul and Barnabas report "the things which God has done among them" (14:27; 15:4). The apostles do not simply "report" but celebrate and proclaim, as if in cultic praise.[6] Not incidentally, the verb is used in 14:27 and 15:4 in the context of the meeting of the ἐκκλησία.

Just as "a prophet is an idealized hero around whom hagiographical legends are likely to cluster,"[7] so Luke idealizes his heroes, Peter and Paul, with stories of the signs and wonders God performs through them.[8] To confirm their status as being "of God," they are protected and guided by angels in extraordinary ways, and they are granted heavenly visions. So great is their power that others occasionally honor them as angels or gods, an honor which they self-deprecatingly decline; but their very refusal of such honors only confirms their status as being "of God."

The work of God done by the apostles signposts God's kingdom. That kingdom is not limited to Israel, but is proclaimed in Samaria (8:12), in Asia (14:22), in Ephesus (19:8; 20:25) and finally in Rome (28:31). "The Lord will be king over all the earth" (Zech 14:9). Conscious of the prophetic expectation of messengers proclaiming the εὐαγγέλιον of Yahweh's universal kingship and salvation (Isa 52:7, 10; 51:4–5; cf. Ps 95:2–3), Luke traces the work of God from Jerusalem to Rome. His frequent use of the verb "to proclaim" (εὐαγγελίζομαι), highlights the heraldic role of the apostles (5:42; 8:4, 12, 25, 35, 40; 10:36; 11:20; 13:32; 14:7, 15, 21; 15:35; 16:10; 17:18). It is a role paralleling that of the angels (Luke 1:19; 2:10) and of Jesus himself (Luke 4:18, 43; 8:1; 20:1). As evangel-announcing apostles, they are the appointed Jesus-witnesses, especially to his resurrection (Acts 1:8, 22; 2:32; 3:15; 5:32; 10:39, 41; 13:31; 22:15).

---

5. Among other Greek writers, Epictetus, for one, also knew the expression ἔργα τοῦ θεοῦ (3.5.10).

6. Cf. Ps 70:17, where the synonymous ἀπαγγελλεῖν is used, with Ps 63:10; Isa 42:9; 44:7; 46:10; and elsewhere, particularly in Psalms and Deutero-Isaiah.

7. Barton, *Oracles of God*, 99.

8. The link between apostles and prophets is a close one for Luke (see Luke 11:49; cf. Eph 2:20; 4:11; Rev 18:20). Aune rightly sees apostles as distinct from prophets and yet can still say: "In many respects the NT apostle was the functional equivalent of the OT prophet" (Aune, *Prophecy in Early Christianity*, 202). The frequent claim that the prophecies have been or are being fulfilled (Acts 3:18–26; 4:24–30; 7:52; 8:28–34; 10:43; 13:27–41; 15:15; 26:22–27; 28:23, 25) implies continuity between the prophets of Israel and the apostles.

The good news announced and taught is of Jesus Christ (5:42; 8:35; 10:36; 11:20), and is a word of salvation (13:26), of life (5:20); of peace (10:36); of God's favor (χάρις) (14:3; 20:32); of the gospel (15:7); and of truth (26:25). So dominant is this message in Luke's mind that he often refers to it simply as "the word," without any qualifying genitive (4:4; 6:4; 8:4; 10:44; 11:19; 13:46; 14:25; 16:6).

The witness-apostles are empowered and authorized by Jesus (1:8) much like the ascending Elijah empowered Elisha with his spirit (2 Kgs 2:9-12). At Pentecost, the spirit of holiness comes upon them (1:8) and they are frequently described as being "full of the Spirit" (2:4; 4:8, 31; 6:3, 5, 8; 7:55; 11:24; 13:9) who controls their decisions and movements (8:29, 39; 10: 19; 11:12; 13:2; 15:28; 16:6, 7). That same Spirit inspires their speech in fulfillment of the prophet-expected plan and work of God (Joel 2:28-32). Not surprisingly, then, the verb ἀποφθέγγομαι, which carries notions of inspired utterances and prophet speech by those "ecstatically transported,"[9] is used of Christian speakers in Acts (2:4, 14; 26:25).

Filling them with the Spirit, God acts through the mouths and hands of the apostles as he had acted through Jesus, so, not surprisingly, the apostles are recognized as having been with Jesus (Acts 4:13).

Because Peter and Paul are "of God," they hear "the voice" (9:4; 10:13; 22:6) as Moses heard "the voice of the Lord" (7:31) and as Elijah heard it at Horeb (1 Kgs 19:12). Ananias tells Paul that "the God of our fathers has appointed you to know his will, to see the Just One and to hear a voice from his mouth" (22:14-15). This direct speech from the Just One to Paul parallels the communication from mouth to mouth that existed between God and Moses (Num 12:8; cf. Exod 4:15-16; Jer 1:9).

In Jewish tradition, the word of God accomplishes the work of God. 4 Ezra encapsulates the relation: "Your word created the work" (6:38) and "Your word went out and the work was done" (6:43). It is not at all surprising, then, that because the apostles are doing the work of God they proclaim the word of God.[10] Luke depicts Peter and Paul primarily as speakers. It is well-known how much material in Acts consists of speeches; and even the posture and body movements of Peter and Paul are those of orators: They

---

9. Behm, "ἀποφθέγγομαι." It is used only in Acts in the New Testament.

10. The relation between word and deed, and the power of the word, was well-known among Greeks. In the fifth century BCE, the sophist Gorgias of Leontini said: "Speech is a great power which performs great divine works through a very insignificant and hidden form" (*Gorgias* 8, my translation). Much closer to Luke's time, Dio Chrysostom addresses the Rhodians and talks of divine men (θεῖοι ἄνδρες) who can speak with such eloquence and who are so highly admired for their oratory (*33rd Discourse* 4-6). Dio felt that his own oratory was not of his choosing, but was by the will of some deity who gave him courage to speak (*32nd Discourse* 12, 21).

stand to speak (1:15; 2:14; 5:20; 13:16; 15:7; 17:22; 21:40; 25:10; 26:6; 27:21); and they motion with their hand (12:17; 13:16; 21:40).

The phrase "the word of the Lord" obviously recalls "the word of the Lord" (λόγος τοῦ κυρίου) that came to the prophets (e.g., 1 Kgs 17:3, 8; Zeph 1:1; Hag 1:3; Zech 8:1). In the Jewish scriptures, almost everywhere it occurs, it is a technical term for the prophetic word of revelation.[11] Like the prophets of Israel, the apostles proclaim a prophetic word of revelation to both Israel and the nations, oracles of judgment and salvation. Peter calls Israel to repent because it is the latter days (2:38–40; 3:19–20; 13:40–41); and Paul calls the nations to turn from "these vain things" to the living God (14:15; 17:30; 19:26).

II

The words of Peter have a power that other mediums must acknowledge. In Samaria, Simon practices as a *magos* (μαγεύειν) (8:9), and is thought to have access to a revelation and a power not available to other mortals. He claims to be someone great (μέγας) (cf. Luke 1:15, 32) and is thought by others to be "the power of God which is called Great" (ἡ δύναμις τοῦ θεοῦ ἡ καλουμένη Μεγάλη) (8:10). But Simon realizes that his greatness fails to compare with the power in the words, signs, and miracles of Philip. He believes and is amazed (8:13). He desires the power, but he misunderstands-and this is crucial to Luke's point. Simon thinks the power is in Peter and so offers to buy the power from him (8:19). Peter reacts indignantly, as was expected of any credible vessel of a god. The marks of a deceiver are that they ask for money[12] and that they claim the power to be of themselves; "the genuine apostle covets nothing."[13] Greek writers generally despised self-aggrandizement, especially in orators and philosophers, and admired self-control.[14]

---

11. Schmidt, "דבר."

12. Like many Greek philosophers, Philo criticizes "the word-catchers and sophists who sell their tenets and arguments like any bit of merchandise in the market" (*Vit. Mos.* 2.212).

13. Schille, *Die Apostelgeschichte*, 125, my translation.

14. See, for example, Plutarch, *Moralia* 81D, 84E. Plutarch also admires Pericles, not only because he had δύναμις as a speaker but also because he was utterly disinterested and superior to bribes (Plutarch, *Lives* 3:15). In his essay "On Inoffensive Self-Praise," Plutarch deals with the matter of an orator's self-praise. In addition, he praises Python of Aenos for down-playing some great deed of his by saying it was the doing of some god, "I did but lend my arm" (Plutarch, *Moralia* 542F; cf. 816E). Peter and Paul would have received Plutarch's praise. Plutarch thinks that orators, in particular, should take every opportunity to quote Homer's "No god am I; why likenest thou me to the immortals?" (543D). The kings who are unwilling to be acclaimed gods or sons of gods are

Luke wants the reader to understand that Peter, by all standards, truly is a man of God and a genuine vessel of divine power. The reader already knows Peter's attitude from an earlier healing episode: "I have no silver and gold," he says (4:6).[15]

Simon recognizes Peter has access to the source of divine power and so he asks Peter "to pray for me to the Lord" (8:24). Intercession was a privilege of angels (e.g., Tob 12:15; 1QH 6:13; 1 Enoch 9:10; 15:2; Dan 6:2) and of the mighty heroes of Jewish tradition such as Abraham, Moses, and Enoch. Simon recognizes the status of Peter as a true man of God; Luke allows him to be placed in the same category as the heroes of Israel, if not of the angels themselves.

There is no doubt that Peter received the power Jesus had promised his disciples (λήμψεσθε δύναμιν) (1:8). Primarily, he is a messenger and proclaimer of words from God in fulfillment of Joel's prophecy (2:16). Filled with the Spirit, his words have power to change hearts (2:37-39); to heal (3:6; 8:34); to bring death (5:5, 10), but also to restore life (9:40); to curse (8:20); and to bring down the Spirit (10:44). As a genuine agent of God, Peter properly indicates that the power (δύναμις) rests not within himself (3:12) but in the God of Abraham, Isaac and Jacob and the fathers (3:13) and in the name of the Lord Jesus-the only name given to humans which can save and heal (4:12). This is a blatant claim to superiority over all other names, all other powers, all other divinely-inspired healers and savior-figures.

The power of Peter's words is seen most strikingly in the episode of Ananias and Sapphira (5:1-11). Peter exposes the deception of Ananias and Sapphira (5:4) who are not lying to mere men but to God whose holy Spirit gives Peter extraordinary perception. The power that is in Peter's words is awe-full. Gabriel, the angel of the Lord, can strike Zechariah dumb (Luke 1:20), and the angel of the Lord can strike Herod with a fatal disease (Acts 12:23), but on hearing Peter's words, Ananias and Sapphira drop dead in his presence. Pesch draws attention to the interesting parallel in the story of Susanna in which two witnesses bring incompatible testimony against Susanna and are told: "You have lied against your own head, for the angel of God has received the sentence from God and will immediately cut you in two" (vv. 55, 59).[16] In Acts, Peter is the angel of God who mediates the sentence of God on Ananias and Sapphira.

---

the ones whom people willingly honor (543D).

15. The use of verbs in 3:6 may well be significant. Peter does not possess (ὑπαρχειν) silver and gold, but he does have (ἔχειν) the name of Jesus to give because it has been given to him (4:12). The name and power of Jesus is not something that can be possessed like money.

16. Pesch, *Die Apostelgeschichte*, 1:196.

Predictably, the people respond with great fear (5:11; cf. Luke 2:9; 5:26; 7:16; 8:37) at what has been a divine epiphany. Some dare not join the apostles (5:12). The dare must be taken seriously. It is not that some decide not to join as if they were declining to take out membership in a local club. The verb (κολλάω) can imply table-fellowship (cf. 10:28). People dare not have fellowship with the apostles because of the power that lies within them (5:12). That this is what is to be understood is made clear from v. 15 where others think that Peter's shadow is power-filled enough to heal those across whom it might fall. Not surprisingly, the people were "magnifying them" (ἐμεγαλύνετο αὐτούς) (5:13) just as later some at Ephesus "magnified the name of the Lord Jesus" (ἐμεγαλύνετο τὸ ὄνομα) (19:17). Somewhat surprisingly, this magnifying of the apostles is allowed to stand without any modification or correction, and without any effort to redirect the praise to God. So thin is the line between God and God's agents that to magnify the agents is to magnify God. For Luke, Jesus (in Luke's gospel) and Peter (in Acts) are filled with the same divine power; and the response to both from the people is the same: amazement (Luke 4:22; 11:14; 24:41; Acts 2:7, 12; 3:10; 4:13; 8:14); and praise of God (Luke 2:20; 4:15; 5:25–26; 7:16; 13:13; 17:15; 18:43; 23:47; Acts 2:47; 3:8; 4:21; 11:18; 21:20; cf. 19:17). Indeed, Peter is depicted with a raw power that has none of the compassion that at least implicitly marks the Lukan Jesus (see Luke 7:13 of Jesus directly; and 10:33; 15:20 in his parables). And that power is in his speech.

The emphasis on Peter's speech and his status also come to the fore in his meeting with Cornelius. The Roman wants to hear Peter's words (ῥήματα, 10:22), and he worships Peter as if an angel (10:25). A little later, Cornelius says: "we are all here in the presence of God to hear everything which has been commanded to you by the Lord" (10:33), thus indicating that he understands Peter to be an agent who has commands (τὰ προστεταγμένα) from the Lord not dissimilar to the commands which Moses received from the Lord (cf. Luke 5:14; Mark 1:44). Peter is the spokesperson for God, the revealer of the will and commands of God.

The word and its speaker are also at the heart of the narrative dealing with Herod's death (12:20–23). Josephus gives a fuller version of that death[17] in which Herod, in a display of power and royalty, dons his royal robes and gives an oration, to which the populace responds: "It is the sound/voice of a god (θεοῦ φωνή), not of a human being" (12:22). In Josephus" account, it is the dress of Herod which astounds the masses and makes them think he is a god. Luke, however, draws attention to the speech of Herod. It is his speech that causes people to think he is the voice of a god; and, unlike the genuine

---

17. Josephus, *Ant.* 19.343-50.

men of God, Herod accepts the divine status offered him. He is struck down by an angel and dies (12:23): with the very next verse Luke states laconically: "And the word of the Lord increased and multiplied" (12:24). The word of the Lord, the voice of God, is heard in Peter's speech but not in Herod's.

III

Not surprisingly, the status of Peter is matched by Paul.[18] As Beker says, "Luke often portrays Paul as a 'divine man' (theios anêr) who incarnates the epiphany of God in this world."[19] So dominant are Paul and Peter in Acts that one could well argue that they constitute Luke's purpose for writing the second book.[20]

Paul is a chosen "vessel" (σκεῦος) of the Lord (9:15) and, like Peter, he is Spirit-filled, with a word of the Lord that all other sources of revelation must acknowledge. So Paul and Barnabas are "sent out by the Holy Spirit" (13:4) and, as if to accentuate their high status, Luke mentions that they have John with them as an "assistant" (ὑπηρέτης) (13:5). On Cyprus, Paul preaches the word and then receives a summons from Sergius Paulus the proconsul who "sought to hear the word of God" (13:7).[21] There is no reason to suggest that Sergius Paulus was "open and eager to hear the word of God" as if in contradistinction to "the duplicity of the Jewish magician and false prophet," as Dunn suggests.[22] It is just as likely that Sergius and Elymas are "in it together."

The emphasis on the word of God in this episode is obvious. Words have power, but that power is increased when spoken by someone of high status. Paul is "full of the holy spirit" (13:9), and so his word is power-full. It is a word which confronts Bar-Jesus (13:6–11) who is expressly called "a magos Jewish false-prophet" (μάγον ψευδοπροφήτην Ἰουδαῖον) as if to draw attention to his claim to have access to the will of God, in other words, to secret, divine revelation (13:6–12). As Bruce says, Elymas "claimed falsely

---

18. The parallels between Peter and Paul (and Jesus) are well-known. See Pesch, *Die Apostelgeschichte*, 145–46; Dunn, *Acts*, xiv.

19. Beker, *Heirs of Paul*, 53.

20. Rather curiously, Dunn does not include this as one of his seven possible purposes for Acts. See Dunn, *Acts*, xi–xiv.

21. Given the context, is it coincidental that Luke uses the verb ἐπιζητέω here? This verb "appears as one of the standard ingredients of the confession texts" in curses, and has the notion of calling on the gods to pursue a guilty party (Versnel, "Beyond Cursing," 78). Is there the suggestion that Sergius used some magic formula calling on divine help to track down Paul and bring him to his court?

22. Dunn, *Acts*, 176. It is unnecessary to give δέ in v. 8 the force of "but."

to be a medium of divine revelation."[23] But in the end, the false seer is led blinded at the word of the power-filled Paul. Like Peter before him (5:4, 9), Paul's word has the power to destroy all deceit. Elymas is told that "the hand of the Lord" is upon him and he will be blind (13:11). Being a Jew, Elymas knew the power of "the hand of the Lord" and has to acknowledge it, just as the magicians in Pharaoh's court acknowledged the "finger of God" (Exod 8:15; cf. Deut 3:24; 4:34; 7:8; Isa 8:11; Jer 15:17; Ezek 1:3 and many other passages). Blindness was one of the threatened punishments on Israel for living in breach of the covenant (Deut 28:28–29). Luke says Elymas "went about seeking people to lead him by the hand" (περάγων ἐζήτει χειραγωγούς) (13:11). The compounds of ἀγ- possibly are used to show that the tables are turned on Elymas. As a magos, he had the power to perform what Eitrem calls "the ἀγωγή ritual" which led victims to follow the wishes of the magic practitioner.[24] Now, Elymas himself seeks to be led.

Sergius, who presumably had previously shared the views of Elymas and possibly even summoned Paul to his court to prove him wrong, is impressed and believes. As proconsul, he knew the power of speech and may well have agreed with Plutarch that leadership of a people is leadership of those who are persuaded by speech (διὰ λόγου).[25] In addition, he undoubtedly knew a world full of seers claiming revelatory and oracular power, and so recognized a man filled with power when he saw him. Luke is again careful to say that Sergius acknowledges not Paul's power but the power of "the teaching of the Lord" (13:12). But the teaching of the Lord is inextricably bound up with the words of Paul. In fact, it is worth noting that when Paul curses Elymas, he does not invoke his God but speaks the curse directly. Sergius would have found this impressive indeed since cursing generally involved invoking the gods or daemons.[26]

He would have recognized, and Luke's audience with him, that Paul is no mere magician, but is in a superior category. His words are performative utterances because he is "of God."

This performative power of Paul's words is central also in the episode of Paul and Barnabas at Lystra (14:8–18). Here too it is the speaking of Paul that attracts attention: The crippled man listened to Paul "speaking" (λαλοῦντος) (14:9). The verb λαλεῖν in Acts often suggests an oracle; it is used of both God and angels (3:21; 5:20; 7:6, 38; 8:26; 10:7; 22:9; 23:9; 28:25); and is also used of glossalia (2:4; 10:46; 19:6). It was Paul's word that heals him

---

23. Bruce, *Book of Acts*, 249.
24. Eitrem, "Dreams and Divination," 175–87.
25. Plutarch, *Moralia* 802D.
26. See, for example, Versnel, "Beyond Cursing," 60–106.

(14:10). At first glance, this is out of character in Acts. In Jerusalem, Peter first invokes the name of Jesus and makes it very clear that he is performing the healing act by Jesus" power and not by his own (3:6, 16; 4:10). This does not happen here, with the result that there is an understandable response from the locals: Paul and Barnabas are the gods come down in human likeness (14:11). Paul does not act as a mediator or petitioner of power, but as the source of power itself. As suggested already, if Paul had called on the name of Jesus, then he would have been considered a magician and not a god. Again, it is not unlikely that Luke wishes to draw a daring distinction between Paul and other known magicians. Paul is not a magician. He is superior to them; and this the local Lystrans perceive.

Luke states that Paul was called Hermes because he was the chief speaker (ὁ ἡγούμενος τοῦ λόγου) (14:12). It is Paul's word—which has the power to heal—which is considered to be of the gods. And Paul makes it clear that the ultimate purpose for his visit is not to heal but to "bring you good news" (14:15). On the surface, the point Luke seems to make is that while Paul's speech is clearly impressive because it has the power to heal, Paul is not a god visiting in human form, but a mortal ambassador empowered and sent by the living God. Like Peter, Paul rejects divine status. But this self-deprecation confirms in the reader's mind that Paul is indeed "of God." Kahl is right to say that "Paul makes it clear that he and Barnabas are mere M[ediators of] N[uminous] P[ower]s, and that his miraculous act should lead them to recognize God as the sole B[earer of] N[uminous] P[ower]."[27] But Kahl's talk of "mere mediators" needs to be understood vis-a-vis God. Paul's rejection of divine status confirms that he is a true mediator of God's power.

Despite the dramatic action expressing disapproval (14:14), so dynamic and effective is Paul's word that the people still need to be restrained from offering sacrifices (14:18). Luke has done what is prescribed and had Paul reject the suggestion that he is a god; and so he does not need to admonish this behavior. Paul is not a god, but the Lystrans are right to perceive his high status as a vehicle of divine power. Luke is saying: "Even the pagans perceive that Paul is "of God." They misunderstand, but they know the divine source of his words and of their power."

Further, Luke leaves no doubt that the traditional gods do not have the same power as the creating God of Israel (14:15-17). The rain-bringing God is the living God of whom Paul is a messenger. Luke may have been familiar with the myth of Orion's birth, in which Zeus and Hermes appeared to Hyrieus, a poor bee-keeper and farmer, who was granted a son after sacrificing

---

27. Kahl, *New Testament Miracle Stories*, 86.

a bull, making water in its hide, and burying it in his wife's grave. The child born was Orion, the bringer of rain.²⁸

The Lystra episode is paralleled on Malta (28:1–6). Paul is immune to the attack of a "viper" (28:3). The Greek word for "viper" is ἔχιδνα. Echidne is also the name of an autochthonous goddess in Greek mythology who Hesiod describes as a half nymph, half huge snake with speckled skin, who eats raw flesh beneath the earth, and who dies not nor grows old.²⁹ Possibly, the locals understood the creature which wrapped itself around Paul's hand to be the embodiment of Echidne. They thought Paul would die—not [only] from the snake's poison but because he was singled out by the feared goddess. When Paul does not show any signs of suffering, the response of the locals is that he is a god (28:6). Luke does not correct the idea. Paul's very body has a power that immunes it against the power of Echidne. Paul has heard from the God "of whom I am" that he will arrive in Rome (27:24); it is his God who determines his fate and not Dike (Δική) as the locals believe (28:4). Paul is "of God" and he possesses a divine power that enables him to both withstand the threat of Echidne and to heal the sick (28:8). The locals are right to honor him with honors (28:10). It is another case of the pagans perceiving the truth about Paul. In this context, it is also noteworthy that the boat carrying Paul to Rome has the figurehead of the Dioskouri, protector-twins of sailors.³⁰ The point again is made: The gods serve the man of God (28:11).

At Philippi, another clash of revelatory power occurs when Paul meets the Pythian oracle (16:16). The meeting takes place as "we were going to the place of prayer" (16:16). Luke draws attention to the two rival loci of revelation: Paul, who goes to pray to find the will of God, and a woman who has a "spirit of divination," a pythonic spirit (πνεῦμα πύθωνα). The woman is a channel for the divine oracles (μαντευομένη); Luke claims Paul is a channel of the oracles of the Lord. As the pagans of Lystra and Malta perceive correctly, so also here the oracle correctly identifies Paul as a messenger of the Most High God (16:17), confirming Luke's point that even the oracles of the pagans know the origin of Paul's power. The woman also knows the divine origin of Paul's proclamation (καταγγέλλουσιν) (cf. 17:18) and identifies it correctly as "the way of salvation" (ὁδὸς σωτηρίας) (16:17). This phrase may reflect the tradition that Apollo followed the wounded

---

28. See Graves, *Greek Myths*, 152. He cites Servius on Virgil, *Aeneid* 1.539; Ovid, *Fasti* 5.537; Hyginus, *Poetic Astronomy* 2.34.

29. Hesiod, *Theogony* 297.

30. Theissen, *Miracle Stories*, 101.

Python as he fled "along the road which we now call the Sacred Way" (κατὰ τὴν ὁδὸν, ἣν νῦν ἱερὰν καλοῦμεν).[31]

Paul (the oracle of God) addresses the spirit (the oracle of Apollo) and commands it "in the name of Jesus Christ" to leave the woman, which it does, as it must (16:18). Her lords (κύριοι, the power terminology can be noted) are naturally upset, but their power is broken and their source of gain gone. The Pythian oracle is silenced. Once again, the two points are made: Paul is "of God"; and other "lords" acknowledge that his word has liberating and healing power.

The high status that Luke grants the apostles is implied further in the episode of Paul and Silas in prison at Philippi. They are depicted at prayer, praising God (16:25) in the middle of the night. This reflects the eternal nightly practice of the angels (T. Levi 3:8) and the behavior of the ideal man like Moses.[32] When there is an earthquake, Paul speaks as one in control of the situation (16:28) while the jailer is alarmed. He acknowledges Paul's control and so addresses him and Silas as "lords" (κύριοι) (16:30-31). This form of address is used elsewhere in Acts only of angels and of Jesus (9:5, 6, 10, 13; 10:4, 14; 11:8; 22:8, 10, 19; 26:15). The jailer acknowledges the status of the apostles;[33] but the boundary is appropriately maintained, and he is immediately directed to believe in the Lord Jesus (τὸν κύριον Ἰησοῦν) (16:31). And once again, Paul speaks the word of the Lord effectively (16:32).

At Athens, where Paul is strangely less effective, he is recognized as a speaker from the gods: "He seems to be a "preacher of foreign divinities"" (καταγγελεὺς ξένων δαιμονίων) (17:18). If the genitive is subjective, it suggests that the foreign divinities have sent Paul as their herald. This would then be similar to the Lystran understanding of Paul. Even if "of foreign divinities" (ξένων δαιμονίων) is better understood as an objective genitive, Paul still is depicted as someone with a revelation about these strange gods. The less flattering identification of him as a babbler or chatterer (σπερμολόγος) also highlights his speech. Through Paul's Areopagus address, Luke has taken the opportunity to claim again that the revelation of the true God comes through the creator God of Israel who has appointed Jesus as judge by the resurrection; and that all other gods are, at best, pale reflections of the true God (17:22-31).

In Acts 19, Luke continues to walk the narrow line between portraying Paul as a source of power himself and as a mediator of God's power. Paul lays

---

31. Plutarch, *Quaest. Rom.* 293.

32. Philo, *Virtues* 72-75.

33. "The jailor perceives in the prisoners divine lords and pays them their due honor" (Schille, *Die Apostelgeschichte*, 348, my translation).

his hands on the twelve disciples at Ephesus and the holy spirit comes on them (19:6); his clothes have healing powers (19:12); and his name is known to the demon (19:15) who overpowers the Jewish exorcists (19:16). These expressions of power are not allowed to stand alone; Luke heads them with: "God did extraordinary miracles by the hands of Paul" (19:11). Paul's hands are "the hand of God." But Paul is blatantly portrayed as power-full.

The frequent references to "greatness" in Acts 19 indicates that Luke perceives a struggle between the greatness of the Lord Jesus (κύριος Ἰησοῦς) and the greatness claimed for Lady Artemis (κύρια Ἄρτεμις) and other traditional powers in Ephesus. Magical writings are destroyed; "the word grew by the might (κράτος) of the Lord" (19:20); and it is the name of the Lord Jesus that is magnified (ἐμεγαλύνετο) (19:17). In the riot of the Artemis cultists, Demetrius expresses the fear that the greatness (μεγαλειότης) of Artemis will diminish as a result of Paul's preaching (19:27). In order to maintain that greatness, the cry "Great (Μεγάλη) is Artemis of the Ephesians" goes up as a ritualistic chant against the threat (19:28, 34). In addition, the *grammateus* calls Artemis "great" (μεγάλη) (19:35). Artemis Ephesia was famous for her epiphanies. An edict of 162 CE mentions that many shrines and sanctuaries and cults of Artemis Ephesia had been erected and founded because of her many manifestations (ἐπιφανίαι).[34] The greatness of Artemis was known throughout the world, as Demetrius rhetorically claims (19:27). But Demetrius also acknowledges that the word of Paul has changed the opinions of many people as to whether gods made by hands are indeed gods (19:26). It is the speech of Paul that is doing the damage. While there is no demise of Artemis at Ephesus, the *grammateus* at least acknowledges the power of Paul's God and allows it to exist side by side with the greatness of Artemis (19:35–40). As a source of revelation, Paul stands with the best of them, says Luke. And he does so because he is "of God."

In sum, Luke intends Paul and Peter to be understood, like Jesus, as heroes in the mould of Israel's prophets and as men of divine power. As Hengel says, "What marked out the wise men and prophets of Israel's earlier history were their "heroic" personalities, which manifested themselves above all in their astonishing miracles."[35] As a mother recognizes Elijah as "the man of God" (ἄνθρωπος τοῦ θεοῦ) because of his power to revive her child (1 Kgs 17:24), so Peter and Paul are intended to be recognized as "men of God" by similar acts of resuscitation (9:41; 20:10). Their words, their actions, and their very bodies are dynamic instruments of the living God.

---

34. Horsley, *New Documents*, 4:74. For a more detailed study of Paul's work in Ephesus, see Strelan, *Paul, Artemis*, 132–43.

35. Hengel, *Judaism and Hellenism*, 1:136.

IV

Because Peter and Paul are "of God," it is to be expected that angels will be on their side. Angels liberate Peter and Paul from prison, and appear to them to give encouragement and direction. For Luke, such angelic activity is a sign of God's kingdom. As is well known, angels feature in the Lukan birth narratives (1:11, 26; 2:9), and some women see "a vision of angels" (ὀπτασίαν ἀγγέλων) at the tomb of the proclaimed-alive Jesus (24:23). Angelophanies are a verificatory sign of God's presence and activity.

In Acts 5:19, the apostles have been imprisoned by the Sadducean high priest in an attempt to prevent the proclamation of the word (4:18), but in the night, an angel of the Lord (ἄγγελος κυρίου) opens the prison doors for the disciples (5:19). There is a delicious irony here. The Sadducees do not "believe in" angels nor in their intervention in human affairs, so Luke relishes telling of an angel inexplicably (to the Sadducees) releasing the prisoners. That the angel comes at night (διὰ νύκτος) is typical in Luke-Acts (cf. Luke 2:9; Acts 16:9; 18:9; 23:11; 27:23) and these nocturnal visits parallel angelophanies in Jewish tradition (Gen 26:24; 31:24; 40:5; 41:11). The angel of the Lord does not appear in dreams,[36] but comes to liberate the apostles and to commission them (πορεύεσθε καὶ σταθέντες) to continue speaking (λαλεῖτε) (5:20). In two brief verses, Luke makes his point: The apostles are "of God" as evidenced by the protection and commission granted them by God's angels.

The same point is made in the second angel rescue (12:6–11) which also has many of the literary and narrative features of angelophanies. Peter is in prison (12:4); security is underlined: The doors are locked, guards attend the sleeping Peter and the doors. The angel of the Lord (ἄγγελος κυρίου) stands in Peter's cell and a light shines. Cells and darkness and guards do not bar the angel of the Lord from immediate access to the man of God. Herod plans Peter's death (12:4), but it is God who controls and directs the lives of his servants. The angel takes the unusual step of striking Peter on the side (πατάξας τὴν πλευράν) the same verb is used of the angel's action against Herod in 12:23 (cf. Gen 8:21; Exod 9:15; 12:23; Num 14:12; Deut 28:22; 2 Kgs 6:18; 2 Macc 9:5).

---

36. It is striking that this is so, given the frequency of dream visitations in Greek literature. In fact, the common nouns for dreams, ὄναρ and ὄνειρος, are rarely found in the New Testament. Matthew uses the first; the second is not found at all. Later Christian writers saw dreams as opportunities for deceiving daemons to appear, claiming to be sent from the true God, so dreams are not to be trusted as being from God (see Justin, *Apol.* 18.2; Irenaeus, *AH* 16.3; Ps-Clern, *Hom* 9.15).

Usually, the verb πατάσσειν implies a severe, even mortal, blow rather than a gentle tap or prod. It probably is meant to indicate the power of the angel that protects Peter.[37] The chains fall from his hands. And with unusual detail, the angel tells Peter to get dressed and to follow out of the prison into the street. The details suggest that Peter has no autonomous power, but his very actions, in fact his being, are determined and dictated by an angel of the Lord. It is possible that Peter experiences a metamorphosis (cf. 8:39) that allows him to pass unseen and unquestioned from his cell into the streets. This suggestion has some merit in that Peter himself did not know what had truly happened: "[H]e thought he was seeing a vision" (ἐδόκει ὅραμα βλέπειν) (12:9); and only later does he "come to himself" (ἐν ἑαυτῷ γενόμενος) (12:11). But he did not imagine the angel or even see it in a vision it was a true and real experience (ἀληθές ... ἀληθῶς) (12:9, 11). Again, whatever is thought to have happened, the point is clear: "The Lord has sent out his angel" to rescue Peter (12:11). The angels are on his side.

The reader of Acts will not be surprised by this. Already the opening chapteris are spiced with references to angels and visions. For forty days, Jesus had been "showing himself" (ὀπτανόμενος) (1:3) to people. The verb is appropriate for heavenly visions (Acts 26:19; Luke 1:22; 24:23) and is related to the noun ὀπτασία which refers to a vision or revelation (cf. 26:19; 2 Cor 12:1). Forty days is the period Moses (Exod 24:18), Elijah (1 Kgs 19:8), and Jesus (Luke 4:2) spent in a context of receiving revelations. There is also angelophanic language used of Jesus in these opening verses: Jesus stands (παρέστησεν) (1:3; cf. 1:10; 11:13; 27:23; Ezek 10:3; Zech 1:11; Luke 1:11; Rev 7:9; 8:2-3; 11:1); and Jesus goes into heaven (cf. Luke 2:15) and is enveloped by the Presence (1:9-10). As heavenly beings came to the shepherds with the announcement of Jesus" birth (Luke 2:9), so at his resurrection (Luke 24:4) and his ascension into heaven, angels come with an announcement. to the disciples (1:10). That the two men of 1:10 are not human figures but heavenly beings or angels is clear from their apparel (cf. Luke 24:4), from their stance; and from the use of "behold" (ἰδού) which Luke uses frequently to indicate the presence or message of an angel (Luke 1:20, 31, 36; 2:9, 10; 24:4, 13; Acts 10:30; 12:7; 27:24). It is not impossible that they are to be understood as Enoch and Elijah-the two prophets and visionaries who in the tradition had become angelic messengers of God. In these very opening verses of Acts, Luke introduces Theophilus to his theme: The disciples are men in the company of God's angels.

---

37. Compare the vision of Jacob concerning Judah that "a powerful angel accompanied me everywhere so that no one might touch me" (T. Judah 3:10).

Angels issue directions. So Philip is directed towards a meeting with the Ethiopian (8:26); Saul is directed to go into Damascus (9:6); and Ananias is directed to meet Paul (9:11). Interesting is the language used in these messages: "Rise and go" (ἀνάστηθι καὶ πορεύου) (8:26) (ἀναστὰς πορεύθητι) (9:11; cf. 9:14); "rise and enter" (ἀνάστηθι καὶ εἴσελθε) (9:6; cf. 26:16); "rise, go down and go" (ἀναστάς κατάβηθι καὶ πορεύου) (10:20). It is the language used to describe the action of angels in Jewish literature (cf. Joseph and Asenath 14:8, 11) and it is the language of the call formula used by God in addressing the heroes and prophets of Israel (e.g., Gen 28:2; 31:13; Josh 1:2; Jer 1:17; 13:6; Ezek 3:22; Jonah 1:2; 3:2).

Finally, an angel appears to Paul with words of encouragement. In Acts 27:23, Paul says he has seen an angel of the God "of whom I am and whom I serve." Paul knows himself to be "of God." As Dunn points out, "the God-centeredness of the brief message is striking, as so often earlier in Acts."[38] Here again the angel characteristically stands next to (παρέστη) Paul and says: μὴ φοβοῦ, Παῦλε. The exhortation, followed by the name, is a common form of address in angelophanies, visions, and oracles (cf. Gen 15:1; Isa 44:2; Dan 10:12; *Jos. Asen.* 14:11; 3 Bar 7:6). So angels serve to assure, to protect, and to direct the men of God.

V

The apostles experience a further sign of God's presence and direction: They see visions. Acts is the only New Testament writing to use the term "vision" (ὅραμα) apart from one instance in Matthew where Jesus refers to the "transfiguration" experience as an ὅραμα (17:9).[39] That the apostles see visions puts them in the same rare category with the heroes of Israel's past. Abraham (Gen 15:1 LXX) and Jacob (Gen 46:2 LXX) both see visions at significant moments in their personal lives and in the history of Israel. Moses" life-changing experience is referred to as an ὅραμα (Exod 3:3 LXX). Samuel, the great early prophet of Israel, had his life shaped by an initial ὅραμα which he is afraid to report to Eli (1 Sam 3:15 LXX). In fact, on a general level, God is said to have rescued Israel out of Egypt not only with his mighty arm but also with "great visions" (ὁράμασιν μεγάλοις) (Deut 4:34; 26:8 LXX). Luke, steeped in his Jewish history and scriptures, has

---

38. Dunn, *Acts*, 340.

39. Artemidoros says a horama is something that is actually seen and not imagined (1.2.5 19). *Horamata* were significant in the actions and decisions of well-known Greek and Romans. Brutus before crossing from Asia into Europe saw a ὅραμα at night in which a φάσμα stood at his side and spoke to him (Appian, *Bell. Civ.* 4.134).

his new heroes experience similar visions and so have their claims to be "of God" validated. To add to the parallels, both Abraham and Jacob have visions accompanied by the message of encouragement: "Fear not!" (μὴ φοβοῦ) (Gen 15:1; 46:3). Paul is similarly encouraged at very significant moments in his life (Acts 18:9; 27:24).

In most modern, Western circles, one would keep such visions to one's self for fear of being regarded as unstable. But in Acts, such visions are acted upon as commands of the Lord. Paul's vision of the man from Macedonia is his call to go to that region (16:9). Cornelius's vision (10:3, 30) means he immediately sends for Peter (10:7). Ananias hesitates at the command to visit Paul (9: 10) but he sees no choice but to obey. Peter's vision (10:17, 19; cf. 11:5) must be obeyed despite its mind-changing demand. That Peter (11:5) and Cornelius (10:30) both repeat and report on their visions suggests that their audience would have been impressed and that it authorized their subsequent actions. The Lord appears to Paul in a vision (ἐν ὁράματι, 18:9) with words of encouragement about the prospects in Corinth with the result that Paul stays eighteen months in that city (18:11). The "heavenly vision" (οὐρανία ὀπτασία), as Luke describes Paul's Damascus experience (22:17-21; 26:19), is also one he cannot disobey. The word of God, received in vision, determines the actions of Paul. Such obedience to the commands of God puts Paul (and Peter) in the category of Philo's virtuous men. As Philo says: "The actions of the wise man are in no respect different from the divine commands . . . the words of God are the actions of the wise man."[40]

Such visions validate Luke's claims that his heroes are "of God" and that God was doing something wondrous in Israel and among the nations. Visions validated the prophets. According to Num 12:6, "If there is a prophet among you, I will make myself known to him in a vision (ἐν τῷ ὁράματι); I will speak with him in a dream." Isaiah refers to some of his oracles as ὁράματα (21:1, 11; 23:1). But it is the apocalyptic Daniel who has visions aplenty (1:17; 2:1, 7, 19, 26, 36, 45; 4:25; 7:1, 13, 15; 8:1, 2, 13, 15, 17, 26, 27; 9:24; 10:1). What is particularly significant about these prophetic visions is that they reveal the word of the Lord to the nations and concerning the nations. In Acts, Peter and Paul have visions precisely when they are given a word to go to the nations. Peter is sent to Cornelius through a vision (10:17) and likewise, Paul is commanded to go to Macedonia through a similar experience (16:9).

---

40. Philo, *Migr.* 129-30.

VI

In Acts, Peter and Paul are vessels of God. Unlike Paul, who, at least in certain contexts, insisted that the power of God worked in very fragile earthen vessel (2 Cor 3:7–12), Luke depicts that same dynamic power present in power-filled vessels-men who are of divine (θεῖοι)[41] status.

This is demonstrated by their performative words and power-laden actions; by the power that is given even to their bodies and clothes and shadows; and it is also demonstrated through their self-deprecating responses to veneration from others and through their refusal to make any financial gain out of the power that is in them; and it is demonstrated by the angelophanies they experience and by the visions they are granted. In a world impressed by power and one in which such power was seen as "divine," Luke offers his (powerless?) audience powerful heroes whose words and work are "of God" and so cannot be invalidated. Rival mediums and rival powers experienced the power of God in these men to their loss. The will and work of God cannot be successfully opposed. Gamaliel's hunch proved correct.

---

41. It is now generally accepted that the category "divine men" (θεῖοι ἄνδρες) was not a known category in the first century CE. See, for example, Holladay, *Theios Aner*. This challenges the earlier work of Bieler, *ΘΕΙΟΣ ΑΝΗΡ*.

The Running Prophet (Acts 8:30)

THERE ARE A NUMBER of physical gestures and movements performed by the central characters in Acts which are easily passed over and ignored by the reader. For example, Peter and Paul both "stare" (3:4; 14:9), Paul speaks in "a loud voice" (14:10), and "shakes his hand" before a speech (21:40). While these are not significant actions in themselves, they are often consistent with and contribute to the overall portrayal of Luke's major characters. To ignore them, as is generally the case in scholarship, may mean that some of the subtlety and depth of Luke's writing goes unnoticed.

In Acts 8:30, Philip is said to have run (προσδραμών) and heard the Ethiopian eunuch reading Isaiah the prophet. This running by Philip is an example of a seemingly innocuous action which, I am suggesting, is complementary to Luke's portrait of him as one who, like a prophet of Israel, carries out a mission under the impulse of the Spirit. Running is characteristic of an inspired and commissioned prophet and of priests and others called to cultic service.

Prophets as Runners

As one would expect, the verb "to run" (τρέχειν and its compounds) is used in the LXX and in the NT in the common sense of moving at a quick pace (e.g., 1 Sam 17:51; Acts 21:32); and it is well-known that the running of an athlete is used by Paul as a metaphor for the Christian life and struggle (1 Cor 9:24, 26), a metaphor taken up by later Christian writers (e.g., Ignatius, *Eph.* 3:2; *Phil.* 2:2). Again as expected, "running" is used to describe the movement of messengers (e.g., 2 Sam 18:19–30) and couriers (2 Chr 30:6, 10). Probably less well-known is that runners (הרצים [Heb]; οἱ παρατρέχοντες [LXX])[1] often accompanied the chariots of war-leaders, kings, and noblemen particularly in war (1 Kgs 1:5; 14:27–28; 2 Kgs 10:25; 11:4). These runners discharged any duty in the leader's service. Along similar lines, runners also featured in festive celebratory processions when they seem to have had the particular role of herald (Gen 41:43; Est 6:11).

---

1. Often translated as "guards."

There is also the running of a prophet, and it is this characteristic to which I draw attention. It is not that the depiction of Philip as prophet hinges on this one verb (προσδραμών); the point is rather that the action of running adds to or at least complements that portrayal. That Luke in Acts 8:26-40 portrays Philip in the mould of the prophets of Jewish tradition can be easily demonstrated.

It is Elijah particularly who seems to be the model. Like Elijah, Philip is associated with Samaria (1 Kgs 18-21; Acts 8:5); both are directed by a heavenly word to go to out-of-the-way places (Philip to the desert road heading to Gaza [8:26]; Elijah to Zarephath [1 Kgs 17:8]), both seem to be able to move with rapid speed (Elijah to Jezreel [1 Kgs 18:46]; Philip to the Gaza road [8:27]; and later to Azotus [8:40]). Both are snatched away, not seen again, but found in a another place (Philip in Azotus [8:39-40]; Elijah into heaven [2 Kgs 2:11]).[2] These parallels have been noted by scholars, especially in the "snatching" by the Spirit: "Die Anspielung auf die Entrückung des Elias scheint klar."[3] Munck also thinks the episode is "recalling the account of Elijah";[4] Dunn suggests that in the snatching by the Spirit, "Luke may have had in mind 1 Kings 18:12 and 2 Kings 2:16 which envisage similar sudden transporation."[5] About the overall episode, Rackham writes: "Like a new Elijah, then, Philip is divinely directed."[6] There is no need to elaborate. Put simply, Elijah was a spirit-inspired prophet, directed by the word of the Lord. So too, for Luke, is Philip.[7]

In Acts 8:26-40, from beginning to end, Philip carries out his mission at the direction and impulse of the Spirit. As Jervell rightly says: "Das Geschehen wird bis ins letzte Detail vom Himmel bestimmt. Nicht aus eigener Initiative handelt Philippus."[8] The episode begins with Philip receiving direction from the angel of the Lord (ἄγγελος κυρίου) (v. 26) who speaks (ἐλάλησεν) to Philip and tells him to "rise and go" (ἀνάστηθι καὶ πορεύου) to the road from Jerusalem to Gaza (v. 26). This command is given with precisely the same verbs as those used in the word of the Lord to Elijah (1 Kgs 17:9 LXX). Suddenly, Philip is on the Gaza road. However he got there,

---

2. Compare also Obadiah's complaint that "the Spirit of the Lord will carry you whither I know not" (1 Kgs 18:12).
3. Jervell, *Die Apostelgeschichte*, 274.
4. Munck, *Acts*, 79.
5. Dunn, *Acts*, 115. The snatching is paralleled in Ezek 3:12.
6. Rackham, *Acts*, 121.
7. Not surprisingly, his virgin-daughters are said to be προφητεύουσαι (Acts 21:8-9). One can also note that Luke twice says the eunuch was reading Ἡσαίαν τὸν προφήτην (8:28, 30).
8. Jervell, *Die Apostelgeschichte*, 272.

whether by a translocation by the Spirit or otherwise, the reader is meant to understand that he did not choose to go there. Like many a prophet before him, Philip does not act as a free decision-making agent.

In passing, there is debate as to whether the phrase κατὰ μεσημβρίαν (v. 26) refers to the direction "south" or to the time of day, "noon." The latter is rejected by some because that time of day is deemed too hot for travel: "der Mittag ist keine Reisezeit."[9] Others, conversely, see that very impractical time for travel as a sign of Philip's calling: God calls prophets to do strange things.[10] Both arguments are weakened by Conzelmann's reminder that the matter of heat and inconvenient time of travel would obviously depend on the time of the year.[11] In any case, there is another, and I think more plausible, reason for taking it as a time reference. In Acts, at least, the noon hour seems to be a time for revelation, and since it was not an hour for prescribed prayer, one might suggest for extraordinary revelation. So Paul, according to his reports in Acts 22:6 and 26:13, receives his revelation and call while travelling at noon (the heat clearly not a problem!). The same noon hour (the sixth hour) is the time of Peter's revelatory vision which leads to the conversion of Cornelius (10:9). Outside of Acts, in John 4:6, Jesus and the Samaritan woman meet at noon, a meeting during which significant revelation takes place, and as a consequence of which the Samaritans conclude that Jesus is "the savior of the world" (4:42). These three examples taken together would suggest that the call to a mission to non-Jews is given at the noon hour. Here is a fourth example: Philip is told to travel at the noon hour because he is to provide a revelation of the scriptures to an Ethiopian.[12]

While many scholars have implicitly or explicitly noted the prophetic, Elijah-like characteristics of Philip, his running is not seen to be related. Instead, Barrett interprets the running literally: "Philip quickened his pace,"[13] which indicates he sees no significance in the movement. Pesch implies a similar understanding: "Dazu muß Philippus 'hinzulaufen,'" that is, in order to catch up with the chariot.[14] The action is ignored by Bruce,[15] Dunn,[16]

---

9. Bauernfeind, *Kommentar*, 128.

10. Barrett, *Acts*, 1:427.

11. Conzelmann, *Die Apostelgeschichte*, 55.

12. For examples of revelation at noon in Jewish legend, see Ginzberg, *Legends*, esp. 3.92. Of course, one might also consider the canonical Gospel references to midday or the sixth hour as the beginning of a period of darkness during Jesus' crucifixion (Matt 27:45; Mark 15:33; Luke 24:44–45; cf. John 19:14; Gos Pet 5:15).

13. Barrett, *Acts*, 427.

14. Pesch, *Die Apostelgeschichte*, 291.

15. Bruce, *Book of Acts*, 175; *Acts*, 191.

16. Dunn, *Acts*, 114.

Lake and Jackson,[17] Haenchen,[18] Jervell,[19] and many other commentators. Earlier scholars tended to see Philip's running as "rightly taken to indicate the eagerness with which Philip obeyed."[20]

But the point is that Philip does not run voluntarily; his is not a willing eagerness or obedience but rather a spirit-compelled running. He is prompted by the Spirit (τὸ πνεῦμα) to run to the chariot of the eunuch (8:29). As Rackham says, it is "under a sudden divine impulse."[21] It is inspired running, the sacred running of a prophet.

Philip's inspired running parallels that of Elijah who runs (ἔτρεχεν) with supernormal speed ahead of Ahab's chariot and reaches Jezreel before him (1 Kgs 18:46). He does so having had "the hand of the Lord" upon him (χεὶρ κυρίου ἐπὶ τὸν Ηλιου) (LXX). Or as Josephus tells it, "the prophet, being inspired by God (γενόμενος ἔνθεος), ran along with (συνέδραμε) the king's chariot to Jezreel" (*Ant.* 8.346). Lindblom believes that the phrase "the hand of the Lord" in the prophetic narratives is an expression for an ecstatic fit.[22] It would seem that Philip's running is of a similar ilk.

The notion that running might be inspired by a spirit is also present in other NT examples. In Mark 5:6, the demoniac runs and worships Jesus. It is no coincidence that "running" (ἔδραμεν) and "worshipping" (προσεκύνησεν) are linked, since running is also regarded as a cultic action in some Jewish traditions, as will be seen below.[23] Mark 9:15 also hints at ecstatic, if not cultic or ritualistic, running as the "whole crowd" was amazed (ἐξεθαμβήθησαν) by a healing performed by Jesus and "running, they greeted him" (προστρέχοντες ἠσπάζοντο αὐτόν)—greeting being a solemn, ritualistic action. On another occasion, a similarly ecstatic crowd (πᾶς ὁ λαὸς ... ἔκθαμβοι) seized Peter and John and ran with them (συνέδραμεν) into the stoa (Acts 3:11).

But to return to the running of a prophet: There are a few passages in the OT which suggest that running is characteristic of a prophet and conveys the notion of carrying out a divine commission. Clear is Jer 23:21: "I did not send the prophets, yet they ran; I did not speak to them yet they

---

17. Lake and Foakes-Jackson, *Beginnings*, 4:96.

18. Haenchen, *Acts*, 311. Haenchen does acknowledge Philip's running by stating that it is possible to keep abreast with a slow-moving carriage.

19. Jervell, *Die Apostelgeschichte*, 272.

20. Knowling, *Acts*, 223; cf. "Running means prompt obedience" (Bauernfeind, "τρέχω ktl."

21. Rackham, *Acts*, 122.

22. Lindblom, *Prophecy*, 48.

23. It is common in English to speak of someone running "like a madman" or "running amok."

prophesied." This quite explicitly understands running and prophecy as synonymous or at least as associated behavior.[24]

In addition, a heavenly commission may include the command to run. This is explicit in Zech 2:4 where an angel is commissioned by another angel to "run and tell" (Δράμε καὶ λάλησεν) (2:8 LXX). Here too the sense is not only that of urgency, but of a divinely commissioned task. This notion is strengthened by the use of the noun δρόμος in Acts. John the Baptist is said to have "fulfilled the course" (ἐπλήρου . . . τὸν δρόμον) (Acts 13:25a) which is said to have been to prepare for the coming one (13:24, 25b); and Paul wants to "accomplish the course" (τελειῶσαι τὸν δρόμον)[25] which is then explicitly interpreted to be "the ministry (τὴν διακονίαν) which I received from the Lord Jesus" (20:24). Both John and Paul are seen as being commissioned to fulfill a "run," that is, a holy service. This notion would also seem to be implied in the reference to Jesus as the "forerunner (πρόδρομος) for us" in Heb 6:20.

Since prophets and other commissioned agents run and have a course to complete, one expects to read that the word of the Lord "runs" and has a course set for it. So Ps 147:15 says that the word "runs swiftly" (ἕως τάχους δραμεῖται ὁ λόγος αὐτοῦ) (147:4 LXX) and the author of 2 Thessalonians asks his readers/audience to pray so that "the word of the Lord should run" (ἵνα ὁ λόγος τοῦ κυρίου τρέχῃ) (3:1). Obedience to that word of the Lord is often then expressed in the metaphor of running, closely paralleling the more common "walk" as a metaphor for the pattern of behavior consistent with the will of God. So Ps 119:32: "I will run in the way of thy commandments" (ὁδὸν ἐντολῶν σου ἔδραμον) (Ps 118:32 LXX). If such running implies following a course of life as a sacred calling, then the sentence "those who wait for the Lord . . . shall run (δραμοῦνται) and not grow weary" (Isa 40:31) can be interpreted as a promise to be sustained in sacred service.[26] It was a metaphor continued by some Christian writers, as δραμὼν ὁδὸν ἀληθείας in Odes Sol. 11:3 clearly indicates.

That running indicates not only prophetic activity but also priestly and cultic behavior can be illustrated from ancient Jewish literature. For example, in Num 16:46-47, because Yahweh threatened to inflict Israel with a plague, Moses commands Aaron to take fire and incense quickly into

---

24. Looking at Jer 23:10 as well, Holladay tentatively suggests running is the "stylized behavior" of prophets. See Holladay, *Jeremiah*, 637.

25. In both cases, it might be best to omit any personal pronoun as if the course were John's or Paul's. The particular δρόμος has been chosen for them. A parallel is in Heb 12:1, which encourages: "Let us run the contest that has been set before us" (τρέχωμεν τὸν προκείμενον ἡμῖν ἀγῶνα).

26. "Waiting for the Lord" also probably indicates cultic activity.

the assembly to make atonement. "So Aaron took it as Moses said and ran into the midst of the assembly" (ἔδραμεν εἰς τὴν συναγωγήν) (Num 17:12 LXX) and the plague was averted. Further, David is said to run (δραμεῖν) to Bethlehem to carry out family sacrifices (1 Sam 20:6). Interesting also is 2 Chr 35:13 which refers to the priests "running" (ἔδραμον) with the sacrificed meat to all the people. And in Hag 1:9, Yahweh complains that cultic duties in his house are ignored while everyone runs (רצים [Heb]; διώκετε [LXX]) to their own house, and so, by implication, neglects the "running" to the Lord's house.

In noncanonical Jewish texts, there is further evidence that running was used as a metaphor—or literally—for cultic service. In the Song of Songs 1:17, the line which reads "our rafters are pine" is interpreted in the Rabbah on that Song: "the place on which the priests *ran* was made of pine."[27] In addition, "running together" (συντρέχειν) is sometimes used to refer to the coming together of the people for a holy festival. So Josephus refers to "an immense crowd running together" (συνέδραμεν . . . πλῆθος ἄπαιρον) from all over Israel at the Pentecost feast (*Wars* 2.43). He also says that the Feast of the Tabernacles "happened to occur at the same time as" (συνέδραμε δ' εἰς τὸν αὐτὸν χρόνον καὶ ὁ τῆς σκηνοπηγίας καιρὸς ἑορτῆς) a Solomonic decree (*Ant.* 8.100). Christians continued the metaphor, as Ignatius well illustrates: "Hasten all of you to come together (συντρέχετε) as to one temple of God, as to one altar, to one Jesus Christ" (*Mag.* 7).

At Qumran, in the cultic Songs of The Sabbath Sacrifices, "running along a path" is used metaphorically for the cultic life of the faithful (4Q 405.23.i.11). And, presumably depicting the Last Days, the same writings foresee that "the armies of heaven and the wonders of all the divine spirits shall run (אלוהים ירוצו) at His command" (4Q 402.iv.9) and the divine spirits will be seen running in the sanctuary (4Q 403.1.ii.6). While the text of these passages is uncertain, the notion of divine messengers or agents running in cultic service is discernible.

From the Talmud, interesting is *Ber.* 6b. According to this tract, one should not take large steps when leaving the synagogue. But then:

> This is only when one goes *from* the synagogue, but when one goes *to* the synagogue, it is a pious deed to run. For it is said: Let us run to know the Lord [Hos 6:3]. R. Zera says: At first, when I saw the scholars running to the lecture on the sabbath day, I thought they were desecrating the sabbath. But since I have heard the saying of R. Tanhum in the name of R. Joshua b. Levi: A man should always run (ירוץ) to listen to the word of

---

27. See Neusner, *Song,* 143.

the halakhah even on the sabbath. R. Zera says: The merit of attending a lecture lies in the running.

This indicates clearly that such running is to be understood not only metaphorically but literally as describing a physical action which is commended as a pious deed, even when performed on a sabbath.

But literal or metaphorical, in sum, running often carried the sense of performing a sacred service or cultic activity. It was used of prophets, of priests, and of others Spirit-called and involved in cultic and sacred actions. Philip's running is that of a prophet-like-Elijah who runs on the impulse of the Spirit to fulfill a specific mission to which he has been called. His running is closely linked to the word of Isaiah that he hears the eunuch reading. Through Philip that word offers the eunuch a sacred calling which he takes up joyfully as he goes "on his way."

Conclusion

Philip's running is consistent with Luke's portrayal of him as a holy man, as a prophet in the mould of Elijah, inspired, and carrying out a commission that is not of his own choice. Philip runs because he is on sacred service and under divine impulse. It is a running very similar to that of Paul[28] who is so concerned lest he "run in vain" (μή πως εἰς κενὸν τρέχω ἢ ἔδραμον) (Gal 2:2; cf. Phil 2:16), a concern expressed in the very context of his revelatory commission. In the context of Acts 8:26–40, the running of Philip takes on greater significance than a casual reading might suggest. And Luke's deceptively simple use of the word illustrates his skill and art in constructing character and in story-telling.

---

28. It may not be at all coincidental that the call of Paul follows immediately after this Philip-eunuch episode.

Tabitha: The Gazelle of Joppa (Acts 9:36–41)[1]

IN ACTS 9:36, LUKE introduces into his narrative a woman called Tabitha, a name which, he says, is translated into Greek as Δορκάς. Both the Greek, δορκάς, and its Aramaic equivalent, בִּיתָא, mean "gazelle," as is commonly noted.[2] In the Septuagint, the word δορκάς is usually used to translate the Hebrew צְבִי or צְבִי א.[3] If commentators remark at all on this name, it is to give its meaning and its Aramaic and Hebrew forms,[4] to note that it is a rare name,[5] often that of a slave.[6] Others suggest that the use of the name in this episode indicates Luke's knowledge of a local tradition[7] and that the story is "assuredly rooted in good historical memory."[8] Some also see a link between the name Tabitha in Acts 9 and the word "talitha" used by Jesus in addressing a dead twelve-year old girl (Mark 5:41).[9] Tabitha has received some notice in order to highlight the importance of widows, while others see her as illustrating the power of communal love that is stronger even than death.[10] But little attention, if any at all, has been given to the possible metaphorical use of the name itself in the Acts narrative.[11]

---

1. I wish to acknowledge the comments and suggestions made by Dr. Richard Fellows (Vancouver) and Dr. David Luckensmeyer (Brisbane) on various drafts of this paper.

2. See, for examples, Fitzmyer, *Acts*; Jervell, *Die Apostelgeschichte*.

3. For example, Deut 12;15, 22; 14:5; Song 4:5.

4. See Fitzmyer, *Acts*, 445, and others.

5. It occurs in the Jerusalem Talmud (*y. Ned.* 1.5 49b, 2.1 49d). The Greek and Latin forms of the name are a little more common.

6. Williams, "Palestinian Jewish Personal Names," 96.

7. So, for example, Jervell, *Die Apostelgeschichte*, 296.

8. Dunn, *Acts*, 129.

9. See, for example, Bruce, *Book of Acts*, 199. The Western text of Mark 5:41 actually reads ταβιθα in place of ταλιθα.

10. Richter Reimer, *Women*; Pesch, *Die Apostelgeschichte*, 1:326.

11. Chrysostom sensed significance in Tabitha's name. He wrote: "It is not without a meaning that the writer has informed us of the woman's name, but to show that the name she bore matched her character; as active and wakeful was she as an antelope. For in many instances there is a Providence in the giving of names, as we have often told you" (Chrysostom, *Acts of the Apostles*, s.v. "Homily 21").

I will argue that the name of the disciple at Joppa, Tabitha, which means "gazelle," not only reflects her character and her status, but can also be read as a metaphor in the narrative for fringe-members, such as proselytes, in the Christian community. There are a number of characteristics and physical attributes of the gazelle that make it a logical choice as a literary metaphor for the proselyte. I will also show that the name of Tabitha's town, Joppa, can be read as symbolic of the issue of the "mixing" that was so crucial in Jewish dietary and ritual law. Both the metaphorical use of the gazelle and the symbolic use of Joppa occur in a narrative that deals with critical and divisive issues surrounding the status of gentiles (and what is expected of them). These issues are central to Acts' understanding of Peter's mission in particular. The story of Tabitha at Joppa introduces the issue of the proselytes, the narrative continues with the sanctification of the God-fearing Cornelius (Acts 10:1–11:18), and gentile issues as a whole are finally resolved in the narrative by the pronouncements of the apostolic council decree in Acts 15. So the episode about Tabitha is part of the wider narrative in which Peter learns that the eschatological holy spirit promised to Israel, and the "repentance unto life" (11:18), are gifts God intends to be given not only to Israel but also to God-fearers, proselytes and other marginal members of the community. The name Tabitha, and her location in Joppa, draw attention to this point to the audience.

People with animal names are reasonably common in the Jewish scriptures alone: for example, Oreb (raven), Zeb (wolf); Caleb, possibly a proselyte (dog); Khamor (wild ass), Ja'el (ibex); Epher and Ephron (fawn), 'Eglon (calf), Akhbor (mouse), Shaphau (cony or rock-badger), and Khezer (swine). Jewish women named after animals are also known: Rachel (ewe), Leah (possibly, cow), and Deborah (honey-bee) are familiar examples. Tabitha has precedence in Zibiah (2 Kgs 12:2) and in the male equivalent, Zibia (1 Chr 8:9), both meaning "gazelle." Nor is it unusual for humans to be depicted metaphorically as animals. In Gen 49, where the various patriarchs of Israel are so described: Judah is a lion's whelp; Issachar a strong ass; Dan a serpent in the way; Napthali is a hind/gazelle let loose;[12] and Benjamin is a ravenous wolf. As is well known, lovers are described as stags and gazelles in the Song of Solomon (2:5; 4:7). Well known also is the Christian use of the lamb (John 1:29; Rev 6:1), and of the lion, bull and eagle (Rev 4:7).

---

12. According to the Numbers Rabbah 2, the banner of Naphtali had a hind in its center.

The Gazelle

In order to appreciate the metaphorical use of the name Tabitha, it is helpful to know some of the features and characteristics of the gazelle and its significance in ancient Jewish (and other) cultures.

The gazelle is an animal known for its striking physical features, especially its coloring, marking, and its eyes. It has white markings and coloring, and attractive large bright eyes. Physically, the dorcas gazelle that still inhabits modern Israel (there are a few other types) is a comparatively small, slender animal. It has a body length of about 90–110 cm (3–3.6 ft) and stands 55–65cm (1.8–2.1 ft) at shoulder height, with a tail 15–20 cm (6–8 in.) long. It weighs 15–20 kg (33–44 lb.). In coloring, its head and back are sandy-red, while its rump and underside are white or beige. It also has an attractive white eye-ring, and a pair of white and dark brown stripes running from each eye to the corners of the mouth. The ridged, lyre-shaped horns in females are much thinner and straighter than in the male, with fewer ridges, and they grow to a length of 15–25 cm (6–10 in.). The white markings on the gazelle are a dominant feature of the animal, along with its delicate but "royal-looking" horns, and make it very attractive. It is also a very agile, speedy animal exuding a springing, leaping vitality. But for all its agility and vitality, it is prone to disease and becomes a hapless victim if it breaks one of its very fragile legs. It was also a hunted animal, and its meat regarded as somewhat of a delicacy (cf. 1 Kgs 4:23).

Gazelles were commonly seen in ancient Palestine in hilly and rocky terrain, but they also inhabited the coastal plains, such as are around Joppa. It was not a domesticated animal, but was found in the fringe areas of human habitations. Female gazelles today are found in herds that vary in size, depending on conditions, with forty being the maximum, but most are in the 5–10 range. They might sometimes be accompanied by adolescent males, but never by adult males.[13]

The Gazelle in Jewish Dietary Law

As stated, the gazelle's habitat was on the borders. It was neither truly wild nor tame, neither of the desert nor of the town. It was a small, fragile, attractive, game animal. In dietary law, it was representative of those animals that could be eaten in circumstances which had little impact on the clean/unclean state of the eater. By translating the name Tabitha into "gazelle," a

---

13. Walther et al., *Gazelles*, 36. For more details on the habitat and habits of various gazelle species in Syria, Jordan, Palestine, and Israel, see Martin, "Gazelle," 13–30.

Jewish audience was given an entrée to the clean/unclean issue that is raised in Peter's later vision in Joppa. Peter sees "all four-footed animals and reptiles of the earth and fowls of the air" (Acts 10:12), and this is symbolic of the issue of his association with the God-fearer Cornelius, because that association is one in which food is shared. It is for sharing food with the uncircumcised that Peter is later criticised (11:3).

The gazelle was a "four-footed" animal and in Jewish dietary regulations belonged in the "clean" category. Peter could associate with Tabitha the gazelle without offending Jewish consciences, including his own. Since the dietary laws were highly important in many forms of Judaism, it can be assumed that at least Jews in Luke's audience were aware of the gazelle's dietary status. Its ritual status was used in the Torah as the standard for correct practice when it came to eating meat in the town or household (in contrast to the foods that were ritually legitimate within the sacred precincts). The gazelle was representative of animals that "both clean and unclean alike may eat." According to Deut 12:15, Moses commanded, "Eat flesh within any of your towns, as much as you desire, according to the blessing of the Lord your God which he has given you; the unclean and the clean may eat of meat, as of the gazelle and as of the hart" (ὁ ἀκάθαρτος ἐν σοὶ καὶ ὁ καθαρὸς ἐπὶ τὸ αὐτὸ φάγεται αὐτὸ ὡς δορκάδα ἢ ἔλαφον).

And again, in Deut 12:22–23, he says, "Just as the gazelle or the hart is eaten, so you may eat of it; the unclean and the clean alike may eat of it (ὡς ἔσθεται ἡ δορκὰς καὶ ἡ ἔλαφος, οὕτως φάγῃ αὐτό, ὁ ἀκάθαρτος ἐν σοὶ καὶ ὁ καθαρὸς ὡσαύτως ἔδεται). Only be sure that you do not eat the blood; for the blood is the life, and you shall not eat the life with the flesh."

According to Deut 15:22, the gazelle, as well as other non-consecrated meat, could be eaten in homes, without its blood; but it was not to be used in sacrifices. The reason for this permission to eat the gazelle is that it belongs to the category of those animals that have cloven hooves and chews the cud. According to Deut 14:4–6, "These are the animals you may eat: the ox, the sheep, the goat, the hart, the gazelle, the roebuck, the wild goat, the ibex, the antelope, and the mountain-sheep. Every animal that parts the hoof and has the hoof cloven in two, and chews the cud, among the animals, you may eat."

So the gazelle was a "clean," non-consecrated, non-sacrificial four-legged animal (τετράπους) that anyone could eat, regardless of their state of purity or impurity. It could be eaten by all, but only outside the sanctuary. It was not a "holy" animal but neither was it profane or unclean. Peter had no grounds to reject the invitation to "eat" the gazelle, as he later objected to eating other four-footed animals seen in his vision (Acts 10:14).

When we turn to the rabbinic literature, the status of the gazelle there is a little more complex. There was a difference of opinion as to whether the gazelle could be eaten at all. R. Akiba, "who maintains that at no time was it ever forbidden to eat flesh at will" saw Deut 12:22 as sanctioning his attitude; R. Ishmael questioned whether the gazelle was "ever permitted to be eaten at all." Only sacrificial meat was allowed to be eaten by Israel in the wilderness, and therefore gazelle was never permitted (*Hul.* 17a).

For the rabbis, the gazelle is clearly a non-consecrated animal, not to be used in Temple sacrifices, but it also appears to be the model for animals that were sacrificial but blemished in some way. In the discussion of what to do with consecrated sacrificial animals that became blemished, the Gemara states, "as a gazelle is exempt from the law of the firstling (being a non-domesticated animal), so dedicated sacrifices which have become unfit for the altar are also exempt." (*Bek.* 15a; cf. 33a). Since the gazelle was exempt from the law of the firstling, it could not acquire the holiness of the firstling (Deut 15:19). However, some rabbis taught that the gazelle had to be ritually slaughtered because it was on the same footing as a blemished consecrated animal (*Hul.* 28a). In other words, the gazelle had a degree of holiness associated with it.

The Gazelle as Symbol in Jewish and Christian Art and Literature

Asa Strandberg argues in a recent doctoral thesis that in Egyptian art the female gazelle is a symbol of the nurturer and life-giver while the male gazelle is the symbol of the hunted and of death.[14] In Jewish literature and art, the gazelle often seems to serve the same symbolic purposes. Most extant art is probably from the third century or later, but there is little reason to suggest the gazelle was not similarly used in earlier artistic and literary symbolism. In the decorations of the synagogue at Naaran, for example, gazelles featured peacefully grazing at a clump of living flora or at a well.[15] Water, of course, is a symbol of life, so the link between water and the gazelle is an obvious one to make. The gazelle is capable of going without water for long periods of time because it stores its own fluids. In addition, Ps 42:1 refers to the desire of the deer for the living waters. In early Christian art, the deer symbolized the spirit and soul of the believer and often was depicted in baptismal churches near the images of pools and springs that symbolized the fountain of life. Deer were also often depicted intertwined among acanthus scrolls, where they symbolized renewed life, life that comes out of death.[16]

14. Personal email with the author, April 10, 2006.
15. See Fine, *Art and Judaism*, 96.
16. See, for example, Najjar and Sa'id, "New Umayyad Church," 547–60. The

Four physical features of the gazelle make the animal a suitable symbol of life. The first are its eyes which are strikingly soft, big, alive, and alert. Life is in the eyes; at death the eyes are closed and the spirit of life moves from the face. When Peter raises Tabitha to life, she opens her eyes (9:40), a feature mentioned in the raising by Elisha of a young boy who "sneezed and opened his eyes" (2 Kgs 4:35). Attention is drawn to the eyes. Because they are open, life must have been restored. The open eyes are a symbol of life, especially of divine life. It is said that the gazelle sleeps with one eye open, and so it was later used as an image of Yahweh. The Aramaic Targum to the Song of Songs, 8:14, says: "In that hour the elders of the Assembly of Israel will say, "Flee, my Beloved, Lord of the world, from this polluted earth, and let your Presence dwell in heaven above. But in times of trouble, when we pray to you, be like a gazelle which sleeps with one eye closed and one eye open."

A second feature of the gazelle is its speed and agility. Not surprisingly, speedy humans were likened to the gazelle (2 Sam 2:18; 1 Chr 12:8). Their speed sometimes allowed them to escape the snares laid for them (Sir 27:20), that is, it allowed them to escape death. The sure-footedness of the gazelle was used metaphorically for the security offered by God: "[God] has made my feet like gazelles and made me stand on my high places" (2 Sam 22:34; Ps 19:34). In the *Targum on the Song of Songs*, the speed of the gazelle is seen as a positive metaphor for the faith of Abraham, Isaac and Jacob "who were swift in worshiping Him, as a gazelle (2:17), and Yahweh himself is said to have "run like a gazelle" in his saving actions in Egypt (2:9). It is possible that speed was the reason that the revolutionary, John, was also called "the son of Dorcas" (Josephus, *Wars* 4.145).

The attractive horns of the gazelle provided a suitable symbol of the sun and of a new day. The rabbis played especially on the reference in Ps 22:1, which is headed "To the chief musician upon Ayelet Hashachar (the Gazelle of Dawn)." *Yoma* 29a says, "Just as that gazelle's horns divide to here and to there, so the dawn comes up here and there." According to the Jerusalem Talmud, Rabbi Chiya, Rava and Rabbi Shimon Ben Chalafta were walking through the Valley of Arbel at dawn and they saw the gazelle of Dawn as its light first appeared. R. Chiya said to R. Shimon Ben Chalafta: "So will the redemption of Israel be, at first little by little but as it continues it will grow continually" (*j. Ber*.1.1.2). The gazelle of Dawn was a sign of hope. The gazelle uses her horns to dig for water, and the rabbis interpreted this activity as an indication of her piety and closeness to Yahweh: "She digs a hole and enters her horns into it, and lows, and the Deep raises water to her, as it is said, 'Like a gazelle, as she moans for streams of water'" (Ps

---

frescoes of San Clemente basilica use the deer motif as a symbol of life.

42:2). When David saw how the Blessed Holiness answers her, he began the arrangement of a psalm with her: "For the conductor, on the gazelle of the dawn." (*Midrash Tehillim* 22:14).[17]

Finally, the gazelle was considered a beautiful, much-loved, and greatly admired animal. In Gen 49:21, Naphtali is identified as a gazelle "dropping beautiful fawns." In the Song of Songs, the lover sings fondly of the lovely features of the gazelle as symbolizing the beauty of the beloved. "My beloved is like a gazelle" or a young stag (2:9); "Your two breasts are like two fawns, twins of a gazelle" (4:5; 7:3; cf. Prov 5:19). O. Keel writes, "both breasts and fawns of a gazelle in particular symbolize the warmth of life, an inspiring and victorious counter-form to death."[18] A dead gazelle was a symbol of the tragedy of death.

This very positive view of the gazelle among the rabbis is enhanced by their claims that the gazelle is the animal "most loved by God . . . because a gazelle harms no one, and never disturbs the peace" (*Midrash Samuel* 9). According to the Zohar, "Our Rabbis have said that she [the gazelle] is the kindest of the animals, and she has more compassion than she has children. When all the animals are thirsty they gather around her, since they know her kind deeds, so that she will raise her eyes on high, and the Blessed Holiness will have compassion for them" (*Midrash Tehillim* 22:14).

The Zohar,[19] referring to Ps 22:1, says,

> What is the gazelle of the dawn? She is an animal who is compassionate; among all the animals in the world, none is compassionate like her. Because, at a time when time is pressing on her and she needs to feed herself and all the animals, she goes into the distance, by a distant path, and brings food. And she does not want to eat until she comes back and returns to her place. Why? So that the rest of the animals may gather to her, so that she may divide that food for them. When she comes back, all the rest of the animals are gathered to her, and she stands in the middle and distributes portions to each and every one. A reminder of this is: "She gets up while it is still night and gives food to her household." . . . And from what she

---

17. Is it coincidental that the next character in the narrative is Cornelius, a name that is derived from the Latin *cornus*, "horn"? The horn was a symbol of strength and power, especially in military symbolism.

18. Keel, *Song of Songs*, 94.

19. The authenticity and dating of this text is much debated. It was certainly known in the thirteenth century, but there are claims that it dates back to the second century CE.

distributes to them, she is satisfied, as if she had eaten more food than all of them . . .

And at a time when the world needs rain, all the rest of the animals are gathered to her, and she goes up to the peak of a high mountain, and conceals her head between her knees and lows, lowing again and again. And the Blessed Holiness hears her voice and is filled with compassion, and takes care of the world. But she descends from the peak of the mountain and runs and hides herself. And all the rest of the animals run after her, but they do not find her. As it is written, "Like a gazelle, as she moans for streams of water." What is "for streams of water"? For water from those streams which have dried up, and the world thirsts for water—then she moans (*Zohar* III.249a–b).

In Jewish traditions, then, the gazelle was often seen as a very positive symbol of love, of life, and even of God. For the rabbis, one of the most positive things to be said of a bride is that she is "as graceful as a gazelle" (*Ketub.* 17a). This very positive view of the gazelle suggests that the name Tabitha was given to a woman who was viewed very positively within the community to which she belonged. In Luke's narrative, Tabitha is characterised by compassion. She was "full of good works and acts of charity" (9:36), the classic actions of the righteous. She fits the image of the gazelle, later (if not earlier) regarded as the most compassionate and gentle of creatures. Physically, there is a certain grace and beauty in the animal, in its shape and form, but also in its movements and behavior towards others in the herd. It might be remembered that Tabitha, the gazelle, is closely associated in Acts with a group of widows, is clearly loved by them, and appears to have had a caring and nurturing role among them. She belongs to a group, a community made up of "saints and widows" (9:41). Her presence was a source of life and strength and hope; her death was something to be mourned as a significant loss to the community. To be named Tabitha, to be called a "gazelle," was very positive and affirming. This affirming status, however, was modified by the ritual status of the gazelle as an animal that was not consecrated for sacrificial service.

The Gazelle as Metaphor for the Proselyte

The characteristics of the gazelle that have been mentioned make the animal a suitable metaphor for the proselyte. The gazelle inhabited the fringes, it was a clean animal but not to be dedicated for sacrifices, and it could be eaten by clean and unclean. The gazelle was an animal of the desert fringes often on the search for water—a suitable metaphor for the proselyte looking for the living water. Understandably, Ps 42, which refers to the deer panting after the living waters, was used by Augustine to indicate the catechumens preparing for baptism, and he says the Psalm was chanted on the occasion of their baptism.[20]

There are later Jewish and Christian literary uses of the gazelle or deer as metaphor for the proselyte. According to Lev 19:34, "The stranger (προσήλυτος) shall be to you as one of your citizens." Rabbi Alexandri (a third-century Palestinian sage) is reported to have commented:

> How loved is the stranger in the eyes of the Lord, who commanded regarding them in forty-eight instances. [The proselyte] is like a deer that joins a shepherd's herd and is favourable in his eyes. He says, "In this one I have not invested from its birth but it joined my sheep therefore I love it." Such are the righteous proselytes. God said, "since he came under my wing, he shall be to you as one of your citizens" (Midrash Ha-chadash on Leviticus, cited in Torah Sheleima).

In the later *Numbers Rabbah* there is the following story:

> The Holy One loves the proselytes exceedingly. To what is the matter like? To a king who had a number of sheep and goats which went forth every morning to the pasture, and returned in the evening to the stable. One day a stag joined the flock and grazed with the sheep, and returned with them. Then the shepherd said to the king, "There is a stag which goes out with the sheep and grazes with them, and comes home with them." And the king loved the stag exceedingly. And he commanded the shepherd, saying: "Give heed unto this stag, that no man beat it"; and when the sheep returned in the evening, he would order that the stag should have food and drink. Then the shepherds said to him, "My Lord, thou hast many goats and sheep and kids, and thou givest us no directions about these, but about this stag thou givest us orders day by day." Then the king replied: "It is the custom of the sheep to graze in the pasture, but the stags dwell in the wilderness, and it is not their custom to come among men in the cultivated land. But to this stag who has come to us and lives with us, should we not be grateful that he has left the great wilderness, where many stags and gazelles feed, and has come to live among us? It behoves us to be grateful." So too spoke the Holy One: "I owe great thanks to the stranger, in that he has left

---

20. Augustine, *Expositions on the Book of Psalms*.

his family and his father's house, and come to dwell among us; therefore I order in the Law: "Love the stranger" (8.3).[21]

The underlying message, taken as a whole, is clear: Protection of the rights of the proselyte is Israel's responsibility and the convert and the descendants of converts are to be integrated fully into the family of Israel.

In Christian literature, there are indications of the deer and gazelle being used as metaphors for the neophyte. In the Barlaam and Joseph narrative, the gazelle is so used. Barlaam tells Joseph:

> A certain rich man once reared the fawn of a gazelle; which, when grown up, was impelled by natural desire to long for the desert. So on a day she went out and found an herd of gazelles browsing; and, joining them, she would roam through the glades of the forest, returning at evenfall, but issuing forth at dawn, through the heedlessness of her keepers, to herd with her wild companions. When these removed, to graze further afield, she followed them. But the rich man's servants, when they learned thereof, mounted on horseback, and gave chase, and caught the pet fawn, and brought her home again, and set her in captivity for the time to come. But of the residue of the herd, some they killed, and roughly handled others.... But this is the will of the Lord concerning time; thou now indeed must be signed with the seal of holy Baptism, and abide in this country, cleaving to all righteousness, and the fulfilling of the commandments of Christ; but when the Giver of all good things shall give thee opportunity, then shalt thou come to us, and for the remainder of this present life we shall dwell together; and I trust in the Lord also that in the world to come we shall not be parted asunder.[22]

Because the gazelle was a commonly seen animal in certain parts of Israel and elsewhere,[23] and because the Torah gave clear indications of its status, we can assume with reasonable safety that any metaphorical use of the animal would have been understood by Luke's original audiences. In addition, it would seem that by translating the name Tabitha into Greek, Luke drew attention to its meaning, "a gazelle." Instead of reading Δορκας as a Greek version of the Aramaic name, I suggest it be read as referring to the animal. In

---

21. Cited in Barrett, *New Testament Background*, 165.

22. John Damascene, *Barlaam and Ioasaph* 18.156.

23. It is still found in good numbers in Syria, Saudi Arabia, Oman, and Jordan. Its horns commonly feature on the headdresses of ancient Egyptian and Syrian deities, especially of Reshep, the Syrian war-god.

that case, Peter addresses her by her name "Tabitha" in 9:40, and the narrator calls her "the gazelle" (rather than "Dorcas") in 9:39.

In sum, the female gazelle is viewed very positively in both Jewish and Christian art and literature. She is a symbol of love, grace and beauty, of service and compassion; and she is a symbol for the proselyte and the neophyte.

Tabitha, the Gazelle-Proselyte, in Acts

I suggest that the Tabitha in Luke's narrative was a proselyte. Female proselytes are, of course, not unknown from Jewish literature and also from inscriptional evidence. Josephus records the well-known cases of Fulvia in Rome (*Ant.* 18.3.5) and Helena, queen of Adiabene (*Ant.* 20.2.3; cf. *Wars* 2.20.2). Beturia Paulla, a rich proselyte of Rome, is known in inscriptions as *mater synagogae*.[24] Luke himself refers to Lydia in Philippi as one who "revered God" (σεβομένη τὸν θεόν) (Acts 16:14).

It is possible that Tabitha was not her birth-name, but a name given to her by the Jewish community of which she was a proselyte. The use of the word μαθητρία (unique in the New Testament) suggests Tabitha belonged to a Christian community, if the use of the masculine forms μαθητής/μαθηταί in the rest of Acts is any indication. She was given her name because it fitted her character. Tabitha had some of the characteristics of a *dorcas*, a gazelle. By translating her name for a Greek-speaking audience, Luke draws attention to that character. The name (and especially re-naming) and character link is well known from elsewhere in ancient Jewish and Christian literature. For example, Abram is called Abraham by Yahweh "because I will make you father of a multitude of nations" (Gen 17:5); Simon, son of John, is renamed Cephas which the narrator says means πέτρος (John 1:42). James and John are renamed Boanerges which is translated υἱοὶ βροντῆς, "sons of thunder" (Mark 3:17); Joseph Justus is given a new name, Barnabas, which means "son of consolation" (Acts 4:36).

But what was Tabitha's status within that community of saints (ἅγιοι) and widows (9:41)? I suggest that the name was given to her not only because of her character but also because she was a proselyte. The gazelle was a suitable name and metaphor for a woman on the fringes of a Christian community—a God-fearer or a proselyte. I suggest this for two main reasons: The gazelle was an animal that inhabited the fringes, and for many Jews was regarded as an undomesticated, wild, animal. It was exempt from the law of the firstling, which meant that it was not a consecrated animal. On the other hand, it was

---

24. See Huskinson, *Experiencing Rome*, 312.

an animal that the "clean" could eat, and it belonged to the category of "clean" animals. So there was a degree of ambiguity about the gazelle. The proselyte also raised questions of ambiguity. Attitudes towards proselytes, and acceptance of them, varied from situation to situation, from rabbi to rabbi, from community to community. Their very existence commonly raised questions. It seems that the gazelle was a suitable metaphor for them. Luke refers to "proselytes" three times in Acts (2:11; 6:5; 13:43), and twice he clearly distinguishes them from "Jews" (2:11; 13:43). He also commonly mentions people (often women) who were associated with the synagogue. They were not Jews, but "God-fearers" (10:2, 35; 13:16, 26) or those who "revered God" (13:43, 50; 16:14; 17:4, 17; 18:7). Luke could be read as having some concern and interest in such people since they were the ones who were attracted to the gospel as Paul, in particular, presented it.

So it certainly need not be assumed that Tabitha was born a Jew, despite the Aramaic name; I suggest she belonged to the class of proselytes and was similar to the God-fearing Cornelius. She is said to have been "full of good works and charity" (πλήρης ἔργων ἀγαθῶν καὶ ἐλεημοσυνῶν) (9:36) just as Cornelius is described as "doing acts of charity" (ποιῶν ἐλεημοσύνας) (10:2). Such actions qualified both to belong to the category of "righteous ones." According to 1 Tim 2:10, "good works" are befitting of women who "profess religion" (ἐπαγγελλομέναις θεοσέβειαν).

Tabitha is also closely connected with the widows in the Christian community of Joppa. This too is a possible indication of her proselyte status since the προσήλυτος is very closely linked with the "orphan and the widow" in the Deuteronomic code (e.g., Deut 24:17–21; 26:12; 27:19). What the proselyte and the widow have in common, at least, is that they both have lost family roots and ties—the one by choice, the other by death. Like the widows, as a proselyte Tabitha was vulnerable, and in her weakness could expect support from and protection in Israel. In Acts, the audience might well ask, "Will the proselyte find protection in the renewed Israel?"

I suggest that Tabitha, the gazelle, represents those located on the fringes of a Christian community, those who were "non-domesticated" and more importantly, "non-consecrated," that is, they had not yet been brought into the community of the holy ones. It is true that she is called a "disciple," but that category is not sufficient to imply full acceptance and full membership among the saints. The strange twelve men of Ephesus, who were "believers" but had been baptised only with the baptism of John, are also called "disciples" (Acts 19:1). But they had not been purified—they had not received the holy spirit (19:2). In Acts, the only authorized conveyors of purification by the holy spirit are Peter (10:44–47; John 8:14–17), Paul (19:6–7), and Aeneas (9:17). Tabitha and Cornelius, despite being closely associated with the people of God, had not yet been purified by the holy spirit. Their purification only comes when Peter is present. It took Peter some time to recognise that God shows no partiality (10:35) and that the promised eschatological purifying spirit was also for the proselyte and the God-fearer. Tabitha's death and subsequent restoration to life are metaphors of the process by which such disciples were accepted as "living ones" into the community of the holy. It is a metaphor for the "repentance that leads to life" (εἰς ζωήν) that God was now giving "even to the gentiles" (καὶ τοῖς ἔθνεσιν) (Acts 11:18). Death as a pathway to holiness and purification is not an uncommon idea. I have suggested elsewhere that Eutychus, the νεανίας of Troas (20:9), is another whose death and restoration by Paul is a metaphor for the transitional process that needs to take place for a "young" member to become a "living son" (παῖδα ζῶντα) in the community (20:12).[25]

From a narrative perspective, Tabitha's meeting with Peter prepares the audience for the apostle's critical meeting in the house of Cornelius, the Roman soldier—a meeting that clearly is of great significance in the Lukan narrative. It is often noted that Luke's narrative operates with pairs of events or characters. Gaventa (and many others) therefore links the raising of Tabitha with the healing of Aeneas.[26] The pairing is admittedly close, but I suggest that the Tabitha episode can also be paired equally closely with the Cornelius episode that immediately follows. Her story is part of the Peter cycle of stories in Acts (9:32–12:19) that concludes with Peter entering into the God-fearer Cornelius" house, accepting his hospitality, eating with the "common and unclean" (κοινὸν καὶ ἀκάθαρτον) (10:14), and witnessing the outpouring of the gift of the spirit of holiness on pagans (10:45). The sanctification of a God-fearer, evidenced by the outpouring of "holy spirit," is the climax of the cycle. Tabitha, "the proselyte-gazelle," her location in Joppa, and her death-to-life experience are all part of leading the audience to that climax. Like Cornelius, Tabitha symbolizes the issue facing the Christian community: what is the status of god-fearers, proselytes, diaspora Jews and other fringe or "risky" associates? Can those with whom "both clean and unclean" may eat be accepted into the community? More importantly, can people like proselytes belong to the "holy ones"? Luke's answer is a clear "Yes, by all means; but they, like all of Israel, need to go through a transforming process."

Peter restored Tabitha to life and "presented" her as a "living one" to the community of "widows and saints" (9:41). The verb "presented"

---

25. Strelan, *Strange Acts*, 251–57. There are a number of striking parallels between the stories of Tabitha and Eutychus.

26. Gaventa, *Acts*, 159; cf. Spencer, *Acts*, 106.

(παρέστησεν) is used with the same sense it has in the episode of Mary and Joseph who "present [Jesus] to the Lord" (παραστῆσαι τῷ κυρίῳ) in the Temple (Luke 2:22). It has a strong sense of dedication and consecration.[27] Language similar to that used by Paul when talking about baptism can be discerned here. The same verb is used in Rom 6:13 where Paul urges Christians to present themselves (παραστήσατε ἑαυτούς) to God as "the living ones from the dead" (ἐκ νεκρῶν ζῶντας). Paul uses this language to describe the life of those baptised into Christ (Rom 6:1–11) and into the community of Christ. Peter presents Tabitha to the community as a "living one" (ζῶσαν) (9:41). Her status changes from death to life, from outside (or from the fringe) to inside the community of the holy ones (τοὺς ἁγίους) (9:41). It is as if she was "born again," and as the infant Jesus was presented, so Tabitha is presented as a new born child to the community. Many of the locals "believed the Lord" (9:42), possibly attracted by the good news that the proselyte is also included in the renewed Israel.

The audience is being prepared for Peter's vision in the very next episode in which he sees all sorts of quadrupeds (10:12; there were ten "clean" quadrupeds, including the gazelle; see Deut 14:4) in a sheet and he is told to kill and eat. It is obviously a vision preparing him for entrance into Cornelius" house and for the change in his thinking that he undergoes there. So the very mention of the name, Tabitha, which by being translated has attention drawn to it, might well conjure up the issue of clean and unclean for an audience alert for such clues. That Luke's audience might be expected to watch for such clues is supported by the fact that the relation between gentiles, God-fearers, and Jews in the Christian communities was a burning issue. So crucial was it that the subsequent decision, spearheaded by Peter's report on his visit to Cornelius, was, as Johnson says, "So unprecedented that the entire section of chapters 10–15 struggles with it."[28] So it is that very issue that forms the immediate context of this section of the narrative. It is apt, then, that the episode immediately prior to the vision of Peter and the acceptance of Cornelius and his household into the Christian community should have a woman whose name means "gazelle," the animal that clean and unclean alike may eat, but is not consecrated or holy.

---

27. I suggest that the verb is also used with that meaning in verse 39. The widows do not merely "stand beside Peter" (RSV) but *present* to Peter the clothes of Tabitha as dedicated objects of the dead woman.

28. Johnson, *Acts*, 179.

Joppa

Another reason for suggesting that Tabitha was a proselyte or someone who represented the fringe members of a Christian community is her location in Joppa. It is apparent that much about Tabitha relates to an issue that caused many headaches for Jewish (and many Christian) communities, namely, the issue of "mixing." The name Tabitha, given in both Aramaic and Greek forms, itself indicates her "mixed" identity. Translating the name into Greek draws attention to the woman's status as "mixed." The gazelle could be eaten by "clean and unclean alike." By associating Tabitha with widows (if she was not one herself), Luke might expect the audience to recall the tensions that existed in Jerusalem between Greek and non-Greeks regarding widows and their care (Acts 6).

Locating Tabitha in Joppa accentuates the issue of mixing and adds weight to the argument that she was a proselyte—that is, a Jew who had gentile origins. As Barrett suggests, the double name fits the mixed demographics of Joppa.[29] It is significant that Joppa is mentioned repeatedly (ten times, in fact) in the Peter cycle of episodes (9:36, 38, 42, 43; 10:5, 8, 23, 32; 11:5, 13)—too many times to be co-incidental in the narrative. Repetition draws attention. In the context, the repetition draws attention to Peter's move to the edges and fringes, where mixing is inevitable and critical decisions need to be made about mixing with "the common and unclean" (κοινὸν ἀκάθαρτον) (10:14). Locating Peter in Joppa, a sea-port town known by the audience to be of mixed, if not predominantly gentile, population prepares the way for his pivotal meeting with Cornelius. Peter is yet to move into the homes of the God-fearing gentiles; but he is willing to go on invitation into a house where there is a dead proselyte disciple in the mixed town of Joppa (9:38-39).

Many Jews in Luke's audience would have known of Joppa. It was a town allotted in the inheritance of Dan (Josh 19:46), located between Caesarea and Gaza, and at a distance of thirty miles northwest from Jerusalem. It was an important seaport that linked Jerusalem and the Mediterranean world. Seaports notoriously consisted of mixed peoples from various parts of the Mediterranean world, resulting often in social behavior that raised eyebrows in more mono-dimensional Jewish communities. Joppa was a fringe town in Israel in that it had a large population of non-Jewish inhabitants and relations between Jews and local citizens were not always harmonious, if the episode reported in 2 Maccabees is any indication. According to that episode, the pagan locals tricked the Jewish population into boarding

---

29. Barrett, *Acts*, 1:482-83.

boats, and when out to sea, drowned two hundred of them (12:3–9). In its recent history, Joppa ("beauty") had been sometimes under Jewish control, sometimes not. For example, under Simon Maccabeus, it was in Jewish control (1 Macc 12:33); Antony gave it to Cleopatra (Josephus, *Ant.* 14.10.6); and Caesar restored it to Herod (*Ant.* 15.7.3).

Joppa belonged to Japheth, and Japheth is said to have had seven sons (Gen 10:2; Josephus, *Ant.* 1.6.1) who in turn became known as the ancestors of the gentiles. According to the Targum Pseudo-Jonathan, Gen 9:27 ("May God enlarge Japheth, And may he dwell in the tents of Shem") was interpreted to mean that the descendants of Japheth will become proselytes and will study the Law in the schools of Shem. In other words, there was a known link between Japheth/Joppa and proselytes. If Luke wanted to locate a proselyte in a town that was symbolic of the proselyte, Joppa would have been an understandable choice.

From a narrative point of view, many in the audience familiar with the biblical narratives would have known that it was from Joppa that Jonah wished to flee to Tarshish and so escape the Lord's commission for the Jewish prophet to call Nineveh to repentance (Jonah 1:3). In that story, Joppa represents "the edge," the point of decision, and crisis time for Jonah. In Acts, along comes another one sent by the Lord, Peter. What will happen as he is called upon by the two messengers "not to delay but to come with us" (9:38) to Joppa? Will Peter do a Jonah? The audience is immediately assured: "Peter arose and went with them" (9:39). It is the first step that Peter takes in the transformation of his own thinking about the status of proselytes and God-fearers in the renewed and purified Israel.

There is another Jewish story that has echoes in this episode and one that also deals with Israel's relation to outsiders. It is the story of Balak, king of Moab (Israel's "cousin," the descendants of Lot), and Balaam, the prophet of Israel. The words used by the messengers of the disciples at Joppa in addressing Peter, "Come to us as soon as possible" (Μὴ ὀκνήσῃς διελθεῖν ἕως ἡμῶν) echo the words of the messengers of Balak to Balaam (Μὴ ὀκνήσῃς ἐλθεῖν πρὸς με) (Num 22:16). In that incident, a foreigner, but a "relative" of Israel, requests a man of God to come. Here in Acts, the disciples of Joppa request the holy man Peter to come to attend to a deceased proselyte, and "Peter rose and went with them" (9:39); this recalls how Yahweh told Balaam to go with the messengers of Balak (Num 22:20).

The idea that Joppa was used by Luke as a symbol of mixing, of borders and fringe-dwellers is reinforced by the sentence that links the episode of Tabitha with that of Cornelius (9:43). According to that verse, Peter stayed in the house of Simon the tanner at Joppa. A little later in the narrative that house is said to be "beside the sea" (10:6). Simon the tanner's house in

Joppa is sandwiched between the house where the dead Tabitha was placed, and the house of the God-fearing Cornelius. As is frequently noted, tanners dealt with "unclean" skins of dead animals in their trade.[30] It is all part of the ambiguity in which Peter finds himself and for which he needs divine revelation to instruct him (10:3–23). Peter quickly learns the significance of the divine instruction as he invites the "men sent by Cornelius" into his house and provides them with hospitality (ἐξένισεν) (10:23).

Conclusion

I have demonstrated that Tabitha and Joppa are names that were used as metaphors for proselytes and for the issue of mixing. The status of gentiles was clearly a divisive issue among many early Christian communities, especially among those with significant Jewish members. In Acts, these gentiles often appear in the narrative as proselytes and God-fearers and those who revered God. Luke employs the names Tabitha and Joppa as metaphor and symbol in his narrative as he builds towards the Jerusalem council's decree regarding the status of gentiles and their obligations. If there is any merit in this reading of Tabitha and Joppa, then it is possible that other names in Acts, both of people and of places, deserve closer attention for the role that they might play within Luke's narrative. It might suggest that certain episodes in Acts call for a closer metaphorical and symbolical reading than those concerned for the historical reliability of the episodes would concede.

---

30. See, for example, Bruce, *Acts*, 200.

Who Was Bar Jesus (Acts 13:6–12)?[1]

According to Acts 13, Paul and Barnabas found in Paphos on Cyprus "a certain man who was a magos, a false prophet, and a Jew, whose name was Bar Jesus" (ἄνδρα τινὰ μάγον ψευδοπροφήτην Ἰουδαῖον ᾧ ὄνομα Βαριησοῦ). This man was with the proconsul, Sergius Paulus, whom Luke calls "an intelligent (συνετός) man" (13:6–7). Fitzmyer believes the description of Bar Jesus "borders on the fantastic,"[2] and scholarship in general has tended to see him in very negative terms. He is depicted as being as far removed from the straight paths of the Lord as any pagan magician or any Jewish opponent to the Christian Way. Haenchen, typically, understands this episode as demonstrating "the superiority of Christianity over magic."[3] However, I will suggest that the point of this episode is not a struggle between Christianity and paganism, but a struggle either within a synagogue community to which some Christians belonged or within the Christian movement itself. At issue between Paul and Bar Jesus were the contradictory understandings of righteousness and the way of God. I propose that it was not his magical practices, but his position on these issues that made him, from Luke's perspective, a threatening opponent of the faith.[4]

---

1. I wish to thank my colleague, Professor Michael Lattke (University of Queensland), and the Rev. Drs. Stephen Haar and John Strelan, for their helpful comments on various drafts of this article.

2. Fitzmyer, *Acts*, 501.

3. Haenchen, *Acts*, 398. Dunn says the episode illustrates "the recognition by one who prized magical powers that he stood before one possessed of greater powers" (Dunn, *Jesus and the Spirit*, 166).

4. It could be argued that Bar Jesus in fact was won over to Paul's side. The similarities noticed by scholars between Paul's conversion and what happens to Bar Jesus might support this reading. Both are depicted as opponents of the way of God, both are confronted with an unassailable word, both are rendered blind for a short time, and both are led by the hand. See Garrett, *Demise*, 84.

1. A Magos

The first description given of Bar Jesus is that he was a *magos* (μάγος). Much has been written about the *magoi* and there is no need to repeat the results of that scholarship.[5] The term, of course, originally referred to a Persian caste; but there is no doubt that in later usage it came to be used almost adjectivally of those who had ideas and customs that were foreign to traditional Greek views and customs. To give just one example, Strabo reports that the magoi "even consort with their mothers" (*Geog.* 15.3.20). Pliny wanted to "expose their untruths" (*Nat.* 30.1). Not surprisingly, then, among the Greeks, a μάγος became synonymous with a γοής, a charlatan and trickster (Dio Chrysostom, *Disc.* 39.41). From Luke's perspective, Bar Jesus is a prophet whose interpretation of the will of God is false, and therefore whose authority is foreign to that of the legitimate prophetic circle as represented by Barnabas and Saul. The latter two have been set apart by the Holy Spirit (13:2), sent out by the Holy Spirit (13:4) and are filled with the Holy Spirit (13:9). Bar Jesus, however, has his authority from the adversary. He is, from Luke's perspective, υἱὸς διαβόλου (13:10).

On the other hand, the identification as *magos* could mean little more than that Bar Jesus was associated with the court of the proconsul as a religious adviser, a position some Jews are known to have held.[6] Josephus makes the specific Jew-*magos* link when referring to a certain Simon, coincidentally also a Cypriot, and one who, like Bar Jesus, had friends in the Roman consular system (*Ant.* 20.7.2). In addition, the role and function of a *magos* and those of a rabbi, at least in later times, were not at all dissimilar. Both were "holy men," both were men of power and special knowledge, both were involved in decision-making within their respective communities.[7] However, for Luke, the point of the term seems to be that Bar Jesus, despite his name, certainly does not belong to Jesus, but is an outsider, having a foreign, and therefore invalid, source of authority. The term as used in 13:6 is to characterise Bar Jesus as a serious opponent of Paul.

---

5. In New Testament studies, this work focuses largely on Simon Magus. For a useful bibliography, see Jervell, *Die Apostelgeschichte*, 258–59. See also the recent work of Haar, *Simon Magus*. The understanding of Simon as a *magos* strongly colors the understanding of Bar Jesus as such in many commentaries.

6. Joseph, Daniel, and Ahikar are well-known examples of Jews holding such positions. See also Josephus, *Ant.* 8.2.5; 20.7.2.

7. See Neusner, "Rabbi and Magus," 169–78.

2. A Jew

Bar Jesus is also said to be a Jew (Ἰουδαῖος). Scholars tend to understand this negatively—even as an example of a Lukan anti-Jewish polemic. So J. T. Sanders claims Luke thinks of Bar Jesus as an "evil Jew" who opposes the mission to the gentiles.[8] Barrett includes the term in "everything that Luke did not like."[9] Bruce calls him "a renegade Jew"[10] because he is a magos; and Garrett says he is someone "who by practicing magic commits what Luke regarded as the worst sort of idolatry."[11] In other words, the man is consistently portrayed as being completely outside the pale. That, as will be shown, is questionable, but for now it is sufficient to say that an individual being "a Jew" is not always, if ever, viewed negatively by Luke. It is true that Luke uses the plural "Jews" to refer to those who are not Christian, and he uses it precisely in that way in 13:5 where Paul is said to be proclaiming the word of God "in the synagogues of the Jews." However, the fact is that on the great majority of occasions in Acts when Luke identifies an individual as "a Jew," he does so of a Christian. Such is the case with Peter (10:28), Timothy's mother (16:1), Aquila (18:2), Apollos (18:24), of course with Paul himself (21:39; 22:3), and possibly also with Alexander (19:34). The only exceptions are Scaeva (19:14; but even his sons operate with the name of Jesus) and Drusilla, the wife of Felix, who is quite keen to hear Paul "speak about the faith in Jesus Christ" (24:24). So I doubt that identifying Bar Jesus as a Jew is meant at all to be an anti-Jewish depiction. Nor is it meant to cast him in the outsider category; to the contrary, since Luke commonly uses the category "a Jew" of a Christian individual, one could theoretically understand that Bar Jesus was a Christian. It is possible to think of him as an "incomplete" Christian, as indeed was Apollos, a Jew who needed to be instructed more accurately in the way of God (18:26), and as were the disciples of Acts 19:1–7. In any case, Bar Jesus was a serious threat, partly because he was so very close to the Jesus movement, and possibly even had an impact on it.

3. A False Prophet

The argument that Bar Jesus was someone bordering closely on the Christian community, if not actually within it, gains momentum from the term "false

---

8. Sanders, *Jews*, 259.
9. Barrett, *Acts*, 1:613.
10. Bruce, *Book of Acts*, 249.
11. Garrett, *Demise*, 81.

prophet." However, rather than seeing this term as identifying him as a genuine prophet, the great majority of scholars read this as an association with paganism and magic. Haenchen, for example, says Luke "must have imagined Bar-Jesus as the proconsul's court-astrologer, who at the same time claimed to know the magic formulae by which the bonds of fate can be broken."[12] Thus he is understood to be not only outside of the Christian pale but even also of the Jewish. Pesch also thinks he is representative of a Jewish-heathen syncretism,[13] a view supported by Barrett who thinks that the double description of him as false prophet and magos suggests "that he stood on the boundary between Judaism and heathenism."[14] Jervell is one of the few who rejects this notion and insists that he was associated with the synagogue, and was "ein jüdischer Wundertäter; das Wort μάγος reicht nicht aus für die Bezeichnung 'synkretismus.'"[15] And Schille at least considers the possibility that "false prophet" might be used in the same way as it is used in the Didache, that is, as referring to early Christian charismatic prophets. But he then rejects that idea and prefers to interpret "false prophet" in the sense of a γόης. He does so because he identifies Bar Jesus as a magician.[16]

Fitzmyer understands the description "false prophet" to mean that Bar Jesus "posed as a prophet."[17] This is misleading and reduces the full impact of this episode. Bar Jesus did not pose as a prophet—he was indeed a prophet, but in Luke's opinion, a false one. A false prophet made the same claims as the true prophet—both appealed to a divine authority for their pronouncements. It must also be remembered that the claim of Luke and other Christian writers that prophecy was alive and active was basically a Christian claim. Most non-Christian Jews believed that prophecy had ceased altogether in the Second Temple period.[18] Josephus, for example, reserved the word "prophet" for the biblical prophets, and had no hesitation in calling those who in his own day claimed to be God's messengers "false prophets" (e.g., *Wars* 6.5.2). For all that, in Jewish tradition, a prophet claimed to have stood in the council of the Lord; he is one who claims to reveal the will of God. Both true and false prophet claimed this status and function. That the word/will of God and its interpretation was at issue in this Bar Jesus episode is implied by 13:7 as Sergius Paulus "sought to hear

12. Haenchen, *Acts*, 398.
13. Pesch, *Die Apostelgeschichte*, 2:21, 26.
14. Barrett, *Acts*, 1:613; cf. Stählin, *Apostelgeschichte*, 346n416.
15. Jervell, *Die Apostelgeschichte*, 366n416.
16. Schille, *Die Apostelgeschichte*, 287.
17. Fitzmyer, *Acts*, 499.
18. See Levison, "Did the Spirit," 35–57.

the word of God." This little sentence is crucial in this episode. It indicates the point of conflict between Paul and Bar Jesus—the understanding of "the word of God." Hearing the word of God is important for Luke (Luke 5:1; Acts 13:44; 15:7) and has blessing attached to it (Luke 8:21; 11:28). It is also characteristic of the prophets of Israel to challenge their audiences with, "Hear the word of God" (e.g., Isa 1:10; Jer 19:3; Ezek 6:3; Hos 4:1).

Relevant in this context is Deut 18:20-22: "But the prophet who presumes to speak a word in my name which I have not commanded him to speak, or who speaks in the name of other gods, that same prophet shall die. And if you say in your heart, "How may we know the word which the Lord has not spoken?"—when a prophet speaks in the name of the Lord, if the word does not come to pass or come true, that is a word which the Lord has not spoken; the prophet has spoken it presumptuously, you need not be afraid of him."

This is particularly relevant because of the link between prophet and Name. All prophets speak in the name of the Lord, but the false prophet speaks words that he has not been commanded to speak, and his word does not come to pass. This is the case of with Bar Jesus. He claims to speak with the authority of the name of Jesus (as his very name indicates), but he does not speak what the Lord has commanded. He perverts it. It is Barnabas and Saul who speak rightly the teaching of the Lord, and that results in believing (13:12).

It is curious that the term ψευδοπροφήτης is used in the Septuagint almost exclusively in Jeremiah. There, the false prophets are those who seize Jeremiah for saying that Yahweh will abandon the Temple (Jer 33:7-8, 11 LXX). In Jer 27:9 LXX, the false prophets are linked with the μαντευόμενοι καὶ οἵ ἐνυπνιαζόμενοι καὶ οἵ οἰωνισμάτοι ὑμῶν καὶ οἵ φαρμακοί, not unlike the way Bar Jesus is here linked with the μάγοι. And Hananiah is a typical false prophet (Jer 35:1 LXX) because he stood in the Temple, but proclaimed falsely the intention of Yahweh. Bar Jesus has been proclaiming the word and will of God in Paphos, but from Luke's perspective, he has interpreted the ways of God falsely. That is the point of this whole episode. The authoritative prophetic word of God comes to Cyprus, according to Luke, only through Paul and Barnabas, the true prophets (13:1). Only they have been validly commissioned by the holy spirit to announce the word of God (13:2-3). And so the "teaching of the Lord" (13:12) is seen in its full power and authority only when it comes through prophets and teachers validated by the holy spirit (13:9). Without that validation, one is a son of the opponent, the slanderer (διάβολος) (13:10), not a son of Jesus, despite the man's name.

Secondly, while early Christian writers used the term "false prophet" of those outside the Christian pale (e.g., presumably in Rev 16:13; 19:20; 20:10), they also used it quite clearly to refer to someone within the broad Christian tradition. Christian communities were warned to be on their guard against false prophets who come in sheep's clothing (Matt 7:15; cf. 24:11, 24). Both 2 Pet 2:1 and 1 John 4:1 imply that the false teachers and prophets come from within the community. Paul does not refer specifically to false prophets, but he is well aware of false apostles (ψευδαπόστολοι) (2 Cor 11:13) and false brethren (ψευδαδέλφοι) (2 Cor 11:26; Gal 2:4), again, obviously internal to the communities concerned. The same is also true of the prophets in Rev 2:2, and of the false teachers of the Pastorals (e.g., 2 Tim 3:6–8). And when the term "false prophet" is used in the Didache, it distinctly refers to those within the Christian communities (11:5–10; 16:3). The only other time Luke himself uses the word "false prophet" is in his Gospel (6:26) where he refers to those prophets who are clearly "insiders" to Israel, not outsiders.

In Acts 13:8, the false prophet is said to have withstood (ἀνθίστατο) Barnabas and Saul. It is precisely that verb that is used in 2 Tim 3:8 to describe the opposition of Jannes and Jambres to Moses, and that of the false teachers to the truth of the Pauline tradition. Those men are described as "men of corrupt mind and counterfeit faith," a description not dissimilar to that given by the Lukan Paul of Bar Jesus (13:10). The same verb is used again in 2 Tim 4:15, where Alexander is said to have "strongly opposed our message" (λίαν ἀντέστη τοῖς ἡμέτεροις), and, as with other false teachers, "the Lord will requite him for his deeds." In other words, the verb ἀνθίστημι is use almost technically for those who oppose someone's teaching or prophecy (see also Gal 2:11; Acts 6:10). In addition, the strong judgment that Luke, through the mouth of Paul, passes on Bar Jesus parallels closely similar judgments made throughout the New Testament on false teachers, false prophets, false brethren and the like (Matt 7:15; 2 Cor 11:13; Gal 1:9; 2 Thess 2:11; 2 Pet 2:1; Rev 19:20). In all cases, if these opponents are not actually within the communities, they are very close to them, and that is what makes them dangerous. And in this episode in Acts 13, Luke appears to be using terminology commonly used in Christian circles when writing about conflicts between false and true teachers or prophets.[19]

It is reasonable to conclude that Bar Jesus was a Jewish prophet, and one seen to be a serious threat to the Christian community, and therefore one in some contact with that community. He was a serious threat because

---

19. Clearly, Bar Jesus is both a prophet and a teacher. The link is commonly made; indeed, Luke has made it in 13:1 (cf. 1 Cor 12:28; Did. 13:2; 15:1).

he represented the word of God falsely and opposed the understanding of it by others coming from outside and also claiming to be prophets, namely, Saul and Barnabas (13:7-8). This episode, then, tells of a battle between prophets, in much the same way as "orthodox" prophets of Israel stood in opposition to those "false" prophets who also claimed authority to teach and reveal the ways of God. Klauck is close to the mark when he says that Luke tells this story to warn against an "all-devouring syncretism that at its worst even usurps Christian substance such as the name of Jesus, and hence threatens the Church from within."[20] Klauck at least implies that Bar Jesus represented an internal threat. I doubt, however, that syncretism is the real problem for Luke; it is rather that this man interprets the way of the Lord wrongly, and so his authority is questionable. Valid authority only comes from those who have been given it by Jesus through the legitimate apostles, teachers, and prophets who through prayer and fasting and the laying on of hands, have been set apart by the Holy Spirit for such work (13:1-3). The acceptable prophets and teachers at Antioch are named by Luke (13:1); their teaching and prophecy are authoritative in Lukan circles.

Further support for this understanding of Bar Jesus comes from the charge brought against him by Paul that the prophet was "making crooked the straight paths of the Lord," and so was "an enemy of all righteousness" (13:10). These two expressions are virtually synonymous. The straight paths of the Lord lead to righteousness (cf. Ps 23:3); crooked paths, conversely, pervert righteousness. It is very common for scholars to think that Paul refers in this charge to Bar Jesus' magical practices and his financial profit from such practices. So, on these charges, Barrett says, "Luke has no love for those who have illicit, and probably profitable, dealings with the supernatural. The magus is roundly cursed."[21] But I suggest his opposition to the faith (13:8) was more sophisticated and potentially more dangerous than that. Bar Jesus claims to be teaching the straight paths of the Lord, but Luke thinks he has made them crooked by his false understanding of righteousness. The strong language used by Paul, filled with biblical terms,[22] suggests this man is a real threat, and that is possibly because he is was having influence inside the fold. By calling Bar Jesus a "son of the devil" (υἱὸς διαβόλου), Luke has Paul expose the prophet for what he really is. He is the adversary (διάβολος) who "comes and takes away the word from their hearts, that they might not believe and be saved" (Luke 8:12).

---

20. Klauck, *Magic and Paganism*, 54.
21. Barrett, *Acts*, 1:617.
22. For the Septugintal language used here, see Jervell, *Die Apostelgeschichte*, 347.

The links between false claimants, Satan, deceit, and unrighteousness, interestingly enough, are also found in Paul's writings. In 2 Cor 11:13-15, he writes, "For such men are false apostles, deceitful workmen, disguising themselves as apostles of Christ. And no wonder, for even Satan disguises himself as an angel of light. So it is not strange if his servants also disguise themselves as servants of righteousness. Their end will correspond to their deeds." And similar links are found in 2 Thess 2:11-12, "Therefore God sends upon them a strong delusion, to make them believe what is false, so that all may be condemned who did not believe the truth but had pleasure in unrighteousness."

Bar Jesus in Acts fits the same bill. He is not a "son of Jesus," as he is named, but rather is on the side of the opposition. But the adversary comes to those within like a wolf in sheep's clothing. That is why Luke calls him "false" and a *magos*. Even the non-Septuagintal term, ῥαδιουργία, used by Luke in Acts 13:10, refers to deceit and chicanery, and unscrupulous fraud,[23] and is indicative of an insider rather than of an outsider. It is his teaching about the way of the Lord that is delusional, not his magical powers or pagan syncretism.

Some of the Septuagintal terms used in this condemnation of Bar Jesus are worth further comment. To pervert (διαστρέφειν) the right ways is a feature of false prophets and of false behavior in general (cf. Mic 3:9; Ezek 13:18; Prov 10:9; Ps Sol 10:3; Philo, *Sobr.* 10), and this is what Bar Jesus is charged with doing. Scholars often point to Hos 14:9 (14:10 LXX) and see it as paralleling Paul's charge.[24] Barrett also notes the parallel but thinks "it is unlikely that the passage is specifically referred to, since Hosea says that the transgressors shall stumble . . . in them (sc. the paths), not that they will pervert them."[25] But that is an unnecessary distinction. From Luke's perspective, Bar Jesus perverts the straight paths of Yahweh; he does not walk in Yahweh's straight paths. This causes him to stumble and so to grope for someone to lead him by the hand (13:11).

The Hosea 14:9 passage is worth citing in full, "Whoever is wise, let him understand these things; whoever is discerning (συνετός), let him know them; for the ways of the Lord are right (εὐθεῖαι αἱ ὁδοὶ τοῦ κυρίου) and the upright (δίκαιοι) walk in them, but transgressors stumble in them."

According to Hosea, the righteous (δίκαιοι) walk the straight paths. Bar Jesus, however, is an "enemy of all righteousness" (ἐχθρὸς πάσης δικαιοσύνης) because he has made those straight paths crooked (διαστρέφων

---

23. See *BDAG* 902.
24. For example, see Schneider, *Apostelgeschichte*, 123n48.
25. Barrett, *Acts*, 1:617.

τὰς ὁδοὺς τοῦ κυρίου τὰς εὐθείας). He belongs to the sinners and so stumbles. On the other hand, Luke says that the proconsul Sergius was συνετός, precisely the adjective used by Hosea of the wise man who follows the straight paths of the Lord. Sergius Paulus recognised the straight path of the word of God brought by Paul and Barnabas, and believed (13:12).[26] One might also note the connection between being συνετός and believing made in Sir 33:3: "A man of understanding will trust in the law" (ἄνθρωπος συνετὸς ἐμπιστεύσει νόμῳ). If Luke is implicitly referring to this passage, then the suggestion again is that the νόμος and its interpretation is at stake in this conflict with Bar Jesus.

Jervell is right to claim that the use of Septuagintal terms suggests that Paul's charge "sind Worte gegen einen Juden."[27] After all, Bar Jesus has already been identified as a Jew (13:6). But more importantly, it suggests that the conflict between Bar Jesus and Paul has been on scriptural matters, not on such things as magic or dream interpretation. If the word or law of God, and its interpretation, has been the center of the debate, as 13:7 suggests, then again it makes sense to understand Bar Jesus as being familiar with that word and as having a particular teaching based on that word. In other words, Bar Jesus belongs close to the tradition, at the very least of the synagogue, if not actually within a Christian community at Paphos. In addition, the fact that it is the teaching of the Lord (διδαχὴ τοῦ κυρίου) (13:12) that astonishes the proconsul and leads to his believing is further evidence that this whole episode is not about magic versus Christianity, but about one teaching (namely, that of Paul) being truly derived from the Lord and based on the word of God versus another teaching (that of Bar Jesus) that has its authentication, as Luke would have it, from elsewhere.

4. Bar Jesus

One reason for thinking that this Jewish prophet was actually within the Christian community is found in his name. It is possible, of course, that Bar Jesus was the man's real name and that he was biologically the son of a man named Jesus. After all, it was common practice for prophets to be identified as the "son of." So, for example, Jehu is "the son of Hanani" (1 Kgs 15:33),

---

26. It is possible to read Sergius Paulus as similar to Cornelius, that is, as a god-fearer who already belonged to the faith (cf. 13:8). In any case, Luke seems to be following the usual pattern: Paul goes first to the synagogues (13:5), he meets opposition from Jews, but some god-fearers believe. Jervell thinks the proconsul belongs to the god-fearers (Jervell, *Die Apostelgeschichte*, 346).

27. Jervell, *Die Apostelgeschichte*, 347.

Elisha is "the son of Shaphat" (1 Kgs 19:19), Isaiah is the "son of Amoz" (2 Kgs 19:2) and Zechariah, the "son of Iddo" (Ezra 6:14). So in order to bolster his claim as a prophet, this man used the self-designation, "son of Jesus." That is possible, but given the context and the significance of the name "Jesus" in Acts, this seems too much of a coincidence. I suggest that we consider the possibility that the man called himself Bar Jesus because he thought himself to be a disciple of Jesus. Or, at the very least, he was like the "sons of" Scaeva (a term which also might refer to Scaeva's students or apprentices rather than to his biological sons) who exorcised in the name of Jesus even though, in Luke's judgment, they did not belong to him (19:13–15). In other words, Bar Jesus claimed to be a follower of Jesus and to operate in his name and with his authority, but from Luke's perspective, he has perverted the truth. Just as the sons of Scaeva had no authority to exorcise in the name of Jesus (19:13–16), so also this man has no authority to call himself a son of Jesus.

That the very name Bar Jesus could mean "a disciple of Jesus" is not a new suggestion. According to Schmiedel, W. C. van Manen suggested it over one hundred years ago.[28] However, it seems that van Manen argued on the assumption that the name Bar Jesus first appeared in a primary document available to Luke that did not include the qualifiers, "Jew," "false prophet," and "magos." That speculation certainly weakened, rather than strengthened, his argument, and, I suggest, such an uncontrollable theory was unnecessary. As I have already indicated, one could claim to be a "disciple of Jesus" and also be a Jew and a prophet.

It is well known that the expression "son of" does not always refer to one's paternity. It is often used idiomatically in Hebrew, Aramaic, and in Greek to indicate that one belongs to a particular group, or that one has particular characteristics.[29] The expressions "sons of God" or "sons of Israel" are obvious examples. Joseph, who was given the name Barnabas, which Luke interprets as "son of encouragement" (Acts 4:36), is an example of the association of name and character, as also is the name Boanerges, "the sons of thunder" (Mark 3:17). Bar Cochba, the name taken by the Jewish revolutionary of about 120 CE is an example of the name indicating what was expected or hoped. It is possible that Bar Jesus derived his name from an eponymous use of Jesus' name. A group of singers might call themselves "sons of Korah" or "sons of Asaph" (e.g., Ps 42:1; 44:1; 2 Chr 35:15), and priestly groups might call themselves "sons of Aaron" or "sons of Zadok" (e.g., Lev 1:5; 2 Chr 35:14; Ezek 40:46). The Jewish Scriptures also

---

28. Schmiedel, "Barjesus," 478–83; 480.

29. See, for example, Brown et al., *Hebrew Lexicon*, 120–21; Payne Smith, *Compendious*, 53.

occasionally refer to the "sons of the prophets," meaning a group of prophets associated with Elijah or Elisha, probably as disciples (1 Kgs 20:35; 2 Kgs 2:3–15; 6:1; 9:1). Luke himself has used that expression earlier in Acts. In his sermon at Pentecost, Peter said, "you are sons of the prophets and of the covenant," and that was said in the context of God raising up Jesus as the prophet promised by Moses (Acts 3:17–26). Did Bar Jesus claim to be one of the sons of The Prophet?

According to Matthew, Jesus warned the Christian community against calling anyone "father" (23:9) in a context where clearly the title refers to a teacher or leader of the community. If some Christians called their teacher "father," it is logical that they should call themselves his "sons." In Luke 11:19, Jesus refers to the disciples of the Pharisees as "your sons (οἱ υἱοὶ ὑμῶν). Peter refers to Markos as "my son" (ὁ υἱός μου) (1 Pet 5:13), and although that may be nothing more than a term of endearment, teachers did address their disciples as "sons" (cf. Heb 12:5; Prov 1:8; 2:1; 3:1). The BDAG also gives a number of examples from pagan literature in which the term "son" is used of a follower or pupil, especially among various guilds.[30] The Syriac church father, Ephraem, calls Bardesan's followers, "the sons of Bardesan."[31] This is evidence enough to suggest that the name Bar Jesus could indicate a teacher-disciple relationship. If that is a valid understanding, then it certainly implies that Bar Jesus claimed to belong inside the Jesus movement.

5. Elymas and Bar Jesus

But what does Luke mean when he refers to "Elymas the magician" and then adds, "for so his name is interpreted" (οὕτως γὰρ μεθερμηνεύεται τὸ ὄνομα αὐτοῦ)? Elymas is a name whose meaning has caused "endless bewilderment."[32] I suggest that Luke is playing both on the name Elymas and the name Bar Jesus. In addition, central to understanding his word-play is his repetition of the noun ὄνομα (13:6, 8).

It is worth remembering that writers at the time delighted in finding meanings for names that today we dismiss as far-fetched, if not downright impossible. Three brief examples will illustrate. Philo thought that the Essenes "derive their name from their piety," believing their name was a variation of ὁσιότης (*Quod Omnis* 75). Luke himself says that Barnabas means "son of consolation" (4:36), a derivation to which very few modern scholars

---

30. BDAG 1024.

31. See Brockelmann, *Lexicon*, 89.

32. Dunn, *Acts*, 176. Fitzmyer categorically says, "No one knows what it means" (Fitzmyer, *Acts*, 502).

would give their assent. For a curious logic, Clement of Alexandria is classic. He claims that when the bacchanals shriek "evoe" (εὐοῖ) they are calling out the name Eva "by whom error came into the world. The symbol of the Bacchic orgies is a consecrated serpent. Moreover, according to the strict interpretation of the Hebrew term, the name Hevia, aspirated, signifies a female serpent."[33] I suggest that a key to understanding this baffling link between Elymas and Bar Jesus and the word magos is Luke's use of this kind of etymological argument.

In 13:8, the choice is between understanding μάγος as a translation of Elymas, and understanding Elymas as a translation of the name (ὄνομα) mentioned in 13:6, namely Bar Jesus. As suggested, the use of the word ὄνομα in both 13:6 and 13:8 might not be at all coincidental. The issue of the sacred Name lurks. After all, the man is called Bar Jesus. Without exception, every time in Acts that Luke introduces a new character into the narrative, he does so by using the dative case, ὀνόματι (5:1, 34; 8:9; 9:10, 11, 33, 36; 10:1; 11:28; 12:13; 16:1, 14; 17:34; 18:2, 7, 24; 19:24; 20:9; 21:10; 27:1). Only with Bar Jesus is the nominative case used; elsewhere, Luke uses the nominative ὄνομα exclusively of Jesus. By using the nominative in this episode to describe Bar Jesus, Luke draws sharp attention to the significance of the man's name, of the Name, and of the relation between the two.

Among recent scholars, it is almost unanimously thought that μάγος in 13:8 is a translation of Elymas. It is suggested that the name Elymas derived either from the Aramaic word hlm or the Arabic alim, both meaning a "diviner" or "dream-interpreter." So Jervell says, "ὁ μάγος wird als Übersetzung des Namens Elymas bezeichnet.... Elymas ist wahrscheinlich die gräzisierte Form des aramäischen: haloma, 'der Magier.'"[34] Schille likewise says, "Lukas hat ... zu entlasten versucht, daß er μάγος als Übersetzung für Elymas versteht.... Tatsächlich kommt aramäisch אלימא = stark bzw. Arabisch alim = gelehrt der Bedeutung 'Traumdeuter' nahe."[35] This too is an old suggestion. The seventeenth-century scholars, Edmund Castell and John Lightfoot, had already suggested the Arabic derivation,[36] and it was certainly still supported by some at the beginning of the twentieth century.[37]

This explanation is held largely because the translation, Bar Jesus = Elymas, is believed to be impossible. Bruce states categorically: "Elymas

---

33. *Exhortation to the Heathen* 2.
34. Jervell, *Die Apostelgeschichte*, 346; 346n424.
35. Schille, *Die Apostelgeschichte*, 287; cf. Schneider, *Apostelgeschichte*, 122; Yaure, "Elymas," 297–314; Hemer, *Book of Acts*, 227; Klauck, *Magic*, 50.
36. Schmiedel, "Barjesus," 480.
37. See Lake and Foakes-Jackson, *Beginnings*, 4:144.

... is probably a Semitic word with a similar meaning to magos; it cannot be an interpretation of "Barjesus."[38] Likewise, Dunn says that Bar Jesus and Elymas have nothing to do with each other. He suggests that maybe Elymas was a nickname, "but if so, its point is too obscure for us."[39] Barrett also thinks it is impossible to translate Bar Jesus as Elymas, because the latter seems not to be a Greek name. He suggests we agree with Bengel who said: "nescio quomodo, synonyma sunt," but he himself then adds, "Failing this, the simplest and probably correct solution is that both names were, in the tradition (or traditions) that Luke used, applied to the man in question, and that Luke assumed that the form that appeared to be Greek must be a translation of the Semitic; cf. 4:36. The assumption is a natural one, though Luke might have reflected that the Latin *Paul* is not a translation of the Semitic *Saul* (v. 9)."[40]

In another attempt to solve this puzzle, some have seized on the alternative reading Ετοιμας that appears in D and similarly in some Old Latin manuscripts. While Kirsopp Lake favoured this solution, he was well aware of its weakness: "This seems the best suggestion yet made, but the combination of a doubtful reading with a somewhat strained etymology is not quite convincing."[41] More recent scholarship has seen a number of problems with the hypothesis and so has abandoned it.[42]

There are other variant readings on the name of this man among which are βαριησοῦ, βαριησοῦς, βαριησοῦν, βαριησοῦαν. As Barrett suggests, βαριησοῦ and βαριησοῦαν may be regarded as alternative transliterations of בר־ישוע and βαριησοῦς and βαριησοῦν may be taken as attempts to improve the grammar.[43] All of these suggest the man's name means "son of Jesus/Jeshua." However, some other variants read "son of the Name." The Syriac Peshitta, for example, reads bar šūmā (in some Greek manuscripts, transliterated, βαρσουμα) and some other Greek manuscripts read βαριησοῦμ. Professor S. Brock (Oxford) says that Baršūmā is not a normal Syriac name, and that -šūmā implies a Palestinian Aramaic pronunciation.[44] In any case, these variants indicate that the man is called "son of the Name." It is not difficult to see how "son of Jesus" might be altered to "son of the Name." After all, in Acts, Jesus is the Name given for salvation (4:12); it is the name

---

38. Bruce, *Acts*, 249.
39. Dunn, *Acts*, 176.
40. Barrett, *Acts*, 1:615.
41. Lake and Foakes-Jackson, *Beginnings*, 4:144.
42. See Barrett, *Acts*, 1:615; Haenchen, *Acts*, 398n2.
43. Barrett, *Acts*, 1:613.
44. Personal email communication, October 14, 2002.

of the heavenly being who speaks to Paul near Damascus (9:5); and it the name into which people are baptised (2:38) and upon whom believers call (2:14). So there is a close relation between Jesus and the Name, so close that it is not unexpected that some might out of devotion to Jesus, in fact call him The Name. As Barrett notes, "in rabbinic use שׁם (name) may stand for God; a Syriac translator who could not bring himself to say bar yesu might make the corresponding substitution."[45] Haenchen claims, "Now anybody with the faintest knowledge of Aramaic knew that Bar-Jesus meant 'son of Jesus' and Luke carefully refrains from alerting other readers also to the fact that this rascal bore the sacred name of Jesus as part of his own."[46] I suggest that Luke is doing precisely the opposite. He wants to show that not only is Bar Jesus a false prophet, but that his very name illustrates his falseness. He is not a son of Jesus. Luke draws attention to the name factor by repeating, in verse 8, the noun ὄνομα that he had already used in verse 6. The Syriac translations appear to have picked up on this repetition by repeating the name Baršūmā, used in verse 6, in verse 8. In addition, by translating the name, Luke is drawing further attention to it. The point for now is that there is a conceptual link between Jesus and The Name, a link made by Luke himself in Acts (4:12). So if one is a son of Jesus, one is also a son of the Name. But, Luke wants to show, the etymology of this man's name is to be found not in Jesus the Name but elsewhere.

To explain this other etymology, Luke constructs word-play links between Bar Jesus and Elymas. The latter appears not to be a Greek name; however, it might be a contracted form of a longer name.[47] Indeed, according to Schmiedel, G. Dalman thought that it is a contracted form of Ἐλυμαῖος and that the name has something to do with the Elamites (associated in Acts 2:9 with the Parthians and Medes). Schmiedel responded to this suggestion by saying, "Philologically this derivation is the simplest of all; but it contributes nothing towards the solution of the riddle."[48] But I propose that Dalman's philological suggestion does, indeed, provide a clue, if not the solution.

The key is found with Josephus, probably a contemporary of Luke. According to him, Elymos (Ἔλυμος) was the son of Shem, and the ancestor of the Persians. He writes, "For Elymos left behind him the Elamites, the ancestors of the Persians" (Ἔλυμος μὲν γὰρ Ἐλυμαίους, Περσῶν ὄντας ἀρχηγέτας κατέλιπεν) (*Ant.* 1.6.4). As noted earlier, the magoi were commonly associated with the Persians. This is significant because with this

---

45. Barrett, *Acts*, 1:613.
46. Haenchen, *Acts*, 402.
47. See Blass et al., *Greek Grammar* §125.
48. Schmiedel, *Barjesus*, 480.

datum we now have a link between Ἔλυμας and μάγος without going via the Aramaic or Arabic route.

Josephus's information also helps in understanding how Luke can say that Bar Jesus is translated or interpreted as Elymas. Elymas is the son of Shem (cf. Gen 10:22, 31; 1 Chr 1:17). The Hebrew name Shem (שׁם) and the Hebrew word for the Name (שׁם) provide an ideal opportunity for Luke to play on them. Both names, Elymas and Bar Jesus, can be interpreted to mean "the son of שׁם." By playing on the name of the father of Elymos (Shem) and the sacred Name (שׁם [Heb]) Luke understands Elymas to be an interpretation of (μεθερμηνεύεται) Bar Jesus. By this word-play, Luke is in effect wanting to say that the meaning of Bar Jesus is not "son of Jesus" [= the Name], but "son of Shem," the ancestor of the *magoi*. The son of Shem and the ancestor of the *magoi* = Persians is Elymos. So, logically it seems to me, Luke can say that the name Elymas is an interpretation of the name Bar Jesus. It might be argued that Luke's Greek-speaking audience would not catch Hebrew word-plays. But there is only one Hebrew word that I am suggesting Luke is playing with, and that is the word שׁם (Name). It is indeed feasible to assume that Greek-speakers would know that one Hebrew word, if they knew no other.

The point is that this man does not belong to the true followers of Jesus nor is he a member of the valid, authentic prophetic circle. Paul and Barnabas are the true exponents of the will and word of God, especially in the matter of righteousness. Bar Jesus, therefore, is not the son of the Name, but the son of Shem, the ancestor of the Persians and of the *magoi*, and so he is a *magos*, a foreigner to the true Christian community and an opponent of the truth.

Finally, I draw attention to the fact that Luke was aware of other false claimants in the communities he knew. In Acts 19:13–16, he exposes the sons of Scaeva who use the Name to exorcise. In his Gospel, he repeats Mark's report that there was a man casting out demons "in the name of Jesus," but he was forbidden by the disciples because he was not "following with us" (Luke 9:49–50; Mark 9:38–40). In addition, even Apollos, already a Christian, needed to have the way of God expounded to him more accurately (18:26). Bar Jesus belonged to a category somewhere between Apollos and the sons of Scaeva. He had the name, "son of Jesus," but he did not follow the correct understanding of the way of God as taught by Paul and Barnabas.

In summary, I have proposed an alternative understanding of Bar Jesus to that given in scholarship. I have argued that Luke represents Bar Jesus in Acts 13 as a serious opponent of the Christian faith, not because he taught or practiced heathen magic, nor because he practiced some kind of syncretism, but because he taught the righteous ways of God in a false way. Bar Jesus claimed to be a prophet, he claimed to live up to his name as a "son of Jesus" who correctly understood the way of the Lord, but the Lukan Paul exposed him as a false exponent of that way. Testing the spirit and distinguishing true prophecy from false were difficult issues in many early Christian communities. But Luke was not afraid to make that judgment. For him, it was Paul, a man filled with a holy spirit who had authority in the teaching of the Lord, and his true exposition of the righteous ways of God convinced the intelligent proconsul who then believed.

Summary

In Acts 13, Bar Jesus is confronted by Paul and cursed by him. This false prophet is generally thought to have been syncretistic and virtually pagan in his magical practices. This article argues that he was in fact very much within the synagogue and that he had been teaching the ways of the Lord. He was also a threat to the Christian community of Paphos and may even have belonged inside of it. Luke regards him as a serious threat to the faith because of his false teaching about righteousness and the ways of the Lord.

Strange Stares: Atenizein in Acts

THERE ARE TEN CASES of "staring" in Acts. The disciples stare into heaven as Jesus ascends (1:10), and Stephen stares into heaven at his stoning (7:55); Peter and Paul stare at men they are about to heal (3:4; 14:9); Paul stares at Bar Jesus before cursing him (13:9), and at the Sanhedrin before addressing them (23:1); the crowd stares in wonder at Peter (3:12) and the Sanhedrin stares at Stephen (6:15); Cornelius stares at a visiting angel (10:4) and Peter stares into a sheet from heaven (11:6). In each case, the Greek verb ἀτενίζειν is used; only once is it the main verb (3:12); once it is used in the periphrastic tense (1:10); and in every other case, the aorist participle is used with the main verb being either εἶπεν or εἶδεν/εἶδον.[1]

This article intends to explore the use and meaning of this verb in the wider literature and so to offer a fuller understanding of these strange stares in Acts. In his lexicon, Spicq observes: "Among the numerous verbs of seeing in the NT the denominative verb ἀτενίζειν merits special attention."[2] Such attention has not been given this verb by New Testament commentators despite the fact that, besides its use in Acts, it occurs twice in the Gospel of Luke (4:20; 22:56), and twice, in the one context, in 2 Corinthians (2 Cor 3:7, 13). The consequence is that commentators work from definitions given by standard lexica and dictionaries, such as "to look intently at someone or something, to gaze earnestly, to stare."[3] In other words, the verb is understood only in its simple sense and seen to be of little significance.[4] As a result, four important aspects of the verb have gone unnoticed.

---

1. These features do not refer to Codex D which, at 3:4, has significant variants as will be noted later.

2. Spicq, "ἀτενίζω," 227. There is no entry for ἀτενίζειν in *Theological Dictionary of the New Testament*. It is not listed in the lengthy article on "seeing" in that work (*TDNT* 5:315–82). *The Exegetical Dictionary of the New Testament* devotes only a few lines to it and simply indicates its primary meaning and the NT references. There is no comment, nor are there references to other primary or secondary literature (1:177).

3. BDAG 119. See also Liddell et al., *Greek-English Lexicon*, 269. German dictionaries offer similar meanings: "Starren; mit unverwandtem Blick hinsehen" (Frisk, *Griechisches etymologisches Wörterbuch*, 1:177); "Gespannt auf etw. oder jmdn. hinsehen" (Bauer, *Griechisch-Deutsches Wörterbuch*, 240).

4. In his recent commentary, *Acts*, Dunn draws no attention to the verb at all.

First, the most common object of ἀτενίζειν, particularly in Jewish and Christian literature, is a holy person or place. Secondly, the verb is used occasionally when the subject is at prayer, or even in some ecstatic, paranormal state. Thirdly, ἀτενίζειν suggests intuition, most often on the part of a holy person. It is an intuition that is penetrative, as the frequent use of the preposition εἰς with the verb indicates. And fourthly, the common construction, found in all the literature, of a participial form of ἀτενίζειν followed by a main verb of seeing or speaking suggests that the main verbs are to be understood in a particular way. The subject speaks or sees "with intuition" or "with special perception."

Those scholars of Acts who do comment on ἀτενίζειν, either describe it as a "favorite word" (*Vorzugswort*) of Luke,[5] or offer a brief note on 1:10, where the verb is understood to mean little more than a prolonged staring into space. For example, Barrett writes: "peering [the disciples] were straining their eyes to see their departing Lord."[6] Some earlier scholars thought the verb indicated poor eyesight and linked it to medical terminology, an optional understanding offered by Bruce.[7] Poor eyesight is also regarded by Dunn as one reasonable explanation for Paul's behavior in Acts.[8] But this is correctly rejected by Ramsay: "A consideration of these passages [in Acts and 2 Corinthians] must convince every-one that the action implied by the word (ἀτενίζειν) is inconsistent with weakness of vision. The power which looks from the eyes of an inspired person attracts and compels a correspondingly fixed gaze on the part of them that are brought under his influence."[9]

Ramsay was aware that when the verb is used in Acts with a person as its object, it ought not to be understood in its simple sense without the notion of "power." Along these lines, some scholars, dependent on Lake and Cadbury's unsubstantiated claim that ἀτενίζειν "is frequent in stories of miracles,"[10] I

Nearly all commentaries ignore it, particularly at 10:4; 11:6; 23:1.

5. For example, Bruce, *Acts*, 71; Lake and Foakes-Jackson, *Beginnings*, 4:286; Barrett, *Acts*, 1:82; Johnson, *Luke*, 78; Schneider, *Apostelgeschichte*, 300n37; Schille, *Die Apostelgeschichte*, 73.

6. Barrett, *Acts*, 1:82.

7. Bruce, *Acts*, 71. For the use of the verb in some medical writers, see Hobart, *Medical Language*, 76. Not mentioned by Hobart is the belief that a vulture (χαραδριός) staring at a sick man and the sick man at the vulture (ἀτενίζει ὁ χαραδριὸς τῷ νοσοῦντι καὶ ὁ νοσῶν τῷ χαραδριῷ) is a sign that the sickness is not fatal. The bird's stare cures the man. See Sbordone, *Physiologus*, 3. περὶ χαραδριοῦ.

8. Dunn, *Acts*, 179, 304.

9. Ramsay, *St. Paul the Traveller*, 39.

10. Lake and Foakes-Jackson, *Beginnings*, 4:33.

believe that the verb "steht in Wundergeschichten öfter für den magischen Blick."[11] Unfortunately, there is no evidence, apart from Acts 3:4 and 14:9, that ἀτενίζειν was used in miracle narratives or associated with magic.

Ἀτενίζειν in Non-Biblical Literature

While it is true that there are "relatively few occurrences of *atenizein* outside of First Clement and the NT,"[12] there are many more than this statement implies. However, it is rarely used more than twice by any one author. It is used in the primary sense of "looking long and hard" by Aristotle who knows that people stare (ἀτενίζουσιν) at the tail of a star that is only faintly visible.[13] Aristotle also expresses curiosity that our vision deteriorates if we stare for long (ἀτενίζοντες) at the colors white and black.[14] Diodorus Siculus notices that a certain mountain has a color which "blinds the sight of anyone who gazes steadfastly (ἀτενίζειν) upon it for some time."[15] Polybius claims that sight (ὅρασις) is "quite incapable of holding its gaze on one object" (ἥκιστα γὰρ δύναται πρὸς ἕν μένειν ἀτενίζουσα) but requires variety and change to captivate it.[16] These uses of the verb indicate little more than a prolonged, hard look.[17]

The verb is also used in a figurative sense, meaning "to examine closely" or "to give close attention to."[18] Sextus Empiricus says of the different barkings of dogs that "if one were to look into this more closely" (καὶ ὅλως εἴ τις εἰς τοῦτο ἀτενίσειεν), one will notice that, in fact, dogs bark differently in different situations.[19] Rather similarly, Polybius speaks of "fixing attention on the power of the consuls" (εἰς τὴν ὑπάτων ἀτενίσαιμεν ἐξουσὰν).[20] Later, he refers to someone being "perfectly incapable of concentrated attention on public or political affairs" (περὶ δὲ κοινῶν ἢ πολιτικῶν πραγμάτων ἀτενίσει. εἰς τέλος ἀδύνατος).[21] In this case, it may

11. Schille, *Die Apostelgeschichte*, 124; cf. Haenchen, *Acts*, 199n4.
12. Fisher, "Let Us Look," 224.
13. Aristotle, *Meteorologica* 1.6.
14. Aristotle, *Problems* 2.31.19. The verb is used twice in this context.
15. *Diodorus* 3.39.1.
16. Polybius, *Histories* 38.5.8.
17. For other examples, see Spicq, "ἀτενίζω."
18. A nineteenth-century philologist gives as one definition of ἀτενίζειν: "curare, ut aliquid peragatur" (Schleusner, *Novus Thesaurus*, 1:391).
19. Sextus Empiricus, *Outlines* 1.75.
20. Polybius, *Histories* 6.11.12.
21. Polybius, *Histories* 23.5.8.

well be that the gentleman being discussed lacked insight or intuition rather than the ability to concentrate attention.

Most commonly in non-biblical Greek, ἀτενίζειν has as its object a divine being or place, and it implies more than an intent gaze or stare, suggesting rather either intuitive, perceptive looking, or contemplation. For example, in Lucian, Hermes says to Charon: "If you look closely (ἀτενίσῃς) you will also see the Fates up above, drawing off each man's thread from the spindle."[22] This implies no simple sense of staring, but rather a special insight, a reflective vision, which sees beyond the ordinary and into the divine. Plutarch uses ἀτενίζειν only once and then in a passage whose genuineness is doubtful. In the context of disputing Plato's belief that God formed the world as an image of himself, the writer asks: "How does God, contemplating himself, create?" (πῶς γὰρ ἑαυτῷ ἀτενίζων ἔπλασεν).[23] This is divine self-contemplation.

The fourth century neo-Platonist, Plotinus, uses the verb seven times in his Enneads[24] and nearly always in the context of the soul's contemplation of the divine. So the soul says: ἐγὼ δ' ἡμῖν θεὸς ἄμβροτος because it has ascended to the divine and gazed upon the likeness (πρὸς τὸ θεῖον ἀναβὰς καὶ τὴν πρὸς αὐτὸ ὁμοιότητα ἀτενίσας). Elsewhere, Plotinus says that the enlightened soul has already ascended (ἤδη ἀναβεβηκώς) and so he advises: "Concentrate your gaze and see. This alone is the eye that sees the great beauty" (ἀτενίσας ἴδε οὗτος γὰρ μόνος ὁ ὀφθαλμὸς τὸ μέγα κάλλος βλέπει).[25] And again: "Behold pure mind and look upon it with concentrated gaze, not seeing it with these [bodily] eyes" (ἴδε δὲ νοῦν καὶ καθαρὸν καὶ βλέψον εἰς αὐτὸν ἀτενίσας μὴ ὄμμασι τούτοις δεδορκώς).[26] It is clear from these passages that ἀτενίζειν is a verb used in a peculiar, possibly technical, sense which denotes an insight almost mystical in nature that contemplates a reality not observable by ordinary looking.

The fourth-century philosopher, Themistius, mentions those who have an intense desire to gaze at God (οἱ σφόδρα ἐπιθυμοῦντες ἀτενίσαι πρὸς τὸν θεόν).[27] Here, too, the desire may well be to have special insight into [the nature of] God as much as it is to gaze at, or even to contemplate, God. Interesting is the body language used in relation with ἀτενίζειν in another

---

22. Lucian, *Char.* 16.
23. Plutarch, *Moralia* 881A.
24. According to *Lexicon Plotinianum*.
25. Plotinus, *Enneads* 1.6.9.
26. Plotinus, *Enneads* 6.2.8.6.
27. Themistius, *Themistii orationes*, s.v. "Oration 4."

oration of Themistius: ὅσῳ ἂν μᾶλλον ἐγκύπτων ἀτενίζω τοῖν ὀφθαλμοῖν.²⁸ "Stooping" (ἐγκύπτων) implies submission, the posture of an unworthy supplicant or worshipper. This is consistent with its use in other literature where the worthiness or otherwise of the worshipper is linked to the action expressed by ἀτενίζειν.

The verb is used very rarely in the Hermetic literature, but when it is, it again refers to a contemplation of the divine which is more beneficial when one is in a paranormal state. In *Tractate* 13, Hermes tells his son Tat that he (Hermes) has been born again in Mind and has put away his bodily shape. He is no longer an object of spatial dimensions and so is alien to "all that you perceive when you gaze with bodily eyesight" (καὶ πάντων ὅσα δὲ κατανόεις ἀτενίζων σωματικῇ ὁράσει).²⁹

While the papyri reveal very few uses of ἀτενίζειν, two of the three occurrences known to me are significant. An unclear sense is found in *Berliner Griechische Urkunden* 1816.25 (60–59 BCE). It is a fragmented text of a submission by a certain Ammonius to Paniskos on the matter of an act of violence. Ammonius demands the death penalty as a deterrence to others and in that context says: "I am worthy to gaze upon the greatness of those previously recounted" (ἀξιῶ ἀτενίσαι εἰς τὸ μέγετος τῶν προεξηριθημένων). While it is difficult to establish the precise sense of the verb here, the object of the gazing, namely, μέγετος, and the appeal to worthiness would suggest that this is no ordinary staring, but suggests, at least, special insight.³⁰

Quite clear is the compound verb in P. Mag. Leid. W. 16.8 which says: "When the god enters, do not gaze into his face but at his feet" (εἰσελθόντος δὲ τοῦ θεοῦ μὴ ἐνατενίζε τῇ ὄψει ἀλλὰ τῆς [l. τοῖς] ποσί). This is part of a magic text, and again, two things are obvious: The verb has the divine as its object; and such gazing, or contemplation, requires appropriate humility.

Interesting is the use of ἀτενίζειν in the so-called "Mithras Liturgy."³¹ The cultic context is significant. Various verbs of "seeing" are used in the liturgy, but ἀτενίζειν is used in a way that suggests that the worshipper sees the holy while in an ecstatic state. But there is a twist to the verb in this liturgy because the promise is that the supplicant will see the immortal and the presiding gods ascending and descending and then "you will see the gods staring at you and rushing upon you" (ὄψῃ δὲ ἀτενίζοντάς σοι τοὺς

---

28. Themistius, *Oration* 2.29b.

29. *Hermetica* 13.3.

30. The editors list ἀτενίζειν among a number of "rare expressions" found in this submission. See Schubart and Schäfer, *Spätptolemäische*, 92.

31. *PGM*, 4:475–835. For Greek text and English translation, see Meyer, *Mithras Liturgy*.

θεοὺς καὶ ἐπί σε ὁρμωμένους).³² This is one of the few occasions that the gods, and not humans, are the subject of the verb. Here, as in Plotinus, the verb is used in the context of ascent and descent, movements often associated with visions and revelations.

The liturgy continues with the instruction: "At the point of seeing the doors open and the world of the gods within the doors, then stand still, draw breath from the divine into yourself and stare intently" (ἀτενίζων).³³ A youthful beautiful god will appear and the supplant is to greet him with a prayer and then will see him walking. "Look intently (ἀτενίζων), make a long bellowing sound, like a horn, releasing your breath and straining your sides; and kiss the amulet and say... 'Protect me, προσυμηρι.'"³⁴ The cultist will then see the god descending, dressed in clothes and with hair reminiscent of figures portrayed in the Jewish and Christian revelatory ascent genre. The prayer is that the god will stay and dwell in the soul. Then the advice is to "gaze upon the god (ἀτένιζε τῷ θεῷ) while bellowing long, and greet him in this manner."³⁵ This text illustrates very well the close relation between the verb ἀτενίζειν and prayer, ascent, vision and revelation. The verb suggests a particular "spiritual" state into which the suppliant enters which enables him/her to see or to contemplate holy things. Ultimately, the devotee is able to gaze even upon the god and the god will gaze upon him/her. This is an intensely mystical experience. In non-Jewish and non-Christian literature, then, ἀτενίζειν is used in three senses: Primarily, to describe long, hard staring; figuratively, to indicate close attention or insight; but most commonly it is used in the contemplation of the divine. The latter sense appears to be particularly dominant in the literature from the first century CE onwards.

Ἀτενίζειν in the Septuagint, the Pseudepigrapha, and Other Jewish Literature

The simple verb occurs only three times in the Septuagint,³⁶ each time in a figurative sense. In 1 Esd 6:27, Darius commands that the temple be rebuilt

---

32. *PGM*, 4:556.
33. *PGM*, 4:629.
34. *PGM*, 4:658.
35. *PGM*, 4:711.
36. The compound verb ἐνατενίζειν is found in 3 Esd 5:30, where the king as extremely angry with Haman and "looking at him, said threateningly" (ἐνατενίσας μετὰ ἀπειλῆς εἶπεν). The typical participle + main verb of speech can be noted. The context suggests that the king had "good insight" into the true character of Haman. The Greek translation of Aquila at Job 7:8 uses ἀτενίσει for the Hebrew verb שׁור.

completely and that special attention be given (ἀτενίσαι) to those who have returned from captivity to Judah. A second passage refers to people who are "intent on fulfilling" the purpose of the king (ἀτενίζοντας εἰς πρόθεσιν) (3 Macc 2:26). Here the verb may well imply "insight." The third case is more interesting. In the Prayer of Manasseh, the staring is directed towards, if not into, heaven: "I am not worthy to gaze and to see the height of heaven because of the large number of my unrighteousnesses" (οὐκ εἰμὶ ἄξιος ἀτενίσαι καὶ ἰδεῖν τὸ ὕψος τοῦ οὐρανοῦ ἀπὸ πλήθους τῶν ἀδικιῶν μου) (12:9). The use of ἀτενίζειν with another verb of seeing (often, as here, ἰδεῖν) is very common. And the now-familiar context of the verb is also here: The suppliant is at prayer; the object of the verb is a divine person or place; and the suppliant's feeling of unworthiness is admitted.

It is this sense that dominates the use of the verb in the Pseudepigrapha where the verb is used just seven times.[37] In each case, the object of the gaze is a superior, nobler, or holier figure in whose presence the one gazing feels unworthy. In the *Testament of Reuben*, Reuben is not bold enough to gaze and look (ἀτενίσαι καὶ ἰδεῖν) into the face of his father (4:2). Reuben has sinned against his father by looking at the nakedness of Bilhah, Jacob's concubine, who was drunk in her tent. Reuben's shame is not dissimilar to the unworthiness confessed in the *Prayer of Manasseh*. In looking into the face of his father, Reuben is looking into the face of a morally superior, one against whom he has sinned.

In the story of Joseph and Asenath, Joseph has righteously declared that he cannot kiss Asenath because he is a Jew and she is not. On hearing this, Asenath is exceedingly distressed, sighs heavily, and "was gazing" (ἦν ἀτενίζουσα) at Joseph with her eyes open and full of tears (8:8). Joseph notices this and blesses her. Two things can be noted: Asenath, like many others who "gaze," is not in a normal emotional state; and Asenath's gaze is directed towards Joseph before whom she feels unworthy. She is in the presence of a righteous man. Later, Asenath meets a heavenly man who takes her by the hair and shakes her. Asenath is afraid because the heavenly man's hand emits sparks as if it were as hot as iron. She "looks, gazing (ἐπιβλέψεν ἀτενίζουσα) with her eyes at the man's hand" and is then told "Happy are you, Asenath, because the ineffable mysteries have been revealed to you" (16:13-15). Asenath has an epiphanic visionary experience which is expressed, as is so common, by a participle of ἀτενίζειν in conjunction with a main verb of seeing.

Such visionary and revelatory staring occurs in the other four instances of the verb in the Pseudepigrapha. In the *Apocalypse of Moses*, Eve

---

37. Denis, *Concordance grecque*.

confesses her sin, and is raised up by an angel who bids her rise because the spirit of Adam is being carried to its Maker. Eve gazes into heaven and sees (ἀτενίζασα ... ἴδεν)[38] a chariot of light borne by four eagles, and she is in the presence of the seraphim and the Holy One (33:2). Again, gazing is co-terminous with seeing a heavenly vision.

The connection with heavenly visions can be noted also in the *Testament of Abraham*. Abraham is taken up by the angel into the heavens: "And Abraham looked and saw (ἀτενίσας ... εἶδεν) two gates, the one small and the other large, and between the two gates sat a man upon a throne of great glory, and a multitude of angels round about him" (8:4). Similarly, Abraham, in the heavens, "looked and saw (ἀτενίσας εἶδεν) men upon the earth" (12:6).

The single occurrence of the verb in the *Testament of Solomon* is in the context of Solomon who has called Ephippas and another demon to transport a pillar to the heavens. The pillar was suspended in the air by the spirits, and "when we looked intently (ἐν τῷ ἀτενίζειν), the lower part of the pillar became oblique, and so it is to this day" (24:5). It is a strange passage, but the object of the verb is holy (the pillar is a symbol of the temple) and in the heavens.

In other Jewish Greek literature, the verb is used very rarely. Philo does not use it; and it is used only twice by Josephus. He writes of some martyred Jews who died "with their eyes fixed on the temple" (ἕκαστος ἀτενίσας εἰς τὸν ναὸν ἀφεώρα).[39] Once again, the participle is used with the main verb of seeing to underline the peculiar kind of seeing that is meant—one focused on a holy place, in this case, the temple.[40] In the second instance, Josephus describes the arrogance of Agrippa who wears a garment made wholly of silver at a festival to honor Caesar, and as the sun shone on it those who "gazed upon" him (ἠτένιζησαν) were filled with a kind of horror.[41] The implication is that the spectators were filled with a sense of awe at this epiphany of a god. It is possible that Josephus knew the verb as a technical term for gazing at a divine figure and so used it ironically to highlight the arrogance of Herod.

---

38. Some manuscripts read ἠτένισεν ... καὶ ἴδεν (Tischendorf, *Apocalypses*, 18).

39. Josephus, *Wars* 5.517.

40. Hippocrates reports the case of a dying man who, staring fixedly with his eyes (ἀτενίσας τοῖσιν ὄμμασιν), died (Hippocrates, *Epidemics* 7.10). This is the death-stare, the stare into a *tremendum*.

41. Josephus, *Ant.* 19.344.

Ἀτενίζειν in Non-Canonical Early Christian Literature

While ἀτενίζειν is used commonly in Christian literature down to the fourth century, at least, it is rarely used more than once or twice by any one writer.[42] When it is used, it commonly has a holy person or place as its object, and so is consistent with its use in other literature. There are few exceptions. One, possibly, is the use of the compound ἐνατενίζειν by Justin who is amazed to meet a philosopher on a lonely beach, and so "I fixed my eyes rather keenly on him" (ἐνητένισα).[43] This stranger is a mysterious figure and possibly that is why this particular verb is used; or, since Justin felt inexplicably attracted to him, the verb might suggest his intuition that a most significant meeting was about to occur. Justin also uses the same verb when advising his readers that they will perceive prophetic utterances correctly when they "pay attention with the mind to what is said" (ἐνατενίσατε τῷ νοὶ τοῖς λεγομένοις).[44] The verb may well suggest "deeper insight." Likewise, Hippolytus, bishop of Rome in the third century, writes "in order that the reader, having insight into the treatises of this man [Elchasai], may be made aware of [his heresy] (ἵνα τοῖς αὐτοῦ ἐγγράφοις ὁ ἐντυγχάνων ἐπιγνοίη)."[45]

Since the verb occurs frequently in the canonical Acts, it should not be surprising to find it also in the apocryphal Acts. There, too, it is used consistently in the familiar construction of a participle + main verb of perception, and with heaven or a holy person, either Jesus or a sainted apostle, as the object; and it is used to highlight the intuitive vision or speech of a sainted apostle.[46] An example of the former is found in the Acts of Peter and Paul as Paul "stares into the height of heaven" and prays (ὁ δὲ Παῦλος . . . ἀτενίσας εἰς τὸ ὕψος τοῦ οὐρανοῦ εἶπεν).[47] An example of the latter is found in the Acts of Barnabas as Barnabas recognised (ἀτενίσας . . . ἀνεγνώρισεν) Heracleius,

---

42. It is used by a number of writers in the sixth century, including John of Caesarea and Maximus the Confessor, consistently in the sense of the contemplation of God, sometimes of the person of Jesus.

43. Justin, *Die ältesten Apologeten*, s.v. "Iustinus Dialogus" 3.1.

44. Justin, *Die ältesten Apologeten*, s.v. "Apologia" 1.42.2.

45. Hippolytus, *Refutatio* 9.13.6.

46. The only occasion where it seems to be used in its simple sense is in Acts of John 113, where John says it would be grievous for him to look at a woman (τὸ ἀτενίσαι γυναικὶ ἐπαχθές). All references from the apocryphal Acts are found in Lipsius and Bonnet, *Acta Apostolorum Apocrypha*. Translations are mine.

47. *Acts of Peter and Paul* 11.

having met him once before. He then appointed him bishop, an action which suggests his recognition was a particularly perceptive, intuitive one.[48]

The sainted apostle Paul is the object of Thecla's stare as she sits at the window and "gazes at Paul as if at some joyful spectacle" (ἀτενίζουσα ὡς πρὸς εὐφρασίαν).[49] Thecla is in a paranormal state—for three days and nights she does not eat or relate to her family; instead, she "devotes herself to a strange man."[50]

The verb also occurs in contexts in which the saint experiences a kind of metamorphosis or there is an epiphany. The martyr Andrew prays to Jesus and the spectators see a reflection (ἀπαύγασμα) like lightning from heaven which surrounds him "with the result that human eyes were not able to look at him" (ὥστε οἱ ὀφθαλμοὶ τῶν ἀνθρώπων μὴ δύνασθαι ἀτενίσαι).[51] Similarly, on a rare occasion when ἀτενίζειν is used as the main verb, "those standing by stared at Thomas" (οἱ παρόντες ἠτένιζον εἰς αὐτόν) and saw his form (εἶδος) change into another shape (μορφή).[52] The *Acts of Philip* report crowds staring at Philip (ἦσαν οἱ ὄχλοι ἀτενίζοντες εἰς αὐτόν) with some saying that he was truly a man of God while others that he was a *magos*.[53] An epiphany context is found in the *Martyrdom of St Matthew* as the saint addresses Jesus who appears in a vision as a child while the former is in the mountains, in solitude, wearing an apostolic robe, barefooted and at prayer.[54] In the same writing, the demon does not dare to look into Matthew's face (οὐδὲ εἰς τὸ πρόσωπον αὐτοῦ τολμῶ ἀτενίσαι) "since he obliterated our whole race by proclaiming the name of Christ."[55]

Finally, in the apocryphal Acts, the construction ἀτενίσας . . . εἶπεν is found a number of times in the *Acts of Peter and Paul*. In these contexts, the verb implies intuition or insight on the part of the speaker who is always a sainted apostle.[56]

---

48. *Acts of Barnabas*, 17.

49. *Acts of Paul and Thecla*, 8.

50. As is often the case, the verb is only used in its participial form in this work. It is used on three other occasions, with Paul, or his words, as the object (10, 20, 21). For further examples of ἀτενίζειν implying a magnetic attraction that the apostles had, see *Acts of Thaddaeus*, 3; *Acts of Thomas*, 8.

51. *Passion of Andrew*, 14.

52. *Acts of Thomas*, 8.

53. *Acts of Philip*, 37.

54. *Martyrdom of St Matthew*, 1.

55. *Martyrdom of St Matthew*, 15. This usage is similar to that in the Joseph and Asenath narrative referred to earlier.

56. See *Acts of Peter and Paul*, 11, 76, 77. The latter two are paralleled in the *Martyrdom of Peter and Paul*, 55, 56; the latter also uses the construction in 52. It is also used in

The verb is used in contexts of prayer and visions in other apocryphal Christian writings. Curiously, in *The Protevangelium of James* it is only used as a main verb and never in participial form. Anna (who has not been able to produce a child) has fasted, put on bridal garments, cleansed her head, and gone into the garden at the ninth hour—the hour of prayer. She sits under a laurel tree and prays to God for a child and while praying, she stares into heaven (ἠτένισεν ... Ἄννα εἰς οὐρανόν) and sees a bird building a nest (3:1). In other passages, Mary meets Elizabeth and hears her news and then stares into heaven (ἠτένισεν εἰς οὐρανόν) and prays (12:2); and Joseph, hearing of Mary's pregnancy, cries: "With what countenance shall I look unto the Lord my God?" (ποίῳ προσώπῳ ἀτενίσω πρὸς κύριον τὸν θεόν) (13:1).

Among later Christian writers, Gregory of Nyssa, in the fourth century, uses both the simple verb and its compound ἀτενίζειν mostly, like Plotinus, as a technical term to describe the soul's contemplation of the divine. So he writes of Moses "gazing in tranquility" (ἐνατενίζειν δι' ἡσυχίας) on invisible realities.[57] And in his allegorical interpretation of the Lost Coin parable, he writes: "All those powers which are the housemates of the soul ... will then be con-verted to that divine delight and festivity, and will gaze upon the ineffable beauty of the recovered one" (τῷ ἀφράστῳ κάλλει τοῦ εὑρεθέντος ἐνατενίζουσαι).[58]

Elsewhere, Gregory twice uses the simple verb ἀτενίζειν with the divine and holy as its object: πρὸς τὴν θείαν ἀκτῖνα ἀτενίσαντες; and πρὸς τὸ θεῖον εἶχε τὴν ψυχὴν ἀτενίζουσαν.[59] His contemporary, Amphilochius of Iconium, uses it to denote a special sense of sight, that which is "with the eyes of the heart" (ὀφθαλμοῖς καρδίας ἀτενίσας).[60]

So in post-canonical literature the usage is consistent: The subject is frequently a sainted apostle or someone at prayer and they are given a vision or experience of the holy; sainted apostles have a peculiar intuition or insight which directs their speech or actions; or, lesser mortals direct their gaze at a sainted figure. In still later Christian literature, the verb is used predominantly to describe a vision that takes place in a contemplative state, a gazing that is of the heart and soul and not of the bodily eyes.

---

the *Acts of John* when the apostle sees a painting of himself, compares it with his image in the mirror, and "says with deep perception" (ἀτενίσας ... εἶπε), that it is not a painting of the "real" John but a dead picture of a dead man (28).

57. *PGM*, 44:456c.
58. *Traité de la virginité* 12.3.35.
59. Cited in Stephanus, *Thesaurus*, 2:2359.
60. Amphilochius, *Orationes* 7.25.

Ἀτενίζειν in 1 Clement

Before turning finally to Luke's use of ἀτενίζειν, it is worthwhile examining 1 Clement since it appears six times in that letter. It would appear to be used consistently in the sense of a mystical contemplation of the divine, often in a liturgical setting. Luke and the author of 1 Clement might well have been contemporaries. At least one scholar would claim that 1 Clement in fact predates Luke-Acts claiming both write in the first decade of the second century.[61] Whatever dates are suggested in scholarship, no one would deny that they were near, if not actual, contemporaries.

Scholars of 1 Clement have, with one exception, ignored the verb. Schneider does not include it in his selected vocabulary.[62] Hagner, who looks for evidence that Clement knew Acts, lists single words common to both yet, curiously, ignores ἀτενίζειν altogether.[63] The one scholar of 1 Clement to notice the significance of the verb is E. W. Fisher, whose article,[64] it appears, has gone unnoticed by Luke-Acts scholars.[65] After examining a number of sources, Fisher concludes that ἀτενίζειν "is a technical term for gazing at God or for gazing at the divine,"[66] and that in the NT it has two chief loci: Epiphany and healing, and that the two are quite related: "[T]he context in which ἀτενίζειν occurs . . . has to do with the manifestation of divine power."[67]

In 1 Clement, the verb is nearly always used in exhortations. So: "Let us fix our eyes on the blood of Christ" (ἀτενίσωμεν εἰς τὸ αἷμα τοῦ Χριστοῦ) (7:4), and "Let us look closely at those who have perfectly served his divine glory" (ἀτενίσωμεν εἰς τοὺς τελείως λειτουργήσαντας τῇ μεγαλοπρεπεῖ δόξῃ αὐτοῦ) (9:2), by whom he means Enoch, Noah, and Abraham. In 17:2, Abraham is said to speak, "Seeing the glory of God" (καὶ λέγει ἀτενίζων εἰς τὴν δόξαν τοῦ θεοῦ). The familiar participle of ἀτενίζειν with the main speech verb again suggests that Abraham speaks from the vantage point of insight into, or a contemplation of, the glory of God. Later, the writer again encourages his readers: "Let us fix our eyes on the Father and creator" (ἀτενίσωμεν εἰς τὸν πατέρα καὶ κτίστην) (19:2). Finally, in 36:2, he claims

---

61. Green, "Matthew, Clement," 1–25.
62. Schneider, *Clemens von Rom*.
63. Hagner, *Use of the Old and New*, 256–63.
64. Fisher, "Let Us Look," 218–36.
65. It is neither mentioned in the recent English translation of Spicq nor does the *EDNT* include Fisher's article as a secondary reference (1:177).
66. Fisher, "Let Us Look," 1.
67. Fisher, "Let Us Look," 222.

"through Christ we fix our eyes on the heights of heaven" (διὰ τούτου ἀτενίζομεν εἰς τὰ ὕψη τῶν οὐρανῶν).

In these passages, the verb clearly indicates either a figurative or a mystical sense of "seeing,"[68] and has as its object something or someone holy. Most scholars of 1 Clement would agree that many of the exhortations to "gaze" are given in a liturgical context. So Knopf, commenting on 19:2, believes the author "lehnt sich in diesem Abschnitt unzweifelhaft auf das stärkste an die Gemeindeliturgie an."[69] And commenting on 36:2, Knoch believes this is part of a Christ-hymn which comes from the Roman liturgy and is similar to material in the hermetic mystical literature, in the mysteries religions, and in gnosticism.[70] 1 Clement uses ἀτενίζειν exclusively in the sense of gazing at the holy and in the context of prayer, liturgy, and devotion. One would assume that readers were familiar with this sense of the verb in this context. This use is consistent with its use in later Christian texts and also in the wider literature. Since 1 Clement was written almost contemporaneously with Acts, its use of ἀτενίζειν is obviously important for understanding it in Acts.

Ἀτενίζειν in 2 Corinthians

That ἀτενίζειν rarely attracts the attention of commentators on 2 Cor 3:7, 13 is understandable since it only occurs there in Paul. Paul refers to the tradition that "the sons of Israel saw the face of Moses, that it had been glorified" (εἶδον οἱ υἱοὶ Ἰσραηλ τὸ πρόσωπον Μωυσῆ ὅτι δεδόξασται) (Exod 34:35 LXX). Paul embellishes the tradition by saying that Israel was unable to "look into" (ἀτενίσαι εἰς) Moses" face because of its brightness or glory (3:7). Collange draws attention to the verb and suggests it has a depth of meaning generally not known.[71] Martin, borrowing from Collange, says the verb "denotes intensity and fixedness set on a heavenly form"[72] and agrees with Collange

---

68. Contrary to Fisher, Lindemann thinks this is not mystical "seeing" in the Abendmahl but rather a figurative looking/focusing attention on death of Christ (Lindemann, Die Clemensbriefe, 44).

69. Knopf, Die Lehre der Zwölf, 74. For a list of other scholars (including Bultmann and Harnack) who basically agree that these exhortations have a liturgical context, see Fisher, "Let Us Look," 220.

70. Knoch, Eigenart, 325.

71. Collange, Énigmes de la deuxième épître, 75–76. French scholars tend to show more interest in the verb. See Gregory Nyssa, Traité de la virginité, 415; Daniélou, Platonisme et théologie mystique, 40–42, who notes its significance especially in Gregory of Nyssa's writings.

72. Martin, Second Corinthians, 62.

that ἀτενίζειν is the key word in 3:13.⁷³ Windisch also rightly senses that the verb has nuances not normally noticed, and that it is used in 2 Cor 3 in the same sense as it is used in the Acts passages and in 1 Clement. He says it is "von pneumatischen Erscheinungen gebraucht."⁷⁴

It is clear that in both verses, the object of the verb is something or someone divine or holy (the face of Moses in verse 7 and τέλος τοῦ καταργουμένου in verse 13); and that the context is one of epiphany or revelation. In other words, its use is consistent with that in other literature.⁷⁵ That Paul uses the verb in such a context throws important light on how it might be understood in Luke-Acts.

Ἀτενίζειν in Luke-Acts

Dependency on lexicon definitions leads commentators on Luke to understand the two occurrences of the verb in his Gospel only in its simple sense. But in the light of its common usage, a deeper sense can be seen. In Luke 4:20, attention and emphasis is given to sight. The verse is better translated: "After rolling up the scroll and handing it to the official, he sat down. And when the eyes of all those in the synagogue were gazing (ἦσαν ἀτενίζοντες) at him, he began to say to them." Reference to the eyes (πάντων οἱ ὀφθαλμοί) together with the use of the imperfect periphrastic creates the sense that those in the synagogue were about to experience something extraordinary; they were to receive an insight into the true nature of Jesus. In fact, Jesus reveals himself as the fulfillment of scripture, as One from God. The verb ἀτενίζειν has pointed to this epiphany. As other literature has shown, ἀτενίζειν is used frequently in such contexts. Luke uses the verb similarly in the episode involving Stephen (Acts 6:15) where again the audience "gazes" at a holy man, one to whom heavenly revelations have been given. In both cases, the audience looks at a revealer. As in 2 Cor 3:7, an appropriate verb for such "gazing" is ἀτενίζειν.

In the case of Luke 22:56, Tannehill's comment, "the light from the fire enables the servant-girl to get a better look at Peter,"⁷⁶ misses the nuance of ἀτενίσασα . . . εἶπεν. Attention has already been drawn to the use of the participle with the verbs εἶπεν and εἶδεν. Here, ἀτενίζειν indicates that the

---

73. Martin, *Second Corinthians*, 68.

74. Windisch, *Der zweite Korintherbrief*, 114.

75. In the Septuagint, the verb ἀτενίζειν appears neither in this context nor in the Pentateuch as a whole. Nor do Philo and Josephus use it when commenting on Exod 34. See Philo, *Mos.* 2.70; Josephus, *Ant.* 3.83.

76. Tannehill, *Luke*, 327.

woman spoke on the basis of an intuitive insight which enabled her to see the true relationship of Peter with Jesus.

In Acts it would appear that ἀτενίζειν is used in two similar but distinguishable ways. Firstly, for staring at holy people—at Peter, at an angel, and at Stephen, (3:12; 10:4 + dative; 6:15 + εἰς); and for gazing into heavenly places or objects (1:10; 7:55; 11:6 + εἰς). And secondly, for the staring of holy men at others, suggesting intuition or deep perception. Peter and Paul stare before performing a miracle (3:4 + εἰς; 14:9 + dative); Paul stares at a hostile opponent and at the Sanhedrin (13:9 + εἰς; 23:1 + dative).

Vision is central in Acts 1:9–11 (βλεπόντων . . . ὀφθαλμῶν . . . ἀτενίζοντες . . . ἰδού). The periphrastic tense used in 1:10 draws attention to the action of ἀτενίζειν. Barrett, while acknowledging that "ἀτενίζειν is a stronger word than βλέπειν," understands the verb to mean that the disciples "were straining their eyes to see their departing Lord."[77] Bruce also implies the disciples are staring into the sky and not into "heaven" and so he sees no connection between their staring and the appearance of angels.[78] Haenchen thinks likewise, claiming that the phrase εἰς τὸν οὐρανόν refers to Jesus' destination, and is not the object of the participle, ἀτενίζοντες.[79] This is not likely. The disciples have been promised power (1:8), and then they experience an epiphany of the highest order as Jesus is lifted up (1:9). They are given a vision into heaven itself from where angels appear and speak to them. The object of ἀτενίζειν in other literature demands that the phrase εἰς τὸν οὐρανόν refers to the object of the disciples" gaze. Given the liturgical context of the verb in 1 Clement, liturgical undertones may also be running through this episode.

Among the strangest stares in Acts is Peter's in 3:4 where there is a focus on the eyes. The crippled man sees (ἰδών) Peter; then Peter "stares" at him and says (ἀτενίσας . . . εἰς αὐτόν . . . εἶπεν): "Look (βλέψον) at us."[80] The use of the aorist participle with the aorist main verb suggests the action is co-terminous and that Peter speaks on the basis of his "staring." Our study

---

77. Barrett, *Acts*, 1:82.
78. Bruce, *Acts*, 38.
79. Haenchen, *Acts*, 149n8.
80. Codex D uses the verb only with the cripple (not Peter) as the subject. For Peter, the verb ἐμβλέπειν is used instead. There does not appear to be any significance in the subject change, although Epp suggests that making the cripple the subject of the "strong word ἀτενίζειν . . . may indicate a more awesome status and a higher regard for the apostles in their role as miracle-workers" (Epp, *Theological Tendency*, 155). Maybe, but Codex D does not make similar changes at 14:9, for example. On the other hand, it is worth noting that variant readings to ἀτενίζειν are reasonably common in the literature. Some compound of βλέπειν is the normal alternative. Besides the Codex D reading at Acts 3:4, see, for example, Mark 14:67 (cf. Luke 22:56) which reads ἐμβλέψασα.

of the verb suggests it implies at least penetrative insight or intuition, but ecstatic vision cannot be ruled out. Calvin may be right: "This stedfast looking upon him was not without some peculiar motion of the Spirit."[81] Modern scholars, however, tend to interpret this staring as the act of a magician. Haenchen claims: "Here as in 13:9, the looking is meant to establish the inner contact necessary for the miracle. Ἀτενίζειν often appears in this sense in miracle stories."[82] He then cites in support Lake and Cadbury who do not give any evidence for such a claim.[83] Stählin also follows this line: "Der Blick ist auch sonst eine Macht . . . hier besonders also das Mittel, das die Heilung anbahnt (vgl. 14,9): die sich begegnenden Blicke bereiten den Boden für die Machtwirkung des Wortes."[84] And Bauernfeind: "Der Blick, namentlich das wechselseitige Anblicken . . . bahnt den Weg für die übernatürliche Wundermacht. Darum liegen zwei der hier ver-wendeten Termini für 'sehen' in einer höheren Sphäre, als das gewöhnliche βλέπειν."[85] Bruce is less dramatic and less power-oriented, seeing the verb in its simple primary sense. Peter fixes his eyes on the man simply to attract his attention.[86] Munck takes a middle road, thinking that Peter "stared gravely."[87] These understandings all miss the mark. The first because there is no evidence that this verb was used to describe the action of a miracle-worker; the second because it is too simple. This is no mere gaze to attract attention. Peter's gazing is preparatory for an epiphany of divine healing power. Munck's suggestion implies it is a special stare, but he is ignorant of its true nature.

In 3:12, the verb is used in a situation not too dissimilar to that in Josephus' account of Herod's arrogance. Peter asks why the crowd wonder (θαυμάζετε) and why they stare (ἀτενίζετε) at him and John as if they had done something from their own power. Nearly all commentaries ignore the verb at this point, presumably because they understand it to mean a simple "stare."[88] But this is no ordinary staring but a gazing at an epiphany of divine power. The crowd is in a mood of wonder and awe which gives them the intuition that Peter and John are holy even "divine" men. Unlike Herod (12:23), Peter and John reject that status.

81. Calvin, *Commentary*, 2:138.
82. Haenchen, *Acts*, 199n4.
83. Lake and Foakes-Jackson, *Beginnings*, 4:33.
84. Stählin, *Apostelgeschichte*, 59–60.
85. Bauernfeind, *Kommentar*, 60.
86. Bruce, *Acts*, 77.
87. Munck, *Acts*, 25.
88. For example, Bruce, *Acts*, 80.

When Stephen appears before the Sanhedrin, the Sanhedrin is said to "gaze" at him and see (ἀτενίσαντες[89] εἰς αὐτόν . . . εἶδον) his face as that of an angel (6:15). As is consistently the case, ἀτενίζειν has as its object a holy figure and the sense is that the Sanhedrin has the intuition that Stephen is an angel of God. Again, commentators miss the nuance. Haenchen writes of an "exact focusing of the eyes";[90] Bruce translates: "fixed their eyes";[91] while Barrett simply says: "looking at Stephen."[92] Schneider translates: "mit Spannung . . . blicken"[93] but hints at the verb indicating an unusual happening: "Das Partizip bezeichnet auch sonst die Erwartung des Hörers gegenüber einem Redner."[94] As noted earlier, this episode parallels closely that of Luke 4:20.

At the end of his trial, Stephen himself "gazing into heaven, saw the glory of God" (ἀτενίσας εἰς τὸν οὐρανὸν εἶδεν δόξαν θεοῦ). Here ἀτενίζειν is used, as it is in other literature, in the context of a martyr-visionary, of one in a paranormal state and at prayer. Stephen is expressly described as being "full of [the] holy spirit" (7:55a). Bruce implies ἀτενίζειν here merely describes the upward look of Stephen;[95] and Haenchen also misses the point by calling it a "heavenward glance."[96] Others at least understand that Stephen's vision "ist für das Martyrologium typisch"[97] and that "der feste Blick zum Himmel . . . charakterisiert hier den Visionär."[98] Even more accurate is Wikenhauser: "Der Geist versetzt ihn in Ekstase."[99] Stephen is in an ecstatic state, full of a holy spirit, and in that state he has a vision into heaven and sees the glory of God.

Commentators simply ignore ἀτενίζειν in 10:4. But once again, this is no ordinary staring. Cornelius has a vision of an angel at the ninth hour of the day (10:5), the hour of prayer; and since Cornelius was a God-fearing man, constantly at prayer (10:2, 4), there can be no doubt that he is at prayer when he receives this epiphany. Nor is it surprising that Luke uses the familiar construction, ἀτενίσας . . . εἶπε. Cornelius becomes ἔμφοβος, and in that state,

---

89. D reads ἠτένιζον.
90. Haenchen, *Acts*, 272.
91. Bruce, *Acts*, 126.
92. Barrett, *Acts*, 1:329.
93. Schneider, *Apostelgeschichte*, 1:440.
94. Schneider, *Apostelgeschichte*, 1:440n61.
95. Bruce, *Acts*, 154.
96. Haenchen, *Acts*, 312.
97. Schille, *Die Apostelgeschichte*, 188. It is used of Stephen as it is used of the martyrs mentioned by Josephus who die with their eyes fixed on the temple.
98. Pesch, *Die Apostelgeschichte*, 1:263.
99. Wikenhauser, *Die Apostelgeschichte*, 92.

he speaks to the heavenly being. He is filled with an awe which creates a sense of unworthiness characteristic of those who "gaze" at holy things.

Cornelius' experience is followed by a similar one for Peter. In 11:5, Peter too is at prayer, and in a state of ecstasy (ἐν ἐκστάσει) he sees a vision (εἶδον ... ὅραμα) of a sheet descending from heaven. Not surprisingly, Peter "stares" into the heavenly sheet and "observed and saw" (ἀτενίσας κατενόουν καὶ εἶδον). Bruce's "when I had looked at it carefully"[100] misses the nuance of ἀτενίζειν. Peter's observation and his seeing stem from an epiphany of heavenly things. He does not see or observe without this experience which Luke describes with the verb ἀτενίζειν.[101]

The verb occurs, again in participial form, in 13:9 when Paul "stares" at Bar Jesus, the Jewish sorcerer in Sergius Paulus" court on Cyprus. Like Stephen, Paul is "full of [the] holy spirit," and like Stephen he "stares" (ἀτενίσας), but the object of this action is not the holy, but, as with Peter in 3:4, a man. Lake and Cadbury suggest this refers to the evil eye,[102] an idea followed by Barrett, who, referring to Talmudic references to the power of the eye, says: "Wherever the wise direct their eyes there is either death or misery."[103] Haenchen disagrees: "ἀτενισας does not mean that Paul possessed the withering glance that Jewish legend attributed to rabbis";[104] as does Schille, who claims the verb belongs in the sphere of magic but does not refer to the evil eye.[105] Both arguments miss the point. By using the verb ἀτενίζειν, Luke depicts Paul as one who speaks (εἶπεν) on the basis of an intuitive vision; he can see into (εἰς) the true character of Bar Jesus as a son of the devil, full of deceit and villainy (13:10).

The use of ἀτενίζειν in 14:9 closely parallels its use in 3:4. Paul, like Peter, heals a crippled man. Paul, "staring" (ἀτενίσας) at the man and seeing that he has faith, speaks to him. Commentators consistently understand the simple sense of the verb. "To fix one's eye upon," says Haenchen;[106] "fixed his eye on the man," is Barrett's translation;[107] Schille talks of "das magische

---

100. Bruce, *Acts*, 220.

101. This also suggests that ἀτενίζειν is not simply a synonym for other verbs of seeing or contemplation.

102. Lake and Foakes-Jackson, *Beginnings*, 4:146.

103. Barrett, *Acts*, 1:616.

104. Haenchen, *Acts*, 400.

105. Schille, *Die Apostelgeschichte*, 288.

106. Haenchen, *Acts*, 425.

107. Barrett, *Acts*, 1:675.

'starren.'"[108] Calvin might be on track when he says: "The cripple's faith was revealed to Paul by the secret inspiration of the Spirit."[109]

Finally, in 23:1, with the typical construction, Luke says Paul "stares" at the Sanhedrin before addressing them (ἀτενίσας . . . τῷ συνεδρίῳ εἶπεν). Haenchen comments: "'Looking steadily,' Paul has no anxiety before the judges."[110] "Fixing his eyes on the Sanhedrin," Bruce translates.[111] Both miss the significance of the action; as, surely, does Dunn's suggestion that Luke refers to Paul's poor eyesight.[112] Paul has better than 20/20 vision and speaks to the Sanhedrin on the basis of that insight. He sees the Sanhedrin, represented by its highpriest, for what it really is. The possibility that Paul was gifted with revelatory insight is later acknowledged by his fellow-Pharisees, who ask, "What if a spirit or an angel spoke to him?" (23:9).

Conclusion

The strange stares of Acts, expressed by the verb ἀτενίζειν, have a depth of meaning that has been missed by commentators. It is reasonable to say, on the basis of the evidence, that the verb is a technical term, used particularly in the context of a divine epiphany or a manifestation of divine power. In Acts, those who stare are at prayer, in ecstasy, or experiencing transported vision (7:55; 10:4; 11:6); they are "full of the holy spirit" and inspired with an intuition or penetrative insight which gives them the ability to see "into" people (3:4; 13:9; 14:9; 23:1); and they have a vision which breaks into the heavenly world (1:10; 7:55). Such dynamic sight makes them, in turn, the object of reverent, awe-inspired stares (3:12; 6:15).

---

108. Schille, *Die Apostelgeschichte*, 305.

109. Calvin, *Commentary on Acts*, 38.

110. Haenchen, *Acts*, 637, cited approvingly in Schneider, *Apostelgeschichte*, 2:330n14.

111. Bruce, *Acts*, 424.

112. Dunn, *Acts*, 304.

Recognizing the Gods (Acts 14:8–10)

LITTLE ATTENTION IS GIVEN to the stare and the loud voice of Paul in the healing of the cripple in Acts 14:8–10. This article examines these two actions and suggests that far from being incidental in the narrative they help to explain how the Lystrans recognized that "the gods have come down" in Paul and Barnabas. In both Graeco-Roman texts and in Jewish literature, the stare and the loud voice are indicators of the action or presence of the gods. In addition, the command "arise" is commonly given by divine beings in Jewish texts.

The cry "The gods having become like men came down to us" and the desire on the part of the Lystrans to offer sacrifices[1] (Acts 14:11–13, 18) are commonly understood to be in response to the healing of a crippled man by Paul. This understanding is mainly based on 14:11: "The crowds seeing what Paul had done" (οἱ τε ὄχλοι ἰδόντες ὅ ἐποίησεν Παῦλος). Bruce, for example, says the Lystrans wanted to sacrifice "seeing the instantaneous cure performed on the lame man";[2] Barrett similarly writes: "A miraculous healing profoundly impresses the local residents";[3] and Haenchen agrees: "It is Paul's mighty work which leads the ὄχλοι into this error."[4] But was it only the cure itself that caused the Lystrans to recognize the gods in Paul and Barnabas? What did the Lystrans actually see Paul doing? They saw him stare (14:9) and heard him speak in a loud voice (14:10). I suggest that it was this behavior of Paul, as much as the resultant healing, that evoked the response.

It was not unknown for healers and wonder-workers among the Greeks to be offered sacrifices and to be acclaimed as gods. According to Diogenes Laertius, sacrifices were offered to Empedocles after he had brought a woman to life who had been in a trance and not breathing for 30 days. He went among the people as "nomore a mortal but an immortal god" (θεὸς ἄμβροτος), he was crowned with fillets and flowery garlands and held

---
1. It is not stated explicitly in verse 11 to whom they wished to sacrifice. However, verse 18 would suggest that Paul and Barnabas were to be the recipients.
2. Bruce, *Commentary*, 291.
3. Barrett, *Acts*, 1:663.
4. Haenchen, *Acts*, 426.

in awe (σεβάζεται) on entering any town. At his death, it is said, a very loud voice (φωνῆς ὑπερμεγέθους) was heard calling his name in the middle of the night, but all that was to be seen was a light in the heavens and a glitter of lamps.[5] Pythagoras was also seen by his followers to be an emissary of the gods (Philostratus, *Vit. Apoll.* 1.1) and the wise healer Apollonius was thought by some to be a god (Philostratus, *Vit. Apoll.* 8.5).[6]

However, there is a difference between honouring a healer as a god or as divine (θεῖος) and thinking that the gods have come down in the form of healers, as in the case of the Lystrans with Paul and Barnabas. Were there any give-away signs that caused them to make this identification? A character in Homer's Iliad says when seeing Poseidon, who came in the guise of Kalchas, the diviner: "No, that it is not Kalchas, the seer. Without difficulty, I recognized from behind the trace of his feet and legs, while he was going away. The gods are recognizable" (*Il.* 13.70–72). So there were ways of recognizing the gods, as Vernant says: "As well-camouflaged as a god may be in the skin of a mortal, there is something 'off,' something in the otherness of the divine presence that remains strange and disconcerting even when the god is in disguise."[7]

Was there something "off" in Paul that helped the locals to identify and acclaim him as a god? Acts 14:8–10 offers four clues which suggest a positive answer. The first is that Paul comes to Lystra as a stranger; the second is Paul's stare; the third, his loud voice; and the fourth, his command to the cripple. I will examine each factor, but the main focus will be on Paul's loud voice as the tell-tale sign that "the gods came down."

Paul the Stranger

"Generally speaking one may say that in Antiquity anyone who did something that was not understood or that was considered miraculous ran himself the risk of being looked upon as a god."[8] While this may be true of "anyone," it was especially true of the stranger (ξένος). Attention is not often given to the fact that Paul and Barnabas come to Lystra as strangers. Luther Martin pays implicit attention to it by noting that Zeus and Hermes are the gods who protect strangers and are their patrons, and that the locals show hospitality to Paul and Barnabas just as the local Phrygian couple Philemon

---

5. Diogenes Laertius, *Lives* 8.62.

6. For the close relationship between prophet, healer, and gods, see Kolenkow, "Relationships," 1470–506.

7. Vernant, "Mortals and Immortals," 43.

8. Mussies, "Identification," 2.

and Baucis did to Zeus and Hermes who came to them as strangers according to Ovid's legendary tale (*Met.* 8.611–725).[9]

While that myth is noted now by almost all commentators on this passage, the significance of the gods coming as *strangers* in the form of Paul and Barnabas is rarely noticed. Strangers were often associated with strange occurrences in a community. Stählin says of the ξένος: "He is a man from without, strange, hard to fathom, surprising, unsettling, sinister," and to such outsiders were often attributed magical powers.[10] That the gods appear in the guise of strangers is a notion classically expressed by Homer: "For the gods disguise themselves as strangers from abroad, and assuming the most varied shapes, wander through the cities" (*Od.* 17.485; cf. also *Od.* 13.311–13; 1.111). Dionysius of Halicarnassus tells the myth of the stranger Hercules whom the locals at Pallantium thought to be divine (θεῖος) because he delivered them from a robber (1.40.1).[11] Many other examples could be given, but Anderson's summary will suffice: "Something in society is going awry; a holy man appears—something of a mysterious outsider, and somehow or other the situation is put to rights: the price of corn goes down, the thief is found, the epileptic is calmed, and that is all part of the way society works."[12]

The stranger Paul comes to Lystra and heals a man crippled from birth. This power of the stranger provides a clue to the Lystrans that Paul is a god come down. But more significant for this identification are Paul's stare and his loud voice.

The Stare

Before examining the significance of Paul's stare, attention to the word ὁμοιοπαθεῖς in Acts 14:15 might illuminate more clearly what the Lystrans meant when they said that the gods came down to them "like humans"

---

9. Martin, "Gods or Ambassadors?," 152–56. Martin's interest is in the apostles' role as ambassadors of God and not in their stranger-ness. The Philemon-Baucis myth is not the only one to be noted. There is also the myth of Zeus and Hermes visiting in disguise the poor, widowed, and impotent bee-keeper Hyrieus who showed them hospitality. As a reward, the gods promised him a child if he were to sacrifice a bull, make water on its hide and then bury it in his wife's grave. He did so, and nine months later a son was born to him, named Orion, "he who makes water/rain" (Ovid, *Fasti* 5.493–544). Given the desire to sacrifice bulls (Acts 14:13) and Paul's sermon about who it is who supplies rain (Acts 14:17), this myth should not be overlooked.

10. Stählin, "ξένος."

11. See also *Catullus* 64.384; Ovid, *Met.* 1.212; Eunapius, *Lives*, 467–69.

12. Anderson, *Sage, Saint, and Sophist*, 219.

(ὁμοιωθέντες ἀνθρώποις) (v. 11). In 14:15, Paul pleads that he is a human with πάθη not like those of the gods but like those of the Lystrans themselves. This suggests that when the Lystrans think Paul is one of "the gods come down to us" they are referring more to his πάθη than to his physical form. Rather than being seen as some kind of "incarnation" of the god or the god in human "form," Paul is instead seen as being possessed by the πάθη of the gods. According to Galen, the πάθη are those emotions, passions, and actions which are external. So, for example, he thinks that exhaling and transpiring (ἐκπνοὴ καὶ διαπνοή) are natural activities but inhaling (εἰσπνοή) is an affection (πάθος, *On the Doctrines of Hippocrates and Plato* 8.719). Galen also defines πάθος; as "a motion in one thing that comes from some other thing" and as "a motion contrary to nature" (6.491-92). He distinguishes between ἐνεργείαι, which are natural motions—like moving the leg—and πάθη, which are not natural motions but are externally caused and related directly to the ψυχή. I suggest that Paul's staring and speaking with a loud voice were understood by the locals as signs that the πάθη of the gods had entered Paul, and this interpretation Paul rejects.[13]

To cite Mussies again: "Above all else it is the eyes of the gods that are described as having a special quality, either bright or shining or frightening."[14] That this includes the stare is clearly stated by Heliodorus who says that the gods look straight ahead and without blinking (τοῖς . . . ὀφθαλμοῖς; . . . ἀτενὲς διόλου βλέποντες καὶ τὸ βλέφαρον οὔποτε ἐπιμύοντες) and that this peculiarity is indicative of their true nature (*Aeth.* 3.13.2-3). According to Acts 14:9, Paul stares (ἀτενίσας) at the crippled man. The locals see this as something "off" in Paul which reveals what they believe to be his true identity as a god or as being possessed by a god.

Paul's stare is generally ignored or passed over with very little comment in the scholarship. Some German scholars sense its significance, but usually interpret it as the sign of a magician or Wundertäter rather than as characteristic of a god. Schille, for example, refers to "das magische Starren" and speaks of its "magische Wirkung."[15] It is a verb used to indicate a significant action and so one that deserves to have more attention paid to it.

---

13. NT Greek verb tenses are complex and the aorist particularly so. Is it possible that the aorist κατέβησαν (v. 11) implies that the Lystrans thought Paul and Barnabas to be gods only while they were in the act of healing; that is, while staring, speaking with a loud voice, and commanding?

14. Mussies, "Identification," 4. For an example, the green eyes of Athena inspired terror (Lucian, *Judgment of the Goddesses* 10).

15. Schille, *Die Apostelgeschichte*, 305. Klauck puts it down to Paul's "prophetische Fähigkeit" (Klauck, *Magie*, 71).

RECOGNIZING THE GODS (ACTS 14:8–10)

In the NT, ἀτενίζειν is used 14 times—almost solely by Luke, who uses it twice in the Gospel (4:20; 22:56) and ten times in Acts (1:10; 3:4, 12; 6:15; 7:55; 10:4; 11:6; 13:9; 23:1). Elsewhere, it is used only by Paul and then twice in the same context (2 Cor 3:7, 13). It is not uncommon in Jewish and later Christian writings. There are four important features of the verb's usage: the subject is a holy person, or a holy one is the object of the verb; the subject is often at prayer or in an ecstatic, paranormal state; there is the suggestion that the subject has suprahuman intuition; and finally, the verb is very often used in aorist participial form followed by an aorist main verb of seeing or saying. Acts 14:9–10 follows this standard pattern. Paul, in Acts, is clearly a holy man "filled with the holy spirit" (13:9, 52). He is the subject in 14:9 who has suprahuman intuition into the crippled man. Finally, the verb is aorist participial inform (ἀτενίσας) followed by an aorist main verb of speech (εἶπεν). What may not be so obvious in this episode is that "the subject is often at prayer or in some ecstatic, paranormal state." But that, I suggest, is the case with Paul in this healing episode. Paul stares because he is possessed or infused—not with Hermes, as the Lystrans think, but as Luke would have it—with the living God (14:15).

Paranormal vision is explicit or implicit in virtually every use of ἀτενίζειν in Acts. The disciples stare into heaven at Jesus' "ascension" (1:10); Stephen, in his dying, prays and stares into heaven and sees Jesus standing at the right hand of God (7:55); Stephen's opponents stare at him and see his face to be "like that of an angel" (6:15). In 10:3–4, a centurion, at an hour of prayer and ἐν ὁράματι, stares at the angel whom he addresses as κύριε as he is in a state of great awe (ἔφοβος). Peter also stares as he is ἐν ἐκστάσει (11:6). The verb is also used in the parallel healing miracle, namely Acts 3:1–10, as Peter heals a cripple in Jerusalem, and as Paul prepares to speak before the Sanhedrin (23:1).[16] In summary, the verb in Acts is commonly associated with holy figures, often with heavenly figures like angels, and frequently indicates paranormal vision which sees another reality, something referred to in recent literature as an ASC, an altered state of consciousness.[17] On the basis of Luke's usage in Acts, it seems reasonable to suggest that here too Paul experiences and demonstrates paranormal vision and this is what attracts the attention of the locals.

That such a state may have affected Paul's whole physical condition is not unlikely. His breathing in particular might well have altered. As Dibelius notes: "The look and the strong breathing (called "sighing" popularly) are

---

16. For a closer study of this verb, see Strelan, "Strange Stares," 235–55.
17. For examples of recent interest in ASCs, see Pilch, "Transfiguration," 47–64; Malina, "Assessing," 351–72.

healing media."[18] The altered breathing of the healer who is possessed by a spirit or demon is well known. Theissen says: "The miracle-worker reacts to situations of distress with his emotions, his pneumatic excitement," and this is reflected in the use of such verbs as σπλαγνίζομαι and ὀργίζομαι in healing activities (cf. Mark 1:41).[19] Deep breathing, sighing, groaning, hissing, and other inhalatory noises are commonly recommended for the magical practitioner according to the papyri.[20]

The look of the healer and his emotional involvement in the healing process are well illustrated in the miracle-working Apollonius of Tyana. The sage comes across a demon-possessed boy and looks at him (ὁρῶντός τε ἐς αὐτὸ τοῦ Ἀπολλωνίου). The narrative continues: "the ghost in him (the boy) began to utter cries of fear and rage, such as one hears from people who are being branded or racked. . . . But Apollonius addressed him with anger (ξὺν ὀργῇ) . . . and ordered him to quit the young man" (Philostratus, *Vit. Apoll.* 4.20).

Since sickness was generally understood as a "pathetic" condition, that is, it involved the spirit of the sick person and the demon or "power" of the disease, it is not surprising that for healing to take place Paul the healer needed to be prepared in his own spirit and thus be able to deal with both the spirit of the cripple and the spirit causing the illness. As Hippocrates said, "opposites cure opposites" (τὰ ἐναντία τῶν ἐναντίων ἐστὶν ἰάματα) (Galen 8.698). For the Lystrans, it is Hermes, the messenger with wings on his feet, who cures his opposite—a man crippled from birth and unable to walk (14:8). Since the soul (ψυχή) possesses the chief cause of sensation—it communicates sensation to the body (*Epicurus to Herodotus* 64)—so in order to relieve the sensation of pain one connects with the soul. The staring of Paul suggests that he enters into another reality which enables him to see into the "soul" of the cripple and to see there the faith to be healed (14:9). Such an ability would have been an indicator to many in Luke's audience of Paul's status: "For the whole range of persons with divine powers . . . knowledge of men's hearts seems to be the one convincing proof. The power is thought divine."[21]

In summary, Paul's staring indicates something is "off" about Paul—to the Lystrans it is an indication that he is really one of the gods. The stare also indicates that Paul has paranormal vision which the Lystrans read as indicative that he is possessed with the passions of the gods.

---

18. Dibelius, *Tradition*, 86.
19. Theissen, *Miracle Stories*, 57.
20. See, e.g., *PGM*, 7:768; 13:946.
21. Kolenkow, "Relationships," 1480.

The Loud Voice (Acts 14:10)

A further distinguishing mark of the gods "was the loud and far-reaching sound of their voice which (is) compared either with the sound of thunder or with that of musical instruments."[22] That this was one of the commonly accepted attributes of a divine being is illustrated by Celsus who says that if a divine spirit (θεῖον πνεῦμα) had been in the body of Jesus, then his body would have had different features from those of others, including a different voice.[23] It is a little curious that the connection between Paul's loud voice and the loud voice of the gods is rarely, if ever, made in the scholarship. Most commentaries on 14:10 virtually ignore the phrase μεγάλῃ φωνῇ. That its significance is probably unknown is illustrated by Dunn's tentative suggestion that it might indicate Paul is "speaking across a listening crowd?"[24]

If any attention is given to the loud voice it tends to be found in German scholarship where, like the stare, it is understood to characterize the magician. Wikenhauser thinks both actions might have to do with "a certain power of suggestion" which made the cripple obey.[25] Others relate it to spirit- or demon- possession. Schille says the loud voice illustrates the charisma of the spirit-bearer,[26] an idea reiterated by Haenchen: "The loud voice often betrays that the speaker is driven by the Spirit or a demon."[27]

Very few suggest the immediate connection of the loud voice with the gods. Betz comes close, as he comments on Acts 14:10: "Along with the healing, the powerful voice may also express the judgment of pagans that they are witnesses of an epiphany."[28] Stählin, almost alone, comes very close to identifying Paul's loud voice as the voice of God: "Daß in diesem Ruf Gott selber spricht, wird erstens darin deutlich, daß er den Ruf aufnimmt, mit dem er Hesekiel berief (Ez 2.1), zweitens, in der Kraft der Stimme, die den Geistträger auszeichnet."[29] Interestingly, Barrett rejects the parallel with

---

22. Mussies, "Identification," 7.

23. Origen, *Cels.* 6.75. As Dölger notes, the voice is listed by Celsus next to greatness (μέγεθος) and bodily strength (ἀλκή) and so indicates a powerful voice (Dölger, "ΘΕΟΥ ΦΩΝΗ," 218–23).

24. Dunn, *Acts*, 190.

25. Wikenhauser, *Die Apostelgeschichte*, 164.

26. Schille, *Die Apostelgeschichte*, 305. See also Pesch, *Die Apostelgeschichte*, 2:57.

27. Haenchen, *Acts*, 425.

28. Betz, "φωνῇ, et al."

29. Stählin, *Apostelgeschichte*, 191. Dölger also believes the loud voice of Paul in Acts 14:10 reflects typical belief in *Götter-Epiphanie* or *Theophanie*, but he seems ambiguous about Paul. On the one hand, he says his voice indicates that he is a great *Wundertäter*, and yet he also realizes that his loud voice parallels closely the voice of Jesus in John 11 which he interprets to be the voice of God (Dölger, "ΘΕΟΥ ΦΩΝΗ," 222).

Ezekiel as justification for Stählin's comment, and says absolutely nothing about Stählin's second reason.[30] I suggest that Stählin is on the right track with the second of his reasons particularly. Paul's loud voice is a direct sign to the locals that the gods have come down.

The Loud Voice in Greek and Latin Literature

The phrase "with/in a loud voice" is commonly used in ancient literature in a number of ways: for attention-claiming, in the desire to be heard, or simply to indicate shouting (e.g., Dion. Halic. 3.24.5; Plutarch, *Lives* 24.2.11; Diod. Sic. 17.84.2; Lucian, *Conviv.* 16; *Alieus* 26; *Demetrius* 3.2.5). In addition, the loud voice lends authority to a command (Plutarch, *Cam.* 32.2.4); it is also characteristic of heralds (Diod. Sic. 12.34.4; Plutarch, *Cor.* 25.3.2); and it is seen as desirable in oratory (Lucian, *Bis acc.* 28).

The loud voice is also common in acclamations of kings and military leaders. So, for example, Tarquinius's daughter saluted her father as king "in a loud voice" and prayed to the gods for the state (Dion. Halic. 4.39.1). Fabius, who evoked wonder among the people, on one occasion had standards planted in front of him and was addressed μεγάλῃ φωνῇ as Father (Plutarch, *Fab.* 13.6.3). Similarly, Sulla welcomed Pompey and greeted him μεγάλῃ φωνῇ as Magnus (Plutarch, *Pomp.* 13.4.5). Pompey also evoked astonishment and awe among the crowds on the occasion when he was solemnly asked whether he had fulfilled all the requirements of military service recognized by law. Pompey replied μεγάλῃ φωνῇ that he had indeed done so, and the crowds broke out in shouts and cries of joy (*Pomp.* 22.6.6).

Prayers or vows were also often performed in a loud voice. Egyptian priests called out to hawks "in a loud voice" during a ritual in which vows were made to the gods for children (Diod. Sic. 1.83.2), and it was the custom for Egyptian priests to pray before the king for the king's health "in a loud voice" (1.70.5). Similarly, Lucian has a character say that at symposia, libations were poured out and prayers offered "at the top of their voices" (μεγάλῃ τῇ φωνῇ) (*Cat.* 11). That the phrase can indicate an altered state of consciousness is suggested by Lucian who uses it as part of the description of behavior when an epidemic hit the community—people became crazy and sang songs and speeches from plays and tragedies μεγάλῃ τῇ φωνῇ (*Hist.* 1).[31]

---

30. Barrett, *Acts*, 1:675.

31. That loud voices were associated in some circumstances with madness is illustrated also by Josephus's example of a certain Jesus who day after day cried out loudly in and against the Temple in Jerusalem. He maintained the cry even after being beaten by the authorities, who concluded that some supernatural force had incited him "as

That a loud and frightening voice was characteristic of the gods can be variously demonstrated from the literature: Apollo's voice terrifies Hector (*Il.* 20.375-80); the people of Ithaca are frightened by the voice of Athena (*Od.* 24.529-35); Jason and the Argonauts "shake with fear" at the voice of Hera (Apollonius Rhodius, *Arg.* 4.640-42). One of Lucian's characters experiences the voice of Zeus as having numinous force that strikes like thunder and evokes great fear (*Icar.* 23).[32] When Jupiter demanded fresh thunderbolts from the Cyclops on seeing the Giants coming to seize heaven, he did so with a loud voice (Silius Italicus, *Punica* 9.306-8). If a loud voice characterizes a god, then it can be anticipated that anyone possessed by a god will also speak in a loud voice. This is often the case, particularly in relation to divine prophecy.[33] Speaking of the inspired prophet, Guthrie says: When the prophet speaks he is not himself. He is wrought upon and changed in a manner sometimes terrifying to behold and exhausting to himself. He is possessed by the god and becomes for the time being only a mouthpiece for the utterance of the divine voice."[34]

Virgil provides a good example:

> The prophetic Delian God breathes into her the spirit's visionary might, revealing things to come . . . suddenly her countenance and color changed and her hair fell in disarray. Her breast heaved and her bursting heart was wild and mad. She appeared taller and spoke in no mortal tones, for the God was nearer and the breath of his power was upon her . . . the cavern made her voice a roar as she uttered truth wrapped in obscurity. (*Aen.* 6.10-105)

Similar examples of persons possessed by the gods and speaking in a loud voice are not difficult to find. The Latin poet Silius Italicus reports a priest standing before the altar of a god in a sacred grove when "suddenly the god entered the breast of the prophet. The trees clashed against one another, and a deep humming noise passed through the resounding grove; and then a voice, louder than any we know, burst forth into the air " (*Punica* 3.697-99). Later, the same writer says that Apollo at Delphi spoke

---

indeed was the case." The Romans declared him a maniac and harmless (*BJ* 6.300-309).

32. Not surprisingly, some emperors and rulers are flattered to be told that their voices are like those of the gods and so create the same awe and response (Cassius Dio, *Hist. rom.* 62.20.5; Suetonius, *Nero* 20; Tacitus, *Ann.* 16.22; Philostratus, *Vit. Apoll.* 4.39; 5.7; cf. Acts 12:22).

33. For some examples, and for a discussion on such speech in early Christianity, see Forbes, *Prophecy*. Forbes shows little or no interest in the loud voice itself.

34. Guthrie, *Greeks*, 199.

with a loud voice through the priestess who was "possessed by the god" (*Punica* 12.322-23). Lucian writes an interesting episode in which Menippus tells of his voyage with a magician (μάγος) Mithrobarzanes. The *magos* at one stage ceased muttering in a low tone and instead "shouted as loudly as he could (μεγάλῃ τῇ φωνῇ), invoking the spirits one and all, at the top of his lungs." His voice was so powerful that "in a trice the whole region began to quake, the ground was rent asunder by the incantation" (*Men.* 9-10).[35] Lucian also reports the false prophet Alexander of Abonoteichus pretending to be in a mantic state by running full speed into a temple, entering the water, and singing hymns in honour of Asclepius and Apollo "at the top of his voice" (μεγάλῃ τῇ φωνῇ) as he besought the god (*Alex.* 14). In another ritual action, the same prophet "entered robed as a priest, amid profound silence, and said in a loud voice (μεγάλῃ τῇ φωνῇ), over and over again, 'Hail, Glycon'" (*Alex.* 39).

In summary, the loud voice is used in a variety of contexts in Greek and Latin literature including that of the enthused state of the speaker. The loud voice can be a sign that the speaker is either possessed by the gods or seeking to be in touch with the divine through prayer and invocation.

The Loud Voice in Jewish Literature

In the LXX, the God of Israel speaks "with a loud voice" only once, namely in 1 Sam 7:10. There, God thunders ἐν φωνῇ μεγάλῃ against the Philistines and throws them into confusion. But not surprisingly, the heavenly figure also "cried with a loud voice" (ἀνέκραγεν ... φωνῇ μεγάλῃ) into the ears of Ezekiel (Ezek 9:1). Nor is it surprising that the Hebrews shared with the Greeks the association of the loud voice with their god. A loud voice (μεγάλῃ φωνῇ) is the sign, along with darkness and fire, of the presence of God at the holy mountain (Deut 4:11; 5:22). Similarly, in Bar 11:3 God's voice is spoken of as φωνῇ μεγάλῃ ὡς βροντή, the thunder imagery being quite common (see, e.g., Exod 19:19; 20:18; Ps 18:7-15; 29:3-9, 45:6).

In the LXX, humans commonly speak φωνῇ μεγάλῃ and predominantly in three related contexts: in the offering of corporate prayers during solemn ceremonies; in the expression of corporate praise and blessing to God; and in the expression of private or individual prayers and praise to God. In other words, it is very commonly used in the context of cultic actions. It is sometimes difficult for modern Western Christians, in particular, to envisage such acts. Many Westerners pray in controlled, stylized,

---

35. This behavior calls into doubt Theissen's claim: "Magicians and miracle-workers always speak softly" (Theissen, *Miracle Stories*, 64).

almost mechanical, emotionally low-key liturgical forms and voice; but not so the ancient Israelites. Prayer and particularly praise were often ecstatic, pneumatic, inspired, "emotional" experiences in themselves, especially in a shared, corporate context. So, during a solemn ritual of confession and repentance, certain Levites in the presence of all Israel "cried with a loud voice" (ἐβόησαν φωνῇ μεγάλῃ) to the Lord their God and called on Israel to bless their God (Neh 9:4-5; 1 Esd 9:10; cf. Deut 27:14; 2 Chr 20:19). Even greater is the intensity of the experience when the foundation of the temple is laid. There is great praise of God, with vestments, cymbals, and songs of praise, with the result that people weep and shout for joy "with a great shout" (ἐκραύγασεν φωνῇ μεγάλῃ) (Ezra 3:10-13; cf. 1 Esd 5:62, 64; Jud 14:9; 1 Macc 2:27; 5:31). When the ark of the covenant comes into the presence of Israel, the people respond by crying out φωνῇ μεγάλῃ; such a holy presence ("a god has come into the camp") evokes ecstatic cries (1 Sam 4:5-7). And when Israel makes a solemn confessional oath to the Lord, they do so ἐν φωνῇ μεγάλῃ and with shouting and trumpets and horns (2 Chr 15:14). Cultic acts involve the use of loud voices. Predictably, then, "all my angels" offer praise φωνῇ μεγάλῃ (Job 38:7).

There are also a number of instances when individuals cry out φωνῇ μεγάλῃ (Esth 4:1; Job 2:12; Ezek 11:13; Dan 6:21; Sus 24, 42; Bel 41; Jud 9:1; 13:14; 14:16; 1 Macc 2:19, 27). In nearly every case, the emotion is intense—the prayers and cries are inspired by sadness, anguish, joy, great praise, and confession. Of particular interest is Sus 45-46 in which "God aroused the holy spirit of a young man named Daniel and he cried φωνῇ μεγάλῃ." Here, the loud voice is obviously associated with "the holy spirit" of Daniel; it is the cry of a holy man and suggests possession or ecstasy of some kind.

Only rarely is the loud voice used in the LXX in the sense of shouting or in order to gain attention, as Potiphar's wife does (Gen 39:14)[36] or in order to be heard from a distance as with Rabshakeh (2 Kgs 18:28; cf. Isa 36:13; 2 Chr 32:18). Belshazzar uses a loud voice in the giving of a command (Dan 5:7) but the context certainly suggests that the king is in a state of fear and anxiety if not in an altered state of consciousness: "His color changed, his thoughts alarmed him, his limbs gave way and his knees knocked together"—typical of the visionary's experience in that his body is affected.

Interesting is the expression "in a loud voice" in 1 Sam 28 which reports Saul's visit to a necromancer at Endor because he wishes to communicate with the spirit of the dead Samuel. The necromancer cries out "in a loud voice" (ἀνεβόησεν φωνῇ μεγάλῃ) on seeing the spirit of Samuel

---

36. Her crying out would appear to be significant in the story since it is mentioned in verses 14, 15, and 18.

(1 Sam 28:12). This is the cry of one caught up in a very power-full and spirit-laden experience and is reminiscent of the loud voice of the *magos* in Lucian's episode.

That a loud voice is associated with frenzied, ecstatic prayer is illustrated in 1 Kgs 18:27, 28 as Elijah tells the prophets of Baal to call out in a loud voice (ἐν φωνῇ μεγάλῃ) "because he (Baal) is a god" (ὅτι θεός ἐστιν). This need not be understood as mockery but that this is what one does in beseeching the gods.[37] And so the prophets of Baal cry aloud and, significantly, "cut themselves after their custom with swords and lances" (18.28). This would suggest that their loud crying indicates not simply an increase in the volume of their voices, but rather a change into another state of consciousness.

This relation between the loud voice and a change in the emotional, "spiritual," and physical state of the speaker is well illustrated in 1 Enoch: "I fell on my face, and my whole body became relaxed, and my spirit was transfigured; And I cried with a loud voice . . . with the spirit of power, and blessed and glorified and extolled. And the blessings that poured forth out of my mouth were well-pleasing to [God]" (1 Enoch 71:11).

Here the visionary has an experience which involves his whole body, indeed, his whole self; and in such a state, he cries out with a "loud voice." So the loud voice is closely associated with the spirit and suggests that it is no longer the visionary speaking, but the spirit's voice using the seer's mouth as a channel.

In summary, in ancient Jewish literature the phrase (ἐν) φωνῇ μεγάλῃ is used largely in the context of prayer, blessing, and praise by both individuals and corporate Israel. It conveys a sense of high intensity involving not merely deep emotions like sadness, anguish, joy and confidence, but the very spirit or being of those involved. In some cases there is an explicit link between the loud voice and the Spirit of God or the spirit of those involved; in other cases, that link is implicit. There are also instances where the loud cry is closely related to an intense spirit-filled experience or vision.

The Loud Voice in Early Christian Literature[38]

"A very important use of μεγάλῃ φωνῇ is in relation to the speech of angels, spirits, or bearers of the Spirit," says Betz, and "because praise is rendered in

---

37. In Ezek 8:18, God threatens not to listen to the prayers of Israel even if they pray φωνῇ μεγάλῃ. In other words, no matter how spiritually intense the prayer, God will not listen.

38. I am only interested in the NT and the Apostolic Fathers.

pneumatic joy, it is uttered μεγάλῃ φωνῇ."³⁹ This pneumatic, ecstatic understanding of the phrase is frequent in the NT. However, the only occasions on which it is used in corporate action is in the angelic liturgies of Revelation (5:12; 6:10; 7:10; 11:15; 19:1).

In the canonical Gospels, Jesus speaks μεγάλῃ φωνῇ on only two occasions—in the raising of Lazarus (John 11:43) and at his own death (Matt 27:46, 50; Mark 15:34, 37; Luke 23:46). At the tomb of Lazarus, Jesus, having being in the state of prayer to the Father (John 11:42), cries "in a loud voice" (φωνῇ μεγάλῃ) that Lazarus should come out (11:43). There is good reason to think that this is meant to be identified as the voice of God, with whom Jesus has been (and still is?) in prayer communion. In other words, Jesus here is in a paranormal state, a state of prayer and union with God. The phrase has parallels in Revelation where an angel from heaven, the presence of God, speaks in a loud voice, often in command or in proclamation (Rev 1:10; 5:2; 7:2, 10; 8:13; 10:3; 11:12; 12:10; 14:7, 9, 15; 16:1, 17; 19:17; 21:3). In these examples, the loud voice indicates heavenly authority and can be identified as the voice of God via the medium of an agent.⁴⁰

Significantly for an understanding of Acts 14:10, in the Synoptics Jesus does not speak in a loud voice when he exorcizes or heals. In fact, the only time Jesus does so speak is in his dying moments. All three Synoptic Gospels use exactly this phrase (φωνῇ μεγάλῃ) in describing his death-cry. All three in their own ways link the loud voice with the *pneuma* of Jesus. So in Luke, Jesus commends his spirit (τὸ πνεῦμα) to his Father (Luke 23:46), while in Matthew and Mark, the cry is closely linked to his "expiring" (ἐξέπνευσεν) (Mark 15:37) (ἀφῆκεν τὸ πνεῦμα) (Matt 27:50). There is at least the suggestion that in his dying Jesus is in a state of prayer or even of possession. A number of manuscripts imply that it is the crying out and the exhaling (ὄυτως αὐτὸν κράξαντα καὶ ἐξέπνευσεν⁴¹) that evoke the centurion's statement that this man is υἱὸς θεοῦ (Mark 15:39). It can be noted that the same loud voice-spirit connection is there in the dying of Stephen whose vision and cry again suggest a paranormal state (Acts 7:60).

This spirit-loud voice link is apparent elsewhere in the Synoptic Gospels. On the one hand, the loud voice appears in the context of exorcisms. The demons, before leaving their occupation of a person at the command of Jesus, cry out "in a loud voice" (φωνῇ μεγάλῃ) (Mark 1:26; 5:7; Luke 4:33; 8:38; cf. Acts 8:7). On the other hand, it is used of those offering praise to God, but

---

39. Betz, "φωνῇ, et al."

40. Authority seems to be the implication of the loud voice in two other Acts passages (Acts 16:28; 26:24).

41. So the Bezae text. Others read (οὕτως) κράξας ἐξέπνευσεν.

only in Luke (e.g., 17:15; 19:37). Particularly relevant is Luke's description of Elizabeth as being "filled with the Holy Spirit" and exclaiming with "a loud cry" (Luke 1:42).[42] Her cry is ecstatic and suggests that Luke believes that a loud voice and Spirit-possession go hand in hand.

The clearest example of the link between a human loud voice, the voice of God, and the Spirit is found in a letter of Ignatius. The bishop writes to the Philadelphians, "I cried out with a loud voice, the voice of God (ἐκραύγασα μεταξὺ ὤν, ἐλάλουν μεγάλῃ φωνῇ . . . θεοῦ φωνῇ): Be loyal to your bishop and clergy and deacons." Ignatius stresses that this cry did not come through human lips: "No; that was the preaching of the Spirit itself" (τὸ δὲ πνεῦμα ἐκήρυσσεν λέγον τάδε) (Phil. 7:1–2). The link that Ignatius makes between his voice and that of God and the Spirit is clear. As Schoedel says: "(Ignatius) shared with many others in the Graeco-Roman world the belief that a sudden loud utterance marked the inrush of the divine."[43]

Before leaving this brief survey of the loud voice, it is worth noting that modern studies in altered states of consciousness show that a characteristic feature of trances in shamanism is a change of voice, often increasing in tone and volume.[44] Goodman gives examples of shamans screaming as the voice gets stronger: "He utters a loud mutter, then disjointed sentences and loud cries," and she also offers examples of spirits" voices sounding from the mouth of the shaman.[45] Evidence is also provided by Eliade who describes a healing seance among the Chukchee of Siberia and says that a spirit "enters the shaman's body, whereupon moving his head rapidly, the shaman begins to cry out and speak in falsetto, the voice of the spirit."[46] In addition, Goodman has shown that shouting is typical in glossolalaic experiences and that there are anthropological reports of locals communicating with the dead in loud voices.[47] It would seem valid to conclude that across time and cultures, the loud voice is a sign of possession and of trance-like states. As Dodds notes: "In all parts of the world the "possessed" are reported as speaking in a changed voice,"[48] or, to quote Hull who, in turn, cites Osterreich: "Change of voice is a feature of possession."[49]

---

42. Better manuscripts read κραυγῇ μεγάλῃ.
43. Schoedel, *Ignatius*, 205.
44. Goodman, *Ecstasy*, 37.
45. Goodman, *Ecstasy*, 139, 142.
46. Eliade, *Shamanism*, 255.
47. Goodman, *Speaking in Tongues*, vii, xvi, 15, 61, 81, 109.
48. Dodds, *Greeks*, 91n61.
49. Hull, *Hellenistic Magic*, 80.

Paul's loud voice is a tell-tale sign to the Lystrans that he is possessed by a god or is a god in human form. It also highlights Luke's desire to portray Paul as being a chosen vessel (σκεῦος) of God.

The Command

If Luke is wishing to indicate that Paul speaks with the voice of "the living God" and not of Hermes, then it might be expected that the very words Paul speaks are words spoken by God in the scriptural tradition known to Luke. This is in fact the case. In the command to the cripple, Paul uses the word Ἀνάστηθι. In Jewish Greek scriptures, this same command is most commonly used by "the Lord" (Deut 9:12; Josh 7:10; 1 Sam 23:4; 1 Kgs 12:24; 17:9; 21:18; Jonah 1:2; 3:2; 6:1; Isa 51:17; Jer 13:4, 6; 18:2; Ezek 3:22; Mic 2:10; 4:13; 6:1; 2 Esd 6:13). If it is not God or the Lord who so commands, it is an angel (Gen 21: 8; 1 Kgs 19:5; 2 Esd 7:2) or a prophet or king (Num 23:18; 2 Kgs 8:1; 1 Chr 22:16; 2 Chr 6:41; Bar 5:5; 2 Esd 2:38). In addition, the Psalms call on the Lord to "arise" (Ps 7:6; 9:19; 10:12; 17:13; 35:2; 44:23; 132:8). In the Pseudepigrapha too it is common for the Lord to issue this command (for example, Test. Abr. B 2.8; 3.6; 4.14). Of particular interest is Test. Job. 3.1–2 where the link between the command and the loud voice is explicitly made as a loud voice (μεγάλη φωνῇ), obviously that of God, calls on Job to arise (ἀνάστηθι).

In Acts itself, the command again appears often in the mouth of a heavenly figure. The angel of the Lord so commands Philip (ἀνάστηθι) (8:26) and the imprisoned Peter (ἀνάστα) (12:7); a voice identified as that of Jesus commands Paul (ἀνάστηθι) (9:6; cf. 22:10; 26:16), and a voice exhorts Peter to "rise, kill and eat" (ἀναστὰς θῦσον καὶ φάγε) (10:13; 11:7) and in 10:20, it is the Spirit who commands: ἀναστὰς κατάβηθι. The Lord gives the imperative to Ananias (ἀναστὰς πορεύθητι) (9:11) who in turn commands Paul to "arise and be baptised" (ἀναστὰς βαπτίσαι) (22:16). As Paul does in the Lystran episode (14:10), so Peter commands the paralysed Aeneas and then the dead Tabitha to "rise" (ἀνάστηθι) (9:34, 40), as he does also the worshipping Cornelius (ἀνάστηθι) (10:26). It would seem that without exception the command[50] is given in the context of holy figures and holy actions. It is ultimately the command of God and there can be only the response of obedience.

---

50. The command is expressed with the verb ἀνίστημι either in an imperatival form or in a participial form + an imperatival form of the added verb.

This command in the mouth of Paul suggests that he is an instrument or vessel[51] of the Lord, or, as Stählin says, his voice is the voice of God, and so his command is a "heavenly" or divine command. The crippled—better, probably, the spirit or demon of crippledness—must obey. Luke almost laconically adds the result in four words: καὶ ἥλατο καὶ περιεπάτει (14:10)

Conclusion

In many ways, Acts 14:8–10 is a unique episode in the NT. It is the only occasion on which an apostle heals without any calling on the name of Jesus (cf. Acts 3:6).[52] Apart from Jesus" raising of Lazarus, it is the only instance in which a healer uses a loud voice in the healing process and it is the only instance which combines staring with a loud voice. Kahl believes that here is the only time an apostle is depicted as a B(earer of) N(uminous) P(ower) rather than a M(edium of)NP and he understands the loud voice as an indication that "Paul himself appears here as an independent BNP who commands the healing with authority (εἶπεν μεγάλῃ φωνῇ)."[53] It would seem that Kahl misunderstands. He claims that in this episode there is "no divine participation,"[54] it is "without divine involvement."[55] But the loud voice, the stare, and the command indicate precisely the opposite. The divine is certainly involved—Paul is possessed by it and is even perceived to be its physical manifestation. He is a medium of numinous power rather than an independent bearer of that power.

In summary, the loud voice and the stare are features in the Lukan narrative of Acts 14:8–10 that cannot be overlooked since they are inseparably linked to the dramatic response of the Lystrans. They are indicators or clues that Paul was possessed by a "divine spirit" in his body, and combined with his stranger-ness and his use of the divine command to "arise," they help to understand the Lystrans" identification of him as a god, and they reinforce Luke's own claim that Paul is a chosen vessel of God.

---

51. Paul is described as a "vessel" (σκεῦος) of the Lord in Acts 9:15.

52. The Western Text adds Σοὶ λέγω ἐν τῷ ὀμάματι τοῦ κυρίου Ἰησοῦ Χριστοῦ, which is a clear parallel to 3:7.

53. Kahl, *New Testament Miracle Stories*, 205.

54. Kahl, *New Testament Miracle Stories*, 86.

55. Kahl, *New Testament Miracle Stories*, 96.

Acts 19:12: Paul's "Aprons" Again

THE TRADITIONAL VIEW OF the σουδάρια καὶ σιμικίνθια worn by Paul according to Acts 19:12 is that they were used by Paul in his workshop. So Bruce: "The pieces of material were presumably those which Paul used in his tentmaking or leather-working—the sweat-rags for tying around his head and the aprons for tying around his waist."[1] The only modification to this view is that offered by Leary that the *semicinctium* was probably not an apron but a belt.[2] Leary concludes that the *semicinctium* "is not a specialist garment worn only by leather-workers, but something worn generally."[3] This may well be the case, but Leary and others ignore the context in which Luke writes about these garments. Paul is in Ephesus, and according to 19:9–10 (the verses immediately preceding the mention of these garments) he has been "teaching" (διαλεγόμενος) daily for two years in the σχολή of Tyrannus. This article suggests that Paul wore these garments not in the workshop but in the σχολή.

The words σουδάρια καὶ σιμικίνθια are transliterated from the Latin *sudaria et semicinctia*. As Leary and others have shown, these two articles of clothing[4] were used in a variety of contexts. For example, sudaria were used in burials, as is demonstrated in John 20:7 where the dead Jesus is said to have had one around his head. The same usage is found in the burial of Lazarus according to John 11:44. It is also known from Petronius that the *sudarium* was worn in the home around the neck and used to wipe dirty hands. So Fortunata wiped her hands on a cloth (*sudario*) which she had around her neck (*in collo*) after dividing the remains of food among slaves (*Satyricon* 67.13). The term is used regularly in Apuleius' *Apologia*, sometimes in a diminutive form (*sudariolum*), and interchangeably, it would seem, with *linteolum* and *involucrum*. In that work, Apuleius is charged with keeping certain objects wrapped in a linen *sudariolum* kept near some

---

1. Bruce, *Acts*, 367.
2. Leary, "'Aprons,'" 527–29.
3. Leary, "'Aprons,'" 528.
4. They are not "rags" as Bruce and others suggest. They were worn on the body. This is important for the sick who want to have clothes taken from the "skin" (ἀπὸ τοῦ χρωτός of Paul, 19:12). Rags would not have the same effect.

household gods (*Apologia* 53). This would suggest at least that a *sudariolum* was appropriate cloth in which to wrap a sacred object. Apuleius is in fact charged with magic, and that is the context in which these wrapped and hidden objects are mentioned. He denies the magic charge but does not explicitly deny that the cloth contained sacred objects.

What is more relevant given that Paul probably wore *sudaria* while teaching in a σχολή is that in the course of Apuleius" defense in court, a *sudarium* was worn for the purpose of removing sweat from the face (*Apol.* 53.3, 39; 55.3, 7–8, 16; 57). It would appear that *sudaria* were worn in court by lawyers, probably as part of the court uniform of that profession. To mop the brow may well have been as much a rhetorical gesture as it was to literally remove the sweat caused by hard work. It was part of the pose of an orator. According to Suetonius, Nero, the poet-orator-singer emperor had someone by his side to warn him to spare his vocal chords and to "hold a handkerchief (*sudarium*) to his mouth" (*Nero* 25.3). Suetonius also writes that Nero often appeared in public and gave audiences in a dinner gown with a kerchief around his neck (*circum collum sudario*) but *sine cinctu* (*Nero* 51). In this passage, the two articles of clothing—the *sudarium* and the *cinctium*—have an implied connection. And since Nero thought himself to be an orator, it is implied that he tried to dress the part. But Suetonius thinks his dress and habits "shameless," and he judged Nero's habit of appearing in public *sine cinctu* as such.

Quintillian mentions a certain Vantinius who, when on trial, habitually wore black as in mourning, and would wipe his forehead with a white cloth (*candidum sudarium*) as a sign that he was alive and eating and expected to remain so (*Instit.* 6.3.60). I assume that the presence of sweat on the brow was taken to be a sign of physical activity and therefore of life. Quintillian, writing for would-be orators, suggests that the dishevelled look makes an additional appeal to the emotions, and he registers surprise that Pliny "should think it worthwhile to enjoin the orator to dry his brow with a handkerchief (*sudarium*) in such a way as not to disorder the hair" (11.3.148). Catullus the poet asks that Thallus return his *pallium*, "saetaban napkin" (*sudarium*), and Bithynian tablets (*catagraphos*) which Thallus was parading around as if they were heirlooms (*Catullus* 25). Again, it would seem that the *sudarium* was part of the poet's attire.

Put together, these passages suggest that the *sudarium* worn around the neck was part of the uniform of an orator and was worn and used for effect as much as it was for practical purposes. This understanding is confirmed by a comment made by Petronius. He was giving an oration to a large audience when his teacher, Agamemnon, came up, curious to see who had attracted such a crowd. "He declined to allow me to declaim longer in the Portico than he had himself sweated in the school" (*Non est passus Agamemnon me diutius declamare in portico, quam ipse in schola sudaverat* [*Satyricon* 3]). The verb *sudaverat* is used metaphorically, and its use in combination with *schola* and *declamare* parallels closely the Greek terms used by Luke (διαλεγόμενος ... σχολή ... σουδάρια καὶ σιμικίνθια).

So I suggest that Paul also wore the sudarium while he was teaching in the σχολή of Tyrannus in Ephesus. This seems to me more likely than the traditional view. In addition, craftworkers were not highly regarded, and a worker with animal skins would not have been thought to possess "power" in his clothing or skin. An orator, on the other hand, was thought to have that essential power or δύναμις. The sophist Gorgias of Leontini said: "Speech is the great power which performs great divine works through a very hidden and insignificant form" (Gorgias, *Encomium of Helen* 8, my translation). Much closer to Luke's day, Dio Chrysostom addresses the Rhodians and talks of divine men (θεῖοι ἄνδρες) who speak with eloquence. Dio felt that his own oratory was not of his own choosing, but was the will of some deity who gave him courage to speak (*32nd Disc.*, 12.21). Luke's audience already has seen the power of Paul's loud voice (14:10). In addition, the sweat of a holy and "divine" man was also thought to be effective in countering the fluids of the evil and demonic powers. As Preisigke says, the sweat from Paul's body saturates the clothing and so the clothing then has the same power that is in Paul's body. Paul's bodily fluid is stronger than that of the demons and so absorbs the power from the other and defeats it. There is a battle between the two fluids—that of Paul's and that of the demons—and since Paul's fluid possesses the greatest power, the evil spirit must disappear.[5]

What about the *semicinctium*, traditionally understood to be some kind of apron? In the *Satyricon*, Petronius threatens to hang himself with a *semicinctium* tied to the bed (94.8). As already noted, Leary reasonably thinks the use of the *semicinctium* for suicide hardly suggests it is an apron, and so he understands it to refer to a belt or sash. It would appear to be nothing more than a thinner version of the *cinctium*, or what the Greeks knew as a ζώνη, the girdle. Such girdles or belts wore worn commonly by both men and women.

There is the suggestion that the girdle was understood by some to either possess some power or to symbolize a life-giving power. For example, Pliny knows of the belief that "if the man by whom a woman has conceived unties his girdle (*cincto suo*) and puts it around her waist, and then unties it with the ritual formula, "I bound, and I too will unloose," then taking his

---

5. Preisigke, "Die Gotteskraft," 210–47, esp. 223.

departure, child-birth is made more rapid" (*Nat.* 28.9). It is also known that women left their girdles in the temple of Artemis in Ephesus after childbirth, and that on one occasion ambassadors visited Artemis" shrine at Sardis and offered tunics to her "according to the custom."[6]

As interesting as is the identification of these garments of Paul, equally interesting is the choice on the part of the Ephesians to want to take these garments and put them on the sick and possessed (Acts 19:12). The *sudarium* was worn around the neck and so was in touch with the "power" of the voice; the *semicinctium* went around the area of the stomach and the genitals and so was in touch with the "power" of that part of the body. That the clothing of a holy man, such as Paul, should be put to such use, and to have such effect, would not have surprised anyone in Luke's audience. That garments of the gods or of "divine" people should be used for magical purposes is also not surprising. One might note the Coptic magic spell which invokes the powers by their names and "by your garments" (*P. Lond. Hay* 10391); and the better known episode in the Gospels in which a woman believes she can be healed by touching Jesus" garments (Mark 5:28).

Paul wore the *sudarium* and the *semicinctium* in the hall of Tyrannus where he debated, dialogued and taught. He wore that clothing because it was the accepted dress of an orator. People wanted access to that particular clothing because the voice and the stomach/genital area of a holy man were considered bodily areas of special power.

---

6. See Strelan, *Paul, Artemis*, 48–49.

Going In and Out: Israel's Leaders in Acts

WHEN A REPLACEMENT IS sought for Judas, according to Acts 1:12–26 the criterion for the selection is that the candidate must have been with the apostles during the time that the Lord Jesus "went in and out" (εἰσῆλθεν καὶ ἐξῆλθεν) among them (1:21). This going in and out of Jesus is commonly understood to indicate no more than the time that he spent with his disciples. Bauernfeind, for example, says the verbs "umfassen den gesamten Lebensgang und es soll nur gesagt werden, dass die Zwölf das Leben des Herrn in allen seinen Wendungen teilten."[1] A similar expression is used in 9:28 where Luke describes Paul as εἰσπορευόμενος καὶ ἐκπορευόμενος εἰς Ἰερουσαλημ. Commentators again take it to mean little more than "the regular conduct of life, whatever that might be."[2] Rackham does suspect something more is implied. Like others, he believes it is a Semitism, but then he adds that in 9:28 "it seems to imply that Saul had already become a shepherd or leader of the people."[3] Bruce, seemingly unwittingly, also implies the verbs used together like this indicate leadership when he says that the phrase ἐφ' ἡμᾶς "may further suggest our Lord's relation to His disciples."[4] It is that implication this article explores.

I

The two verbs εἰσέρχομαι and ἐξέρχομαι occasionally appear in tandem in the Acts narrative to describe the travel movements of Peter and of Paul. Two clear examples of this linkage are found in 10:23–24 and 14:20. The former says of Peter that "the next day he got up and went out with them, and some of the believers from Joppa accompanied him. The following day, they went in to Caesarea" (Τῇ δὲ ἐπαύριον ἀναστὰς ἐξῆλθεν σὺν αὐτοῖς, καί

---

1. Bauernfeind, *Kommentar*, 29.
2. Barrett, *Acts*, 1:470.
3. Rackham, *Acts*, 139.
4. Bruce, *Acts*, 79.

τινες τῶν ἀδελφῶν τῶν ἀπὸ Ἰόππης συνῆλθον αὐτῷ. τῇ δὲ ἐπαύριον εἰσῆλθεν εἰς τὴν Καισάρειαν).

And of Paul it is said that after his stoning, "when the disciples gathered about him, he rose up and went into the city; and on the next day he went out with Barnabas into Derbe" (κυκλωσάντων δὲ τῶν μαθητῶν αὐτὸν ἀναστὰς εἰσῆλθεν εἰς τὴν πόλιν. καὶ τῇ ἐπαύριον ἐξῆλθεν σὺν τῷ Βαρναβᾷ εἰς Δέρβην).

Nearly all translations ignore the force of the prepositional prefixes in ἐξῆλθεν and εἰσῆλθεν. That is because they read Acts only at a narrative level. It is natural to read these passages as descriptions of Peter and Paul's travel, but the narrative reading can conceal the fact that the two verbs εἰσέρχομαι and ἐξέρχομαι also carry a technical sense, especially when used in tandem as they are in these passages. When used in that technical sense, the verbs add to the depiction of Peter and Paul as leaders of the restored Israel. It is a usage Luke knows from the Septuagint, where the verbs are used, independently and in tandem, of Israel's leaders, especially in their military or priestly capacity. For example, in Num 27:17, Moses requests God for a leader for Israel who "shall go out before them and come in before them, who shall lead them out and lead them in" (ὅστις ἐξελεύσεται πρὸ προσώπου αὐτῶν καὶ ὅστις εἰσελεύσεται πρὸ προσώπου αὐτῶν καὶ ὅστις ἐξάξει αὐτοὺς καὶ ὅστις εἰσάξει αὐτούς). Joshua, a man "in whom is the spirit" (27:18) is commissioned by Moses to fulfill that role. Moses makes this request because, as he says in another passage, οὐ δυνήσομαι ἔτι εἰσπορεύεσθαι καὶ ἐκπορεύεσθαι (Deut 31:2). Given the context, and the use of these verbs in combination elsewhere, Moses means more than "I am no longer able to get about," as the NIV translates it. Rather, he means he is no longer able to lead Israel, especially in the military conflicts awaiting them. The military sense is demonstrated clearly by Joshua himself when he says, "I am still as strong today as I was when Moses commissioned me. I am still strong enough now to go in and out of battle" (ἔτι εἰμὶ σήμερον ἰσχύων ὡσεὶ ὅτε ἀπέστειλέν με Μωυσῆς, ὡσαύτως ἰσχύω νῦν ἐξελθεῖν καὶ εἰσελθεῖν εἰς τὸν πόλεμον) (Josh 14:11 LXX; cf. 1 Macc 9:29 LXX). The two verbs are also used in tandem of David. He had been appointed commander in Saul's army and had great success. It is said that all of Israel and Judah loved David because αὐτὸς ἐξεπορεύετο καὶ εἰσεπορεύετο πρὸ προσώπου τοῦ λαοῦ (1 Sam 18:16 LXX). Clearly, the verbs here are used metaphorically of David's military leadership and do not simply describe his travel movements. Nor do they simply mean David spent time with the people. In another example where the two verbs are used in tandem, they are used to describe a protecting and providing role. Tobias is about to leave his home, and his mother weeps because she sees him as the "the staff of our hands as he goes in and out before us" (εἰσπορεύεσθαι αὐτὸν καὶ ἐκπορεύεσθαι ἐνώπιον ἡμῶν) (Tob 5:18 LXX).

In addition to the combination of verb forms the Septuagint also uses the nouns ἔξοδος and εἴσοδος in combination. The blessing of God is promised on Israel's "coming in and going out" (εἴσοδος καὶ ἔξοδος) if they keep the commands of God: "Blessed shall you be in your coming in and blessed shall you be in your going out" (Deut 28:6). That this blessing covers Israel's military movements is suggested by the next verse. The promise is that "the Lord will cause your enemies who rise against you to be defeated before you; they shall come out against you one way and flee before you seven ways" (Deut 28:7). The two nouns are also used together in a military sense in 1 Sam 29:6 LXX, where Achish, the leader of the Philistine army, says to David, "You should go out and in with me in the campaign" (καὶ ἡ ἔξοδός σου καὶ ἡ εἴσοδός σου μετ' ἐμοῦ ἐν τῇ παρεμβολῇ). So also in 2 Sam 3:25 LXX, where Abner is reported to have joined David so that he could learn his "comings and goings" (τὴν ἔξοδόν σου καὶ τὴν εἴσοδόν σου). The nouns are used together of the actions of a ruler in 1 Kgs 3:7 as Solomon, having become king to replace David, prays to God for wisdom because "I do not know how to go out or come in" (καὶ οὐκ οἶδα τὴν ἔξοδόν μου καὶ τὴν εἴσοδόν μου). Again, the military dimension cannot be ruled out; the expression certainly is used of Israel's leader. Such is also the case in 2 Kgs 19:27 LXX where the Lord says through Isaiah to Hezekiah: "I know your going out and your coming in" (καὶ τὴν ἔξοδόν σου καὶ τὴν εἴσοδόν σου ἔγνων) (cf. Isa 37:28). In these two passages, as commonly elsewhere, the expression "going in and going out" is a technical term for the movements of a leader of Israel.

There are other passages where the term has a less clear military or leadership inference. According to 2 Chr 16:1 LXX, King Baasha of Israel built Ramah "to prevent anyone from going out and going into (ἔξοδον καῖ εἴσοδον) the territory of King Asa of Judah (cf. 1 Kgs 15:17, where ἐκπορευόμενον καὶ εἰσπορευόμενον is used instead). It is not impossible that King Baasha wanted to prevent military action. In any case, there are also a few occasions in the Septuagint where the two words are linked to mean "all the events in one's life," as most commentators understand the expression in Acts. In Wis 7:6 it is said that all humans enter life by one way and they depart it by one way (μία δὲ πάντων εἴσοδος εἰς τὸν βίον ἔξοδός τε ἴση). In Ps Sol 4:14, the wish is expressed on someone's life: Γένοιτο, κύριε, ἡ μερὶς αὐτοῦ ἐν ἀτιμίᾳ ἐνώπιόν σου, ἡ ἔξοδος αὐτοῦ ἐν στεναγμοῖς καὶ ἡ εἴσοδος αὐτοῦ ἐν ἀρᾷ|.

Better known is Ps 120:7–8 LXX. This passage is not insignificant for understanding the strange incident involving Paul's stoning in Acts 14:19–20. That Acts passage talks of Paul going in and going out. In the Psalm, the pilgrim's going in and going out is promised the protection of God: κύριος φυλάξει σε ἀπὸ παντὸς κακοῦ, φυλάξει τὴν ψυχήν σου. κύριος φυλάξει τὴν εἴσοδόν σου καὶ τὴν ἔξοδόν σου ἀπὸ τοῦ νῦν καὶ ἕως τοῦ αἰῶνος. In Acts 14:19-20, Paul's life is certainly guarded, and his going in and going out are certainly under divine protection and blessing.

The promised blessing on the going in and going out of a pilgrim suggests another use of the two verbs in the Septuagint. They are commonly used of leaders and participators in the cult. In Lev 9:23, Moses and Aaron go in (εἰσῆλθον) to the tent of meeting, then come out (ἐξῆλθον) and bless the people. In Num 4:3, 23, 30, 35, 39, 43, 47, the expression ὁ εἰσπορευόμενος λειτουργεῖν ποιῆσαι πάντα τὰ ἔργα ἐν τῇ σκηνῇ τοῦ μαρτυρίου is used, sometimes with minor variations. The term ὁ εἰσπορευόμενος appears to be a technical term for someone performing a liturgical role. In Ezekiel, the prince goes with his people in and out of the temple during the appointed feasts (καὶ ὁ ἀφηγούμενος ἐν μέσῳ αὐτῶν ἐν τῷ εἰσπορεύεσθαι αὐτοὺς εἰσελεύσεται μετ' αὐτῶν καὶ ἐν τῷ ἐκπορεύεσθαι αὐτοὺς ἐξελεύσεται) (46:10). In Luke's Gospel, Zachariah is said to go into the temple (εἰσελθὼν εἰς τὸν ναὸν) (1:9) and then to go out again (ἐξελθών) (1:22). Priests are those who go in and out of the Temple on their sacred duties. In the Damascus Document of Qumran, the expression "going in and going out" is used specifically in association with sabbath observance. So "no man shall carry perfumes on himself whilst going and coming on the sabbath. . . . No man minding a child shall carry it whilst going and coming on the sabbath" (CD 11:9-11). This would suggest that "going and coming" is a term used to describe a ritual or cultic action.

In 1 Chr 27:1 LXX, it is not clear whether a military or cultic context is to be understood. Possibly both are meant since ἄρχοντες τῶν πατριῶν, χιλίαρχοι καὶ ἑκατόνταρχοι καὶ γραμματεῖς are listed alongside οἱ λειτουργοῦντες τῷ λαῷ. These leaders serve εἰς πᾶν λόγον τοῦ βασιλέως κατὰ διαιρέσεις, εἰς πᾶν λόγον τοῦ εἰσπορευομένου καὶ ἐκπορευομένου μῆνα ἐκ μηνός. According to 2 Chr 15:5 LXX, Israel was "for a long time without the true God, and without a teaching priest and without the Law," and in those times "there was no peace τῷ ἐκπορευομένῳ καὶ τῷ εἰσπορευομένῳ|. Here, the reference might be simply to the day-to-day movements of people but it could mean there was no peace for the military leadership since the next verse says "nation warred against nation and city against city" (15:6). In 1 Macc 3:45, οὐκ ἦν ὁ εἰσπορευόμενος καὶ ἐκπορευόμενος ἐκ τῶν γενημάτων αὐτῆς probably means little more than that Jerusalem was deserted, but again it is quite possible that it was deserted in the sense that no cultic actions took place. This is suggested by what follows in the same verse: "the sanctuary was trampled down." It could also mean that Jerusalem had no leadership; there was no one who was "going in and going out" before them.

Priestly and military leadership are, of course, not incompatible in Jewish historical experience. The Levites, for example, were to have weapons in their hands and be with the king in his "comings and goings" (καὶ ἔσονται μετὰ τοῦ βασιλέως εἰσπορευομένου καὶ ἐκπορευομένου) (2 Chr 23:7 LXX). David can function as both priest and captain; and one of the major concerns of some Jews in the Maccabean period was the combination of military ruler and priest. In the Qumran texts there are examples of priests taking active leadership roles in the eschatological war.[5]

Before returning to look at the expression in Acts, if one assumes a common authorship of Luke and Acts, then one might expect to find the expression also used in the Gospel. The verbs do appear there in tandem but not markedly so. The disciples, in their commissioning by Jesus, are assumed to go in and out (εἰσελθῆτε . . . ἐξέρχεσθε) (9:4). Given the context of their commissioning as leaders with power and authority (9:1) and the fact that they go in and go out of a house (9:3) (οἰκία probably refers to a Christian community), it is reasonable to see the two verbs used in this passage as a technical marker of leadership. A similar thought is found in a parallel commissioning in (ἐξελθόντες) if they are not welcomed. Going in and going out seems to describe the basic activity of a commissioned disciple of Jesus.

In a more general way, Jesus himself is frequently described in Luke's Gospel as going in and going out. So, for example, he went in to (εἰσῆλθεν) the house of Simon (4:38) and then at daybreak, he went out (ἐξελθών) and went into the desert (4:42). Jesus is said to "go out" in 5:27; 6:12; 8:27; 22:39. And 9:31 speaks explicitly of his exodus (τὴν ἔξοδον αὐτοῦ). He is also said to "go in" many times (6:6; 7:1, 36; 9:52; 10:38; 17:12; 19:1). While the verbs may not be used in tandem when referring to Jesus, they are used enough times separately to be able to say that the life of Jesus is characterised in Luke as one of going in and going out. They are the actions of a leader of Israel, and for Luke Jesus is the leader appointed by God to rescue and sanctify Israel. In Acts 5:31, Jesus is described as leader and savior (ἀρχηγὸς καὶ σωτήρ).

II

In recent years, a number of scholars have recognised that Luke understands Christians to be either the restored or the new Israel.[6] The restored Israel needs leaders, and to those leaders God promises to supply power (1:8). Since the Septuagint commonly uses the two verbs "to go in" and "to go out" in tandem and in connection with its leaders, we might expect that Luke

---

5. See especially *The War Rule*.
6. Jervell, *Luke*.

would do the same when speaking of Peter and Paul (and Jesus) who are obvious leaders in the Christian communities. If that leadership is characterised by "going in and going out," then we might expect that they go in and out in the company of others. We might also expect that their going in and going out be in the context of a community. Linguistically, we might expect the verbs to be used with the prepositions σύν and μετά,) And that it indeed the case. In 1:21, where the expression "he went in and out among us" is used of Jesus, Peter is addressing the brethren (ἀδελφοί) who need to find, as a replacement for Judas, one who had been with them (συνελθέντων) (1:22) from the baptism of Jesus by John through to his ascension. In the case of Paul in 9:28, it is explicitly said that he went in and out with disciples (καὶ ἦν μετ' αὐτῶν εἰσπορευόμενος καὶ ἐκπορευόμενος εἰς Ἰερουσαλήμ). This sense of Paul as a leader with followers, by the way, might help to explain the otherwise surprising reference to "his disciples" (οἱ μαθηταὶ αὐτοῦ) in 9:25.

When Peter goes out of Joppa (ἐξῆλθεν) (10:23) and goes into Caesarea (εἰσῆλθεν) (10:24), he makes these moves in the company of others. He moves with those who come from Cornelius" house. It is also said that some of the brethren from Joppa went with Peter (τινες τῶν ἀδελφῶν τῶν ἀπὸ Ἰόππης συνῆλθον αὐτῷ) (10:23). Given the common military use of these verbs in the Septuagint, is it coincidental that the verbs are used of Peter when he meets a representative of the Roman army? Is the subsequent falling to the knees by Cornelius (10:25) an action expected by the reader who has been told—by Luke's choice of vocabulary—that Peter is a leader in Israel?

The two verbs are used in a similar way of Paul in 14:20. There, Paul goes into Lystra (εἰσῆλθεν) and goes out to Derbe (ἐξῆλθεν). As noted above, the protection promised by the Lord in Ps 120 LXX on the pilgrim's going in and going out might well be the point of the two verbs being used here of Paul. And like Peter, Paul too goes out in company with others (with Barnabas). That Paul moves as a leader in a Christian community is implicit not only in the use of the two verbs commonly associated with such leaders, but also in the context. Acts 14:19-22 uses a cluster of "disciple" words. After Paul is dragged out of the city, presumably dead, the disciples gather around him (14:20). They are *his* disciples! In 14:21, Paul and Barnabas go to Derbe and "make many disciples" there, and in the next verse, they are said to strengthen "the souls of the disciples" (14:22). This grouping of "disciple" words in 14:20-22 is probably intentional. If Paul and Barnabas are leaders in Israel who "go in and go out" before the people, they must have a community to lead. In 14:22, Paul and Barnabas are also said to "encourage" the disciples—another act of leaders (cf. Deut 3:28).

A very similar pattern can be observed in 16:40 as Paul and Silas go out of the jail at Philippi and go into Lydia's home where they encourage the group and then go out again (ἐξελθόντες δὲ ἀπὸ τῆς φυλακῆς εἰσῆλθον πρὸς τὴν Λυδίαν καὶ ἰδόντες παρεκάλεσαν τοὺς ἀδελφοὺς καὶ ἐξῆλθαν).

The same two verbs also appear together in 21:8 as Paul and his companions are said to go out of (ἐξελθόντες) Ptolemaeus and to go into (εἰσελθόντες) the house of Philip in Caesarea. Once again, the movement from out to in leaves Paul in the company of a Christian community. There are other occasions when Paul is said to go in and out, even if not in relation to the one place. For example, in 18:19 Paul is said to go into the synagogue at Ephesus and then in 18:23, he is said to go out from Antioch. It is enough to suggest that Luke uses these verbs not simply to report on Paul's movements, but to depict him as one who goes in and goes out before the community, that is, as a leader of the new Israel.

III

Peter and Paul, like Jesus before them, are chosen by God and given a spirit which empowers them to lead the people of God. This leadership is not military in its expression and it would not seem that they are leaders in a holy war. But they do lead people to a new way of holiness. To create this image of these holy leaders, Luke uses terminology familiar to ears attuned to the Septuagint, especially to the story of God's great salvific actions known in Exodus, Leviticus, Numbers, and Deuteronomy. Such an audience knew of the leadership of Moses who went in and out before Israel, and of his successor, Joshua, who prepared Israel for entrance into Canaan. Like Joshua, Peter and Paul, as successors to Jesus as leaders in a restored Israel, go in and go out in the company of others.

Midday and Midnight in the Acts of the Apostles[1]

SOME SIGNIFICANT EVENTS ARE the consequence of experiences that take place at midday and at midnight in the Acts of the Apostles. Philip is told by an angel to go along the road at midday (κατὰ μεσημβρίαν)[2] (8:26), and this audition results in the baptism of the Ethiopian (8:38) and also in the movement of "the word of the Lord" beyond the borders of Israel and Samaria. Later in the narrative, Peter goes to pray on the rooftop where, "about the sixth hour" (περὶ μεσημβρίαν) (10:9), he is in ecstasy and has a vision that results in a non-Jewish household being incorporated by baptism into the renewed Israel (10:47–48) as "Gentiles [to whom] God has also granted repentance unto life" (11:18). Paul's visionary experience near Damascus is said, in two accounts, to have occurred at midday (περὶ μεσημβρίαν; ἡμέρας μέσης) (22:6; 26:13), and the significance of that vision for the mission of Paul to the gentiles is obvious. It is also at midnight (κατὰ δὲ μεσονύκτιον) (16:25) that Paul and Silas experience an earthquake and the possibility of escape from prison. The episode ends with the jailer and his household believing in God and being baptised (16:33). So midday and midnight visions and auditions, and wondrous events at either of these times, result in the incorporation of gentiles into the people of God.

There is another midnight incident in Acts included in this study, and that is when Paul restored Eutychus to life after the latter had fallen three storeys while asleep (20:7–12). There is the suggestion that Paul did this at midnight, since he had prolonged his speaking "until midnight" (μέχρι μεσονυκτίου) (20:7). While there is no baptism in this episode, it does echo some baptismal language, and it shares some interesting symbolic parallels with the Philippi episode, as will be seen.

---

1. It is a great honour and privilege to contribute to a *Festschrift* for Professor Michael Lattke, my erstwhile teacher and *Doktorvater*, and now my respected colleague and valued friend.

2. Others understand this phrase to refer to the southerly direction, which is possible. This is discussed below.

For the sake of completion, there is one other reference to midnight in Acts, but it seems not to carry any significance. The sailors on the ship carrying Paul conjecture "about the middle of the night" (κατὰ μέσον τῆς νύκτος) (27:27) that they are nearing land. Even in this case, it is possible that the midnight hour provided the sailors with a revelation that they were nearing land.

In general, commentators have understood the references to midday and midnight in Acts merely as time-markers and as having no other significance. But they do in fact have another significance that should not be overlooked. Speyer has noted that in the Greco-Roman world "the midday hour was held to be the preferred time for the appearances of gods and demons and for a vision of the beyond" (*Jenseitsschau*).[3] He has also shown the same to be true of the midnight hour.[4] It was not only visions that occurred then, but gods and other spirit-powers often acted in decisive ways at these particular times. This widespread understanding appears to be known to the writer of Acts and presumably also therefore to his audience. If this was the case, then when Luke refers to midday or midnight in the instances mentioned above, many in the audience might well have heard them as cues for a heavenly being to appear in a vision with a significant message, or for that divine being to do something wondrous and decisive. The baptism of gentiles, their incorporation into the people of God, and the outpouring of the holy Spirit on to them, were significant and distinctive features of the Christian movement, according to Acts. Such significant action needed justification. The writer of Acts uses the sudden appearances of heavenly agents at midday and at midnight as evidence that God directed, and so approved, the actions of the apostles, especially that of incorporating gentiles into the people of God.

Midday and Midnight in Greek and Latin Literature

Like with most critical points in time or space, there was some ambiguity about midday in Greek and Roman literature. It was commonly considered a dangerous time,[5] and malevolent or frightening powers were believed to be particularly active at that time. For example, it is at midday, when the sun "from his zenith had drawn the shadows to their shortest compass," that Circe worked her magical and poisonous charms against

---

3. Speyer, "Vision," 330, my translation.
4. Speyer, "Mittag," 340–52.
5. Even today in some Greek circles it is called the "the evil hour." See Green, *Argonautika*, 342.

Scylla (Ovid, *Metam.* 14.53–55). Lucian tells of Eucrates who was walking through a field at midday (μεσούσης ἡμέρας) when suddenly there was an earthquake and thunder, and he had a frightening vision of a terrifying woman, probably Hecate, gigantic in height and Gorgon-like in appearance (*Philops.* 22). On the other hand, benevolent forces were also known to be active at midday, appearing in visions with positive messages. For example, Tacitus writes about a certain Curtius Rufus, who, before he was appointed proconsul, was loitering by himself in an arcade at midday (*per medium diei*) "when a female form of superhuman size rose before him, and a voice was heard to say: 'Thou, Rufus, art he that shall come into this province as proconsul'" (*Annals* 11.21).

Similar is the vision that Jason, of Argonaut fame, experienced in the middle of the day when the sun was at its hottest, and while he was at rest. The chthonic nymphs associated with Athena "stood over my head nigh at hand," gave Jason an assuring message, and then disappeared as suddenly as they had appeared (Apollonius Rhodius, *Arg.* 4.1312–1363). Themistocles had a similar experience, also at midday (μεσημβρίας), and also while asleep, when the mother of the gods appeared to him in a dream (ὄναρ) warning him of a threat to his life (Plutarch, *Them.* 30.1). A further example of divine inspiration coming at midday and in sleep is offered by Pausanius. He knows of a story in which a shepherd was sleeping at midday (περὶ μεσοῦσαν μάλιστα τὴν ἡμέραν) against the tomb of Orpheus, and during his sleep he began to sing the poetry of Orpheus in a loud and sweet voice (*Descr.* 9.30.1).

So midday was the time for both malevolent and benevolent beings to communicate with humans and to influence their lives. Speyer thinks the midday experiences tend to bring blessings and were life-giving; the midnight experiences tend to point to one's death and were life-taking. This is partly because the day belongs to the heavenly gods, while the night belongs to those of the underworld. But certainly the reverse is also to be found, as Speyer acknowledges.[6]

Why was midday believed to be a critical, ambiguous, and dangerous time? There are at least three rather obvious reasons. The first is that midday is the turning point in the day; from midday on the sun proceeds downwards in its course across the sky and light moves inexorably towards darkness. So midday marks the critical point. A second reason has to do with the fact that at midday there is no shadow, or at least shadows are at their shortest. Shadowless times were regarded with some dread.[7] This dread is

---

6. Speyer, "Mittag," 341.
7. See van der Horst, "Peter's Shadow," 208.

clearly expressed in the poetry of Lucan who says of a certain sacred grove, "when the sun is in mid-heaven or dark night fills the sky, the priest himself dreads the appearance of the god and fears to surprise the lord of the grove" (*Bell.* 3.423-26). It was also a common belief that the gods and other demons, not having corporeal existence, cast no shadow.[8] The Pythagoreans, at least, thought spirits of the dead were shadowless (Plutarch, *Quaest.graec.* 39). In addition, Pausanius knows of reports that the shadows of both men and beasts were not visible when they entered the Lycaean temple of Zeus (8.38.6). It is an idea known earlier to Theopompus, but dismissed by Polybius as a sign of blunted intelligence (16.12.7).

A third reason is that midday marked for some the end of business for the day. Plutarch says that "a Roman official does not make treaties or agreements after midday" (μεσημβρία), and that for most people "serious business" and business transactions are never done after midday (*Quaest. rom.* 284). After all, midday was siesta time, the time for sleep and rest, as many a summer tourist will still discover when visiting the southern Mediterranean world. Not only was it rest time for humans, it was also rest time for some of the gods. Theocritus has a goatherd say that he must not play the flute at noon for fear of disturbing the rest of Pan (1.15.8). Ovid speaks of Faunus resting in the field at noon (*medio cum premit arva die*) (*Fast.* 4.761-62). Homer says Proteus, the old man of the sea, comes out of the sea at midday and lies down to sleep in a cave (*Od.* 4.398-461). The fourth-century Ausonius says that at midday the Satyrs and sister-Nymphs meet beside a stream to play and dance "set free from mortal company" who, it is implied, are asleep at that time (*Mosella* 178-80).

Sleep at midday was sometimes transformative for humans. I have already drawn attention to midday visions and inspiration that occurred during sleep. In addition to those examples, Diogenes Laertius cites Theopompus as saying that a young man went to sleep at midday and woke up twenty-seven years later (*Epimenides* 1.109). Pausanius says that weariness and sleep overtook the young Pindar at noon when he was on a journey. He fell asleep and bees put wax on his mouth, so making him a lyric poet (9.23.2).

This association of rest and sleep with midday is a crucial reason for midday being a time for the appearance of a heavenly being. Some Greeks and Romans considered sleep and the point of death as the most likely times when the gods came in visions or dreams because in sleep, as in dying, the soul of a person is receptive to such appearances. At those moments, the soul is purified from all distractions and can enter into another reality

---

8. Is this reflected in James 1:17?

unencumbered, and that reality is the world of the gods and their messengers. This view implies that visions of the gods, and the messages communicated through them, come especially to those who are pure, that is, those who are not befuddled by physical passions and emotions and are in a sense "spiritual" or in a spiritual state. Plutarch, speaking of the soul's power to prophesy, says that this power is displayed often in dreams, and in the hour of death, because it is at these two times that "the body becomes cleansed of all impurities and attains a temperament adapted to this end, a temperament through which the reasoning and thinking faculty of the souls are relaxed and released from their present state as they range amid the irrational and imaginative realms of the future" (*Def. orac.* 432C).

Sleep was commonly used as a metaphor for death, and the two were seen as referring to very similar states of consciousness. Sleep was called "the neighbor of death" (ὕπνος γείτων τοῦ θανάτου);[9] and Homer called sleep and death twin brothers (*Il.* 16.672). That Stephen had a vision of the heavens opening and of the Son of Man standing at the right hand (Acts 7:56) would not have surprised many in a contemporary audience. Facing death sharpened his sight and purified his mind of all physical and material passions, thus enabling him to see into the heavenly world. Luke describes Peter and Paul and Philip as men who are ready receptacles for heavenly visions. That Peter falls into ecstasy at midday, that Philip is told by an angel to go somewhere at midday, and that Paul has a pivotal and radical vision at midday is befitting of men who are filled with a holy spirit, purified men set free from vision-preventing passions.

Since visions from the gods frequently occur during sleep, it is natural to expect the very middle of the time of sleep, namely midnight, to be the ultimate time for such visions to come to humans. This is simply stated by Horace who claimed that Quirinus appeared to him "after midnight when dreams are true" (*post mediam noctem . . . cum somnia vera*) (*Sat.* 1.10.33). Nightly visions, whether in sleep or otherwise, and night-actions of the gods are very common in both biblical and non-biblical literature, as indeed they are in Acts itself (e.g., 5:19; 12:6; 16:9; 18:9; 23:11; 27:23). Some examples will make this clear.

Plato tells of souls that "had all fallen asleep, and it was in the middle of the night (μέσας νύκτας). There was a sound of thunder and a quaking of the earth (σεισμὸν γενέσθαι), and they were suddenly wafted thence, one this way, one that, upward to their birth like shooting stars" (*Repub.* 10.621b). According to Diogenes Laertius, Empedocles heard an exceedingly loud voice calling him in the middle of the night (μέσων νύκτων). He got up and

---

9. Eunus VI (Gow and Page, *Greek Anthology,* line 2329).

saw a light in the heavens and a glitter of lamps but nothing else. Empedocles was gone; "he was now a god" (*Diog. Laert.* 8.67). It was at midnight (*medio noctis*) that Io appeared in a vision to Telethusa who was assured by the goddess that the child she was carrying was a girl, and that she should keep the child even though her husband wished otherwise (Ovid, *Metam.* 9.685–703). Plutarch reports that on the night before a battle, as Caesar went at about midnight to visit the watch, men saw a great firebrand in the sky that came over Caesar's camp, and fell down in Pompey's camp (*Caes.* 43). He also records an experience of Brutus "at deepest night" (νὺξ βαθυτάτη) when an apparition of his evil genius appeared to him (*Brut.* 36.3–4).

In his *Metamorphoses*, Apuleius tells of his initiation into the rites of Isis. The night before, he spent in the sanctuary. He says, "I came to the boundary of death. . . . I travelled through all the elements and returned. In the middle of the night I saw the sun flashing with bright light. I came face to face with the gods below and the gods above and paid reverence to them close at hand" (11.23). Earlier, Apuleius related another experience which took place "about midnight," when "suddenly the doors were opened with a violence far greater than any burglar could have produced. In fact the pivots were broken and completely torn from their sockets and the doors thrown to the ground." This happened "automatically" (*sua sponte*). Two witches appeared. On their departure "the doors swung back unharmed into their original position: the pivots settled back in their sockets, the bars returned to the doorposts, and the bolts ran back into the lock" (1.11.14). Midnight is also known as "the bewitching hour" by Lucan who says that Erichtho works on special unknown spells and incantations at midnight (*Bell.* 6.570–824).

The adventures of Apuleius with the sudden and automatic opening of doors at midnight are not unique. Apollonius of Tyana is said to have gone to the temple of Dictynna by night, passed the very savage dogs, was arrested by the guards as a wizard and robber, and imprisoned. "But about midnight he loosened his bonds . . . and ran to the doors of the temple which opened wide to receive him, and when he had passed within, they closed afresh, as they had been shut" (Philostratus, *Vit. Apoll.* 30). Apollonius was believed to have been taken up to the gods and to have become immortal. These two episodes have a clear parallel in the midnight experience of Paul and Silas while in prison (Acts 16:25).

Midday and Midnight in Jewish Literature

Jewish literature, of course, often reflected the cultural and social context in which it was written. In other words, many, if not most, ideas and notions were common to both Jews and non-Jews and were expressed in a common language. And that certainly is the case with notions about midday and midnight. Visions and angelophanies are experienced at both of these critical times. Abraham saw three angels coming towards him at the hottest time of the day (Gen 18:1–2). Jeremiah takes a rest during "the burning heat of the day," presumably midday, falls asleep, and has a vision (4 Bar 5:1–33). According to Ps 90:6 LXX, God offers protection against the midday demon (δαιμόνιον μεσημβρινόν). On Carmel, the prophets of Baal cry to their god from morning to midday. "Midday came" (καὶ ἐγένετο μεσημβρία) (3 Reg 18:27) but "there was no voice and there was no answer" (18:26); Elijah mocks them, inviting them to call out louder because maybe their god is asleep (18:27). So, here too is the notion of the gods sleeping at midday, but also implicit is the idea that if there is no action from the god at midday, then there is not likely ever to be any response.

Since noon was commonly considered an ambiguous and dangerous time, it is not surprising that the righteous of Israel might offer prayer then. So Ps 55:18 LXX says, "Evening and morning and at noon (μεσημβρίας) I utter my complaint and moan and he will hear my voice." Peter, in fact, goes to the rooftop to pray at noon (Acts 10:9). In passing, I might also draw attention to significant events that take place "at the sixth hour" in the Christian Gospels. Jesus rests, then meets and converses with the Samaritan woman when ὥρα ἦν ὡς ἕκτη (John 4:6); and at Jesus' crucifixion, "when the sixth hour had come, there was darkness over the whole land until the ninth hour" (Mark 14:33).

Turning to midnight visions and midnight dramatic acts from the heavenly world, it is at that time that the powerful, destructive actions of the angel of God strike the Egyptian firstborn (Exod 11:4). It is "at the sixth hour" of the night that Jeremiah and Baruch are in the temple, weeping at the altar area. Angels appear from heaven and take them to the walls of the temple and deliver a message to them about the future of Jerusalem and of Israel (4 Bar 2:9–3:13). There is a tradition regarding Samuel, reflected in Ps-Philo, in which it is said that it was at midnight that Samuel heard a voice out of heaven calling him (LAB 53:3). Again, since midnight was an auspicious time, to pray at midnight was regarded as the mark of the righteous. So, for example, Ps 118:62 LXX, "At midnight (μεσονύκτιον) I rise to praise you, because of your righteous ordinances." It is then, at midnight, that Paul and Silas are praying and singing hymns to God (Acts 16:25).

Midday and Midnight in Acts

Turning to look more closely at the midday and midnight experiences in Acts, the significance of those times of day in the narrative is now more apparent. Philip is a prophet, a man of God who is open to the revelations of God. Such a man belongs to those "full of spirit and wisdom" (6:3) and he himself is said to be "full of faith and a holy spirit" (6:5). The episode with the eunuch reinforces these characteristics in two ways. In the first place, Philip acts as he does because of a heavenly audition and not of his own initiative (8:26). Secondly, as a messenger of God, Philip acts precisely at the time when messengers of the gods were expected to act—at midday. Scholars miss the point, and enter into fruitless discussion, when they debate whether or not such a time of the day was suitable for travel.[10] As a result, some prefer the translation "to the south." Typical is Bruce, who is aware that in the Septuagint, "μεσημβρία regularly means "noon" except at Dan 8:4, 9 where it means 'south.'" He concludes, "But here southward is the more natural sense."[11] Lake and Cadbury claim that since midday was not the time for travelling, the meaning "midday" for κατὰ μεσημβρίαν is "so improbable a sense in this passage that it must be rejected."[12] Bauernfeind had argued the same: "die Mittag ist keine Reisezeit."[13] It is an argument Conzelmann counters by saying it depends on the time of the year![14] Such rather fruitless discussion detracts from the literary clue that "midday" in fact provides. It is the time when the gods and their agents are active. While arguing for the sense of "midday" primarily on the basis of the Septuagint and Luke's own usage of the word, van Unnik comes close to its significance. He suggests Philip is told to travel at midday precisely because it is an unexpected time to travel, and so is part of die göttliche Überrraschung.[15] It is the line also taken by Barrett[16] and Marshall.[17]

The point of midday is also sometimes missed in Peter's vision in Acts 10. His vision is said to be "at the sixth hour" not simply "to explain Peter's hunger."[18] Nor is his vision in ecstasy the consequence of some projected

---

10. They seem to forget that Paul was travelling at midday!
11. Bruce, *Book of Acts*, 173n53.
12. Lake and Foakes-Jackson, *Beginnings*, 4:95.
13. Bauernfeind, *Kommentar*, 128.
14. Conzelmann, *Die Apostelgeschichte*, 55.
15. van Unnik, "Der Befehl," 181–91, esp. 187.
16. Barrett, *Acts*, 1:427.
17. Marshall, *Acts*, 161.
18. Johnson, *Acts*, 183.

wish on Peter's part. The sixth hour is an hour of prayer, if not of obligatory prayer, and prayer, especially when combined with fasting, often leads to visionary or auditory revelation. It might also be noted that ecstasy "came upon Peter" (ἐγένετο ἐπ᾿ αὐτὸν ἔκστασις) (10:10). This underscores the point that what eventuates is not the result of Peter's initiative but comes from outside of himself. As with Philip's move towards the Gaza road, Peter's movement into the house of the god-fearing Cornelius and his subsequent baptizing of the gentile's household come at the initiative of God. That is why the heavenly instructions come at midday, the time of day when an audience expects God to be active in communicating significant, and often radical, things to humans.

The significance of Paul's midday vision (22:6; 26:13) is now straightforward. But again, it is not uncommon for scholars to speculate as to the point of the reference. As Dunn notes, "The information has stimulated speculation about the effects of the midday sun in the vision Paul saw."[19] I suggest, rather, that an audience might well have heard this time reference as a sure indicator that Paul was indeed a chosen vessel of God who acted not under his own power nor by his own initiative but under the direction and impulse of the living heavenly Lord. The hallmarks are all present. Paul, like Philip, is moving about precisely at that time of the day when others might well be resting and asleep, and so it is almost inevitable that he comes into contact with a heavenly being that is active at midday. Like Philip, and especially like Peter, he receives a heavenly audition telling him to act in a way that was against his previous judgment and will.

The same point is made again in the midnight drama that culminates in the baptism of the Philippian jailer and his household (Acts 16:25–34). Paul and Silas are in prison praising God at midnight, as the righteous Psalmist exhorts. But the point is not to highlight the righteousness of the apostles—"Fancy that! Not only praising God while suffering but actually doing so at midnight!"—as is suggested by Marshall who says, "Here we have a concrete depiction of the Christian ideal of 'joy amid suffering.'"[20] Dunn uses the exclamation mark—Paul and Silas pray and sing to God "at midnight!"[21] What is missed is that the reference in the narrative to midnight draws the audience's attention to the anticipated activity of God, not to the piety of Paul and Silas. Even though there is no divine appearance in the Acts narrative, the shaking of the ground and the loosening of doors while a petitioner is at prayer were commonly understood to be a favourable

19. Dunn, *Acts*, 294.
20. Marshall, *Acts*, 271.
21. Dunn, *Acts*, 222.

signs of a god's protective presence or of the god's acceptance of the prayer. For example, according to Ovid, Telethusa prayed to Isis:

> Tears emphasised her prayer; the goddess seemed
> to move—in truth it was the altar moved;
> the firm doors of the temple even shook—
> and her horns, crescent, flashed with gleams of light,
> and her loud sistrum rattled noisily (*Metam.* 9.782).

Ovid also tells of a delegation to the Delphi oracle. They entreat the god for aid, and then:

> While ground, and laurels and the quivers which
> the god hung there all shook, the tripod gave
> this answer from the deep recesses hid
> within the shrine, and stirred with trembling their
> astonished hearts (15.669–78).

The same envoys are then in the temple and praying to the god. Ovid continues:

> They prayed the god to indicate for them,
> by clear celestial tokens, in what spot
> he wished to dwell.
> Scarce had they ceased the prayer
> for guidance, when the god all glittering
> with gold and as a serpent, crest erect,
> sent forth a hissing as to notify
> a quick approach—and in his coming shook
> his statue and the altars and the doors,
> the marble pavement and the gilded roof (15.723–34).

Jewish literary traditions also knew of earth-shaking as a sign of God's presence. According to Sir 43:16, "at his [God's] appearing the mountains shake" (ἐν ὀπτάσια αὐτοῦ σαλευθήσεται ὄρη). And earlier in the same writing, "heaven and the highest heaven, the abyss and the earth tremble (σαλευθήσονται) at his visitations; the very mountains and the foundations (τὰ θεμέλια) of the earth quiver and quake when he looks upon them" (16:18–19).

The great trembling (σεισμὸς μέγας) which shakes the foundations (σαλευθῆναι τὰ θεμέλια) of the prison at Philippi is in response to Paul's and Silas's prayer. It is similar to the episode Virgil narrates when Aeneas visits a temple on the island of Anius where he asks Apollo for a sign to show him the way to his homeland. Hardly had he finished speaking when everything seemed to shake, "the doors and laurels of the god; the whole hill shook round about and the tripod moaned as the shrine was thrown open. Prostrate we fall to earth, and a voice comes to our ears" (*Aen.* 3.84–94). So the earthquake at midnight in Philippi is a literary and narrative clue to the audience that God is about to act in a wondrous way for the deliverance of his agents. Midnight appearance and action was a well-known feature of a god in both Jewish and pagan literary traditions.

The final midnight experience narrated in Acts that I wish to look at briefly involves Paul and Eutychus in Acts 20. Once again, the significance of midnight is presumably unknown to scholars, who resort to jokes about the length and quality of Paul's sermons and concern themselves with the inability of Eutychus to stay awake in "the stuffy atmosphere."[22] Maybe the lamps emit odour-inducing sleep, suggests Marshall.[23] How could Eutychus fall asleep when he was sitting by the window where the air is freshest? "Perhaps he had put in a hard day's work from dawn to sunset," speculates Bruce.[24] Marshall and Haenchen speculate whether those inside the room would drop off to sleep before someone sleeping by a window.[25] "Surely we have here a piece of eyewitness information,"[26] is a questionable claim, but it underscores what drives some scholarship. The obsession with historical verification means other significance is lost and sometimes results in non-productive speculation.

No more helpful is Pervo who describes this event as a "delightful little episode of the boy who could not stay awake in church even with the great Paul in the pulpit," a story that evokes a "smile, even if guiltily."[27] Strangely, he finds it "quite religious (*sic*!), an edifying account of a cultic miracle with a good moral about staying awake and out of dangerous places."[28] But Pervo is not alone in this rather dismissive attitude

---

22. Bruce, *Acts*, 385.
23. Marshall, *Acts*, 326.
24. Bruce, *Acts*, 385.
25. Haenchen, *Acts*, 585n2; Marshall, *Acts*, 326.
26. Marshall, *Acts*, 326.
27. Pervo, *Profit*, 65.
28. Pervo, *Profit*, 66.

towards the story. Dunn thinks it a "tragi-comic episode";[29] Johnson calls it a "charming episode"[30] with a "nice touch," but Luke's "dramatic sense seems to have abandoned him completely."[31]

But this episode is not told for comic relief. It deals with the fundamental problem of death in the Christian community, an issue beyond the scope of this article. For now, "midnight" is the literary marker drawing the audience's attention to the possibility of a wondrous action by the agent of God, an action that delivers from death. Midday and midnight were "dangerous" times; in some cases, the "demons" active at those times could prove fatal. In the Acts of Andrew, for example, it is said that in Nicea there "were seven devils living among the tombs by the wayside, who at noon stoned passersby and had killed many" (Acts Andr 6). Here at Troas, Eutychus falls to his death at midnight, overcome by the power of Sleep. In this regard, the episode has some interesting parallels with the earlier Philippi prison experience of Paul. Both events take place at midnight, the time when the audience might expect God or the agent of God to be active in a dramatic way. Unlike the death-producing actions of heavenly beings at midnight against the firstborn of Egypt in Israel's mythology, the actions of Paul, the vessel of God to the gentiles, are life-producing and provide rescue from death. The jailer's life is spared at the word of Paul (16:28), and Eutychus is declared to be alive by the same Paul (20:10). Both episodes have death and sleep at midnight as a central motif. Eutychus is overcome by sleep. The noun ὕπνος is used twice, and both times with words that denote very deep sleep (καταφερόμενος ὕπνῳ βαθεῖ... κατενεχθεὶς ἀπὸ τοῦ ὕπνου). The use of the preposition κατ- in the compound participles denotes some aggression! Eutychus is utterly overwhelmed by Sleep, and it is the sleep of death as he falls out of the window to the ground below. "He was taken up dead" (ἤρθη νεκρός) (20:9). The jailer at Philippi was aroused from his state of sleep (ἔξυπνος) and threatens to kill himself on finding the prison doors open, and thinking his prisoners have escaped (16:27). Both men face death at midnight as a result of their sleeping; both are rescued by the agent of God who is awake and at worship at midnight. In both narratives, there is a "rebirth"—the jailer and his household are baptised (16:33), and the young man (νεανίας) Eutychus, after being "taken up dead" (20:9) is led away "a living son" (παῖδα ζῶντα) (20:12). In both narratives, light also features. In the Eutychus episode, Luke seems to draw conscious attention to them, "There were many lights (λαμπάδες) in the upper chamber

29. Dunn, *Acts*, 268.
30. Johnson, *Acts*, 356.
31. Johnson, *Acts*, 358.

where we were gathered" (20:8); at Philippi, the jailer calls for lights (φῶτα) (16:29). It is no coincidence, it seems to me, that the motifs of midnight, lamps, sleep, and death also feature in the parable of Jesus found in Matt 25:1–13. Midnight is the critical time, the time of death and rebirth, of light and darkness, the time when God and his agents offer life and prevent death. It suggests to me that the reference to midnight in the Eutychus episode (20:7) is not without its significance.

Conclusion

In summary, the modern reader of an ancient text like Acts can derive great benefit from understanding the literary techniques and skills used by its author. If it is assumed that the audiences were familiar with other texts (in a manner not too dissimilar to a modern English-writer who might assume the audience is familiar with Shakespeare), then there is something to be gained by looking for literary clues and markers in the narrative of Acts that might have some significance to an ancient audience. This essay has suggested that Luke used "midday" and "midnight" as temporal markers in his narrative to draw even closer attention to his claim that Peter and Paul and the other Christian characters act under the impulse and direction of God. In addition, the inclusion of gentiles into the Christian community through the act of baptism receives its justification from heavenly visions and auditions given and received at these crucial times of the day. Luke's audience was most likely familiar with literary and mythological traditions that understood these midday and midnight experiences as critical moments when the gods and their messengers were most active. Such time-references provide the audience with further proof that the heroes of the narrative are totally under the control, direction and protection of the living and ascended Lord.

Luke's Use of Isaiah LXX in Acts

Introduction

IT IS WELL KNOWN that Luke, like many the other NT writers, wanted to claim that what he believed God had done through Jesus was consistent with the activity of God in Jewish Scriptures, and that, indeed, God's actions through Jesus were the fulfilment of those very scriptures. The death of the Christ, especially, was believed to be "in accordance with the scriptures" (κατὰ τὰς γραφάς) (1 Cor 15:3; cf. Acts 17:2-3), or, as "Moses and the prophets" had said (Luke 24:27, 44; Acts 26:22; 28:23). A prophetic word is, by definition, a word that is capable of being fulfilled, and its veracity or otherwise depends on that fulfilment. Luke uses prophetic words as basic building blocks in his narrative construction.

Since interpretation of "Moses and the prophets" provided many points of contention between Paul and other Jews in various local synagogues, according to Luke in Acts, we might expect that Isaiah played a significant role within those debates and discussions. Along with the Psalms, Isaiah is the most-cited Old Testament writing in early Christian literature. This is true not only of the canonical New Testament writings. A glance through Justin's *Dialogue* indicates that Isaiah is, along with Psalms, the major prophetic text discussed and cited in that dialogue. So close did Justin see the link between Isaiah and the Christian apostles that he could say, "Isaiah speaks as if he were personating the apostles" (ὡς ἀπὸ προσώπου τῶν ἀποστόλων) (*Dial. Tryph.* 42.2). It would also seem that Isaiah was important for the communities who wrote and used the texts found at Qumran, since some twenty copies of that prophet (second only to copies of the Psalms) have been found there. In addition, about seventy references to, or citations of, passages from Isaiah appear in the non-biblical Qumran texts, which include fragments of five "commentaries" on Isaiah (4Q161–65). There is probably no argument that in many dialogues between Jews and Christians in the first centuries on interpretation of scriptures, Isaiah was at the very center.

I would not want to give the impression that Luke draws on Isaiah more than the other New Testament writers do; or, that he draws on Isaiah far more than any other biblical text. Neither is in fact the case. Exodus and

Psalms are cited directly or implicitly just as often in Acts. And Matthew and Revelation cite or allude to Isaiah at least as much as Luke does. I say this for the sake of perspective.

It has been known for some time that Luke-Acts is dependent on a Greek text of the Jewish Scriptures rather than on a Hebrew text. This Greek text is commonly called the Septuagint (LXX), but that term is becoming increasingly problematic. Letting it stand for now, W. K. L. Clarke[1] has shown that 88 percent of the vocabulary of Acts is found in the LXX (a percentage slightly lower than the four Gospels; again, just to keep perspective). Of the 58 words found only in Luke-Acts in NT, 51 appear in the LXX. "Luke uses a number of rare words which also occur in the LXX."[2] Of 69 characteristically Lukan words and phrases, 68 occur in the LXX.[3] Such statistics would suggest that Acts is saturated with the vocabulary of the LXX.

The Texts

There are many complex questions to be confronted when dealing with the LXX. What we call the LXX is, of course, a constructed text, just as are the NT and MT texts. What is meant when we say that Luke follows the LXX rather than the MT, for example? Did he have a choice, and so preferred one to the other? It is impossible to say precisely what "text/s" he knew. What is the relation between the LXX and the MT or any other Hebrew text, for that matter? What are the roles of the Aramaic Targumim, the Samaritan Pentateuch, and the Dead Sea texts in efforts to trace textual histories? The tradition of categorizing texts into three recensions, families or groups—MT, LXX, and SP—is quite problematic in itself. These are all important and crucial questions and issues.[4]

The matter is also complicated by the fact that the LXX and the Aramaic Targum on Isaiah appear to have some important features in common, features not present in the MT. For example, Brockington has shown that the LXX Isaiah inserts the idea of salvation that is not explicit in the Hebrew text; the Aramaic Targum on Isaiah does the same. But there is no proof of borrowing or influence between the Targum and the LXX.[5] Does the relation between Lukan writings and the Aramaic Targumim need to

---

1. Clarke, "Use of the Septuagint," 66–105.
2. Clarke, "Use of the Septuagint," 70.
3. Clarke, "Use of the Septuagint," 71.
4. For the relation between 1QIsa and LXX Isaiah, see Ziegler, "Die Vorlage," 34–59; van der Kooij, "Old Greek of Isaiah," 195–213.
5. Brockington, "LXX," 80–86.

be reconsidered? There have been those who have suggested that Luke was familiar with an Aramaic text. Torrey[6] argued that Luke knew Aramaic and that Acts 1–15 is Luke's translation of an Aramaic document written by a Jerusalem Christian. These suggestions have long been dismissed, but they might be worth a revisit, especially in the light of the DSS discoveries and of more advanced work in the Targumim.

There would be no one who would seriously argue that Luke was working from a Hebrew text—it seems that his Greek is too closely imitative of the LXX.

This paper basically will ignore the Codex D text of Acts. The MT texts referred to in this paper are from the *Bible Works 5* computer program that uses the *Biblia Hebraica Stuttgartensia* (WTT) (4th edition), Rahlf's 1935 LXX text, and the NA27 text of the NT.

Luke's Use of Isaiah LXX

What does "use" mean? The tendency is to examine those passages in Acts that are clear quotations from Isaiah. Much of that work has already been done, especially by Gert Steyn in his work on the use of the LXX in the Petrine and Pauline speeches in Acts.[7] As Barrett said in his review of Steyn's work,[8] it is also necessary and "more interesting" to examine the Isaianic allusions, hints and paraphrases. We know that a reader can sense the influence of biblical texts in a NT writing, even though those texts are not directly cited, and even though exact words or phrases do not appear. The *Revelation* is a good example of this. And I suggest that Acts may be another example, better than is even acknowledged. Selwyn's theory that *Joshua* was used as a map for some missionary journeys in Acts[9] may have little to support it, but at least it indicates the sense that Selwyn had about the use of the OT in Acts.

We know from Qumran texts, as well as from other NT writings, that Jewish interpreters used the scriptures in a variety of ways, including the conflation of passages from various writings and the techniques of midrash, pesher, allegory, etc.[10] Luke also uses some of these interpretive techniques in Luke-Acts. In the final analysis, Luke is not interested in the text or the person of Isaiah per se; he is more interested in "prophetic

---

6. Torrey, *Composition*. See also Black, *Aramaic Approach*.
7. Steyn, *Septuagint Quotations*.
8. Barrett, "Review," 194–96.
9. Selwyn, "Christian Prophets," 29–38.
10. See Gertner, "Terms," 1–27.

words," and ultimately more interested in the source of prophecy, namely, God. The practice of conflating prophetic words is possible partly because Luke recognizes that God is the common source of all prophetic words. It is also known that "context," as it is understood as a modern literary category, was understood quite differently by Jewish and early Christian hermeneutes. As Miller says, "context" for them meant "the whole of Scripture and contemporary needs."[11]

Possibly, it is worth asking whether Luke found the LXX in some ways more conducive to his arguments than any Hebrew texts he might have known or had access to. Nearly a century later, some Jewish teachers did not accept the Greek translation, while the Christian apologist, Justin, almost seems to regard it as better than any Hebrew! Justin says,

> But I am far from putting reliance in your teachers, who refuse to admit that the interpretation made by the seventy elders who were with Ptolemy of the Egyptians is a correct one; and they attempt to frame another. And I wish you to observe, that they have altogether taken away many Scriptures from the translations effected by those seventy elders who were with Ptolemy, and by which this very man who was crucified is proved to have been set forth expressly as God, and man, and as being crucified, and as dying; but since I am aware that this is denied by all of your nation, I do not address myself to these points, but I proceed to carry on my discussions by means of those passages which are still admitted by you. For you assent to those which I have brought before your attention, except that you contradict the statement, "Behold, the virgin shall conceive," and say it ought to be read, "Behold, the young woman shall conceive." And I promised to prove that the prophecy referred, not, as you were taught, to Hezekiah, but to this Christ of mine: and now I shall go to the proof. (*Dial.* 71.1)

Generally, the rabbis were sceptical about vernacular translations. Of the LXX, they said that the day of its appearance was "as intolerable for Israel as the day the golden calf was made." According to *Meg.* 9a, Rabbi Judah said, "When our teachers permitted Greek, they permitted it only for a scroll of the Torah," and it seems that he forbad the translation of the prophets into Greek. Do we have the beginnings of a debate over texts and translations already in the NT? Were some of the issues debated between Paul and other Jews, according to Acts, text-related and/or translation questions? When

---

11. Miller, "Use of the Old Testament," 66. Miller's article is still helpful on many issues relating to early Jewish and Christian interpretive techniques. See Miller, "Use of the Old Testament," 29–82.

the Alexandrian Apollos was instructed "more accurately" by Prisca and Aquila in Ephesus (18:26), did that include such issues?

This raises a related matter: Who is Luke? By that, I mean to ask what status or authority did Luke have? There is the assumption, both in popular thought as well as among some scholars, that Luke was a reporter, almost as if he were embedded in the mission party of Paul to report on those missions. Others, with possibly more sophistication, see Luke as a historian, and they point to Luke 1:1–4 as indicating this role. Of course, there have been those who suggest that Luke is first and foremost a theologian.[12]

I would like to suggest that Luke is much more than a reporter and a historian, and even more than a theologian (or is that is the highest compliment that can be paid him?). There are signs in Luke-Acts that he sees himself as a teacher, if not also as a quasi-prophet; and that he regards himself as an interpreter of the prophetic word. Luke does not simply cite or recite the prophets, but he *interprets* them. To do that implies that he thought he had some status and authority in his own right. He might have identified with the title "Teacher of Righteousness"; possibly, as a (Levite) *maskil*. Luke links the two dimensions of teaching and prophecy in Acts 13:1,[13] and in that same chapter, the conflict between the prophets, Saul and Barnabas, and the false prophet, Bar Jesus, appears to be over "teaching" that involved the interpretation of "the word of God." Overall in Acts, the apostles are depicted as teachers, in the Jerusalem cycle of chapters 1–7 (4:2, 18; 5:25, 28, 42), as also is Paul (15:35; 18:11; 21:21, 28; 28:31). It is a link that is commonly made in the Aramaic Targum of Isaiah, if not in the LXX. The notion that Luke is a teacher is implied by James Sanders, who says, rather romantically, "What an insistent teaching elder Luke must have been in the instructional life of his own congregation."[14]

In general, there is little doubt that the *interpretation of the scriptures*, and especially of the prophetic word, is a big issue in Luke-Acts. Typical is Acts 17:2-3, in which Luke says that Paul "debated" (διαλέξατο) with synagogue Jews in Thessalonica, "from the scriptures" (ἀπὸ τῶν γραφῶν), "explaining and proving" (διανοίγων καὶ παρατιθέμενος) that the Christ should suffer and rise. The language implies that it was interpretation that

---

12. So Marshall can call his book, *Luke: Historian and Theologian*.

13. A reasonably ancient tradition that Lucius of Cyrene, one of the prophets and teachers along with Barnabas and Paul in Acts 13:1, is Luke, the author of Luke–Acts, is worth at least noting here (see Cadbury, "Lucius"; Lake and Foakes-Jackson, *Beginnings*, 5:489–95).

14. Sanders, "Isaiah in Luke," 19. See Sanders, "Isaiah in Luke," 14–25.

was debated. On that matter, the use of the verbs ζητέω and its cognates in Acts deserves closer attention.[15]

The import of all this is that Luke uses Isaiah (and the other prophets) in much the same way as do the Targumim. That is, he claims to articulate not only what Isaiah the prophet said, but what he meant to say, or even what he should have said. In fact, Luke does that not only with Isaiah, but also with the new prophets in Israel, Peter and Paul. When Luke constructs the addresses of Peter and Paul, he does so as an authoritative interpreter of their words and as a teacher of Theophilus. In brief, I suggest that Luke is far more proactive in his use of Isaiah (and other scriptures) than is often supposed.

All this raises the broader issue of the purpose and method of citing Isaiah (or other Scriptures) in Acts. *Why*, *how*, and *when* does Luke cite Isaiah, for example? Is it as proof text? Is it as polemic? Is it a claim about the Christian interpretation of scripture vis à vis other Jewish interpretations? More importantly, who was authorised to use the scriptures in this way? And I am particularly interested in the question: is Luke claiming something about himself as an interpreter of scripture?

It is worth keeping in mind that Isaiah is referred to by name in only two passages in Acts (8:28, 30; 28:25), and in both cases he is also identified as "the prophet." Such an identification is made elsewhere (John 1:21; Matt 1:22; 3:3; 4:14; etc.), and not only of Isaiah (Luke uses it of Samuel in 13:20). Otherwise, in 7:48 for example, a citing of Isaiah is introduced simply with "as the prophet says," without any naming of the prophet. Here, too, it appears that Luke is doing what the Targumist also does. The latter frequently inserts "the prophet" or "prophecy" into the text where it is absent in the MT (and in the LXX). There is no doubt that the point of the Targumist is that Isaiah per se is not significant; what is essential and central is the prophet, and the prophetic words, and that means that they can be—and are to be—brought as a new message to Israel. Luke thinks likewise.

Passages Showing Substantial Agreement between Acts and Isaiah LXX

There are four passages in Acts that are direct, substantial, quotations from Isaiah. Only one of them explicitly states that the passage quoted is from that particular prophet. There is a fifth passage that introduces words as spoken by God; some of those words seem to be from Isaiah. I have arranged the passages in the order of their appearance in Acts.

15. As Gertner notes, sometimes the interpretation could hang on the vowel used to read a consonantal text (Gertner, "Terms," 1n4).

1. Acts 7:48-50

Stephen, in his speech to the Sanhedrin, has outlined briefly how God had instructed Moses to construct the Tabernacle "according to the *topos* that he had seen" (7:44), and that Tabernacle was used in the land until Solomon built "a house for him" (7:47). Stephen then argues that "the Most High does not dwell in houses made with hands" (ἀλλ' οὐχ ὁ ὕψιστος ἐν χειροποιήτοις κατοικεῖ). Luke's use of the word χειροποίητος echoes its usage in Isaiah, where the prophet always used the adjectival noun with reference to either the idols or the temples of the heathen (Isa 2:18; 10:11; 16:12; 19:1; 31:7; 46:6). It would seem that Stephen is being provocative in using that word of the temple in Jerusalem (cf. Acts 17:24-25).

Stephen supports his argument with reference to Isa 66:1-2. The two passages read as follows:

> ἀλλ' οὐχ ὁ ὕψιστος ἐν χειροποιήτοις κατοικεῖ, καθὼς ὁ προφήτης λέγει, Ὁ οὐρανός μοι θρόνος, ἡ δὲ γῆ ὑποπόδιον τῶν ποδῶν μου·ποῖον οἶκον οἰκοδομήσετέ μοι, λέγει κύριος,ἢ τίς τόπος τῆς καταπαύσεώς μου; οὐχὶ ἡ χείρ μου ἐποίησεν ταῦτα πάντακαθὼς ὁ προφήτης λέγει. (Acts 7:48-50)

> Οὕτως λέγει κύριος Ὁ οὐρανός μοι θρόνος, ἡ δὲ γῆ ὑποπόδιον τῶν ποδῶν μου· ποῖον οἶκον οἰκοδομήσετέ μοι; ἢ ποῖος τόπος τῆς καταπαύσεώς μου; πάντα γὰρ ταῦτα ἐποίησεν ἡ χείρ μου, καὶ ἔστιν ἐμὰ πάντα ταῦτα, λέγει κύριος· καὶ ἐπὶ τίνα ἐπιβλέψω ἀλλ' ἢ ἐπὶ τὸν ταπεινὸν καὶ ἡσύχιον καὶ τρέμοντα τοὺς λόγους μου. (Isa 66:1-2)

The MT reads,

> כֹּה אָמַר יְהוָה הַשָּׁמַיִם כִּסְאִי וְהָאָרֶץ הֲדֹם רַגְלָי אֵי־זֶה בַיִת אֲשֶׁר תִּבְנוּ־לִי וְאֵי־זֶה מָקוֹם מְנוּחָתִי׃1

> וְאֶת־כָּל־אֵלֶּה יָדִי עָשָׂתָה וַיִּהְיוּ כָל־אֵלֶּה נְאֻם־יְהוָה וְאֶל־זֶה אַבִּיט אֶל־עָנִי וּנְכֵה־רוּחַ וְחָרֵד עַל־דְּבָרִי׃2

Some Observations

The text of Acts largely agrees with that of the LXX, which, in turn, is not significantly different to the MT. However, besides the difference in introducing the saying, there are minor differences between Luke and the LXX. For example, the ποῖος τόπος of the LXX is expressed as τίς τόπος by Luke (although the D text follows the LXX), who also has the last statement in the form of a rhetorical question. It appears that the Targum of Isaiah does the same, "All these things my might has made, did not all these things come to be?" says the Lord (66:2).[16]

Justin cites this passage, but writes: Ἡσαίας λέγει, Ποῖον οἶκον οἰκοδομήσετέ μοι; λέγει κύριος. ὁ οὐρανός μοι θρόνος καὶ ἡ γῆ ὑποπόδιον τῶν ποδῶν μου (*Dial.* 22.11). Barnabas (16:2), in criticism of the Temple, quotes Isaiah 66 (along with Isa 40:12), ὁ οὐρανός μοι θρόνος καὶ ἡ δὲ γῆ ὑποπόδιον τῶν ποδῶν μου ποῖον οἶκον οἰκοδομήσετέ μοι ἢ τίς τόπος τῆς καταπαύσεώς μου, which is virtually the same as the Acts text.

In the Acts passage, Isaiah is not mentioned by name, but simply is referred to as "the prophet." In fact, whereas Isaiah introduces the saying as a word of the *Lord* (οὕτως λέγει κύριος—the standard LXX translation of the common Hebrew expression, כֹּה אָמַר יְהוָה), Luke instead introduces it as a word of the *prophet* (καθὼς ὁ προφήτης λέγει). Only part way through the quote, does he insert λέγει κύριος. The Lord speaks through the prophet.

This difference in structure, and the use of the word "prophet" by Luke (rather than the name "Isaiah"), might be intentional. The point is that Israel is against the *prophetic word*. Luke, through Stephen, is claiming that Christians are the true interpreters of the prophets vis à vis "you stubborn people . . . which of the prophets did not your fathers persecute?" (7:51–52). Earlier, Stephen had referred to God's promise of a prophet like Moses (7:37), to Israel's refusal to listen to Moses (7:39), and to God's abandonment of Israel, "as it is written in the book of the prophets" (7:42). In other words, the context is that of Israel's attitude towards and response to the prophets. By referring to this word as a prophetic word, Luke reinforces that the prophets and Israel are at loggerheads, whereas Christian interpreters (Stephen, for example) and the prophets are in agreement. Christians expected followers to "believe the prophets"; so Paul asks Agrippa, πιστεύεις τοῖς προφήταις; (Acts 26:27).

Thornton has made the suggestion that Luke may have been familiar with the tradition reflected in an Aramaic midrash of uncertain date that Isaiah spoke these words against Manasseh, claiming that God was not pleased with the Temple. The midrash says that Isaiah was executed by Manasseh in response to his words against him. As Thornton claims, this helps explain the temple-prophet-martyrdom link and allows for a smooth transition between 7:50 and 7:52.[17]

---

16. Is there something about the use of a question here that is significant? Questions demand answers, they can be rhetorical and make a point, and they seem to be used commonly in debate (Paul and Isaiah also frequently used questions).

17. Thornton, "Stephen's Use," 432–34.

It would seem that Christians saw Isaiah as an ally in their debates over the understanding of God's activity. The Targum of Isaiah underlines the prophetic word against Israel, and Israel's opposition to that word, more than the MT does (30:1, 3, 10, 11; 58:1–6).

It would seem that Isaiah is nearly always cited directly in Acts in a situation of conflict with some Jews, and so polemically. Here, too, the claim is that the temple made with hands in not where the Most High dwells, and Isaiah is cited as supporting that claim. Most scholars today agree that Isaiah was not attacking the temple. Luke, however, possibly understood Isaiah to be doing so, or—and this is the more likely—he uses Isaiah's words as an attack on the temple and attitudes towards it. Like the Targumist, he claims to know what Isaiah should have said, or at least what the prophet really meant to say.

2. Acts 8:32–33

Philip has been instructed by the Spirit to meet the carriage in which the Ethiopian eunuch is travelling. The eunuch is reading from the scriptures, and Philip asks him if he understands what he is reading. The eunuch says he needs someone to show him the [W?]ay (ὁδηγήσει), so Philip is invited to sit with him. The passage that the eunuch is reading is then given; it is introduced by ἡ δὲ περιοχὴ τῆς γραφῆς ἣν ἀνεγίνωσκεν ἦν αὕτη and continues: Ὡς πρόβατον ἐπὶ σφαγὴν ἤχθη καὶ ὡς ἀμνὸς ἐναντίον τοῦ κείραντος αὐτὸν ἄφωνος, οὕτως οὐκ ἀνοίγει τὸ στόμα αὐτοῦ. Ἐν τῇ ταπεινώσει [αὐτοῦ] ἡ κρίσις αὐτοῦ ἤρθη· τὴν γενεὰν αὐτοῦ τίς διηγήσεται; ὅτι αἴρεται ἀπὸ τῆς γῆς ἡ ζωὴ αὐτοῦ.

This is a direct quotation of Isa 53:7–8 LXX:

> ὡς πρόβατον ἐπὶ σφαγὴν ἤχθη καὶ ὡς ἀμνὸς ἐναντίον τοῦ κείροντος αὐτὸν ἄφωνος οὕτως οὐκ ἀνοίγει τὸ στόμα αὐτοῦ. ἐν τῇ ταπεινώσει ἡ κρίσις αὐτοῦ ἤρθη· τὴν γενεὰν αὐτοῦ τίς διηγήσεται; ὅτι αἴρεται ἀπὸ τῆς γῆς ἡ ζωὴ αὐτοῦ, ἀπὸ τῶν ἀνομιῶν τοῦ λαοῦ μου ἤχθη εἰς θάνατον.

The MT reads,

נִגַּשׂ וְהוּא נַעֲנֶה וְלֹא יִפְתַּח־פִּיו כַּשֶּׂה לַטֶּבַח יוּבָל וּכְרָחֵל לִפְנֵי גֹזְזֶיהָ נֶאֱלָמָה וְלֹא יִפְתַּח פִּיו

מֵעֹצֶר וּמִמִּשְׁפָּט לֻקָּח וְאֶת־דּוֹרוֹ מִי יְשׂוֹחֵחַ כִּי נִגְזַר מֵאֶרֶץ חַיִּים מִפֶּשַׁע עַמִּי נֶגַע לָמוֹ׃

Some Observations

In this passage, the Greek texts in Acts and in LXX Isaiah are almost exactly the same, although the Isaiah text continues with an extra sentence (as does the MT). Conzelmann suggests the final sentence in Isaiah is omitted by Luke because "it is anti-climactic if αἴρειν, 'taken up,' is understood as referring to the exaltation."[18]

Some minor Acts mss read ἐν τῇ ταπεινώσει αὐτοῦ. The κείροντος / κείραντος variant is found in manuscripts of both LXX and Acts.

Both Isaiah LXX and Acts differ from the MT at 53:8. The MT (+ 1QIsa; Targ. Isa.) read, "from [out of, as a result of] distress/prison and judgment, he was taken away" (וּמִמִּשְׁפָּט לֻקָּח,מֵעֹצֶר) while the LXX and Acts (and 1 Clem 16:8) read, "in humiliation, his judgment was taken away" (ἐν τῇ ταπεινώσει [αὐτοῦ] ἡ κρίσις αὐτοῦ ἤρθη). In addition, the Hebrew texts reads, "For he was cut off from the land of the living (כִּי נִגְזַר מֵאֶרֶץ חַיִּים) while LXX and Acts read, "For his life is taken away from the earth" (ὅτι αἴρεται ἀπὸ τῆς γῆς ἡ ζωὴ αὐτοῦ).

In LXX Isaiah, ταπείνωσις and its cognates are used over thirty times. Often, they describe the action of God in bringing down the proud (2:12), and in elevating the poor and those who have been humiliated (49:13). So its use here might be the result of exposition on the part of the Greek writers rather than the result of translation. The humility/humiliation motif is also found in the Thanksgiving Hymns of Qumran (1QH 5:13, 16, 18, 20–22; 14:3). It is also a motif that Luke adopted, especially in the hymns that mark the opening to his Gospel (Luke 1:48, 52). Luke has a Jesus who teaches that everyone who exalts himself will be humbled and the humble will be exalted (14:11; 18:14). He also sees Paul's ministry as marked by one who "served the Lord with all humility" (Acts 20:19). Is it possible that here the Christians found the Greek text more helpful than the Hebrew? Jesus' humiliating death needed explanation—the Greek text of Isa 53 went a little way towards providing an explanation. The addition of auvtou/ would support that. According to Clement of Rome, "the holy spirit" said of Jesus that he came in "humbleness of mind," and he then cites Isaiah 53 (1 Clem 16).

It is not clear whether the introductory words in Acts (ἡ περιοχὴ τῆς γραφῆς) refer to the passage of scripture that the eunuch was reading or to the wider content of the passage. I suspect that Luke intends the whole context and content of Isaiah 53–55, rather than simply that particular passage which is used as a starting point by Philip (8:35). Once again, the role of

---

18. Conzelmann, *Acts*, 68.

prophet as teacher (= interpreter of the prophet) in Acts can be seen, a role that the Targum of Isaiah also gives to the prophets.

Is it worth asking why it is this particular passage that is being read and interpreted? Is it because Isaiah is the prophet who indicates more than others a status and place for gentiles and for the scattered of Israel in the promises of God? Or, did it provide Luke with an opportunity to show how *he* interpreted this passage as referring to Jesus *vis à vis* the [current? common?] interpretation that said it referred to the prophet himself? And particularly, did it give him the opportunity to interpret this passage in the light of the suffering (not "death," specifically) and resurrection of the Christ, the fundamental understanding of the Christ that Luke drew out of the Scriptures? Isaiah, with his "suffering servant," provided a good source for Christians to explain and justify the suffering of their Christ. The fact that Luke does not continue the passage as Isaiah does allows the text to be read as referring to Jesus' suffering and exaltation.

In any case, Luke says that Philip used this passage as the starting point (ἀρξάμενος ἀπὸ τῆς γράφης ταύτης) to speak of the good news of Jesus (εὐηγγελίσατο αὐτῷ τὸν Ἰησοῦν) (8:35). "Announcing good news" is an Isaianic word (e.g., Isa 55:7; 60:6; 61:1). The suffering/death of Jesus (as the Isaianic suffering servant) is taken as the starting point of the good news about Jesus. In Luke 24:27, the appearing Jesus begins with Moses and the prophets to interpret in all the scriptures the things about himself, especially that "the Christ should suffer these things and enter his glory" (24:26).

Besides this direct citing of Isaiah, there are a number of clues that suggest this eunuch episode is shaped, almost in midrashic style, by a reading of Isaiah.

The eunuch is said to be from Ethiopia (the word is used twice in Acts 8:27). LXX Isaiah is not disinterested in Ethiopia. According to 11:11, God will ransom the remnant of his people from areas including Ethiopia (כוש [Hebrew]; Αἰθίοψ [LXX]). Later, he announces that the "traders of Cush" (ἐμπορία Αἰθιόπων) (LXX) will submit to the anointed Cyrus, and acknowledge that there is no other God, but "the God of Israel, the saviour" (45:14). And I will soon show that Isaiah's words about eunuchs are not insignificant in reading this episode.

Acts 8:26 sets the scene for Philip to meet the eunuch on "a deserted road" (ἐπὶ τὴν ὁδὸν τὴν καταβαίνουσαν ἀπὸ Ἰερουσαλὴμ εἰς Γάζαν, αὕτη ἐστὶν ἔρημος). It would appear that the description of the road as deserted is deliberate on Luke's part—he draws attention to it. An audience listening with Isaiah in their heads might expect the Lord now to do a new thing, since the scene Luke has created echoes Isa 33:8 LXX: ἐρημωθήσονται γὰρ αἱ τούτων ὁδοί· πέπαυται ὁ φόβος τῶν ἐθνῶν, καὶ ἡ πρὸς τούτους διαθήκη αἴρεται, καὶ οὐ μὴ λογίσησθε αὐτοὺς ἀνθρώπους.

The eunuch and Philip find water along this road through the desert (8:36). This recalls Isa 43:19 LXX, ποιήσω ἐν τῇ ἐρήμῳ ὁδὸν καὶ ἐν τῇ ἀνύδρῳ ποταμούς. The narrative in Acts says, ἦλθον ἐπ᾽τι ὕδωρ. This is reminiscent of the prophetic invitation in Isa 55:1 LXX, πορεύεσθε ἐφ' ὕδωρ. Some mss of Acts (P74 326) in fact read τὸ ὕδωρ, which Barrett thinks "does not make good sense and must have originated in a simple slip."[19] But if an audience is listening with Isa 55:1 in its head, then the definite article might almost be expected. I would suggest, too, that if one so reads this episode, then questions as to what body of water this could possibly refer to become irrelevant.[20]

The eunuch's question, "What prevents me (τί κωλύει με) from being baptized?" (8:37) is an allusion to Isa 43:6, ἐρῶ τῷ βορρᾷ Ἄγε, καὶ τῷ λιβί Μὴ κώλυε· ἄγε τοὺς υἱούς μου ἀπὸ γῆς πόρρωθεν καὶ τὰς θυγατέρας μου ἀπ' ἄκρων τῆς γῆς. Λιβί, (dative of λίψ) refers to the SW wind, and probably here means "Africa." Many Greeks and Romans envisaged Ethiopians as living right across Africa, from west to east.

Finally, there are other hints of Isa 55–56 in the eunuch story. The eunuch is obviously a wealthy man, being in charge "of all the Candace's treasure" (8:27). Isa 55 talks of spending money on what is not bread, "your wages on what fails to satisfy" (55:2), and offers life as a free gift, and membership in the everlasting covenant among peoples that include "a nation you never knew" (Isa 55:4-5). In addition, Isa 56:3-4 indicate that eunuchs, in particular, are not excluded from the covenant: μὴ λεγέτω ὁ εὐνοῦχος ὅτι Ἐγώ εἰμι ξύλον ξηρόν. τάδε λέγει κύριος Τοῖς εὐνούχοις, ὅσοι ἂν φυλάξωνται τὰ σάββατά μου καὶ ἐκλέξωνται ἃ ἐγὼ θέλω καὶ ἀντέχωνται τῆς διαθήκης μου.

It would seem that this episode is a good example of how a prophetic text, like Isaiah, can shape the Acts narrative. There may be few direct quotations, but the influence and use of Isaiah can be distinctly recognised and traced.

---

19. Barrett, *Acts*, 1:432.

20. *Pace* Barrett, *Acts*, 1:433; Bruce, *Book of Acts*, 177; Conzelmann, *Acts*, 69, and others who can't help themselves from at least suggesting a known geographical location.

3. Acts 13:34

Paul is preaching to Jews in Antioch of Pisidia, outlining God's actions in Israel's history and linking Jesus to that action. The good news promised to the fathers God fulfilled by raising Jesus from the dead, as Ps 2:7 had said. That Jesus was raised is also seen as a sign of the promise that "I will give you the holy and sure [blessings] of David," ὅτι δὲ ἀνέστησεν αὐτὸν ἐκ νεκρῶν μηκέτι μέλλοντα ὑποστρέφειν εἰς διαφθοράν, οὕτως εἴρηκεν ὅτι Δώσω ὑμῖν τὰ ὅσια Δαυὶδ τὰ πιστά.

The final phrase seems to be a direct reference to Isa 55:3,

προσέχετε τοῖς ὠτίοις ὑμῶν καὶ ἐπακολουθήσατε ταῖς ὁδοῖς μου· ἐπακούσατέ μου, καὶ ζήσεται ἐν ἀγαθοῖς ἡ ψυχὴ ὑμῶν· καὶ διαθήσομαι ὑμῖν διαθήκην αἰώνιον, τὰ ὅσια Δαυιδ τὰ πιστά.

And the MT,

הַטּוּ אָזְנְכֶם וּלְכוּ אֵלַי שִׁמְעוּ וּתְחִי נַפְשְׁכֶם וְאֶכְרְתָה לָכֶם בְּרִית עוֹלָם חַסְדֵי דָוִד הַנֶּאֱמָנִים

Some Observations

The MT of Isa 55:3 speaks of "the sure mercies of David" (חַסְדֵי דָוִד הַנֶּאֱמָנִים). Luke agrees with the LXX with, "the holy and sure things of David."

The words οὕτως εἴρηκεν ὅτι introduce the words of God. This precise form of introducing a biblical passage is not used elsewhere in Acts (cf. 17:28, where the same verb is used of Greek poets; cf. 2:16; 13:40, where the verb is used of the prophets).

This quote is sandwiched between a quotation from Ps 2, which is introduced with ὡς καὶ ἐν τῷ ψαλμῷ γέγραπται τῷ δευτέρῳ (13:33), and one from Ps 16, which is introduced with διότι καὶ ἐν ἑτέρῳ λέγει (13:35). In addition, Paul then closes his speech with a warning from "what has been said in the prophets" (τὸ εἰρημένον ἐν τοῖς προφήταις) (13:40). It might be noted that when the three passages are cited one after another, the common speaker is said to be God.

In the second and third quote, the emphasis seems to be on what God has said (εἴρηκεν) rather than what is written in a text, as in the first. This could partly explain the addition of Δωσω ὑμῖν in Acts. Barrett thinks Δωσω ὑμῖν simply replaces διαθήσομαι ὑμῖν διαθήκην αἰώνιον of the Isa 55:3 LXX.[21] That might be the case, but I doubt whether it is "simply" that. Luke

---

21. Barrett, *Acts*, 1:647.

excised "everlasting covenant" language elsewhere from a biblical passage he cites (cf. 13:47). He uses the word "covenant" only twice (3:25; 7:8 in relation to circumcision). This contrasts with the use of Isa 55:3 in 1QS 4:22; 5:5-6; 1QSb 1:2-3; 2:25 where, in each case, it is precisely "the everlasting [Davidic] covenant" that is important.

Others suggest that Δωσω ὑμῖν is "attracted" by Ps 15:10b LXX, οὐδὲ δώσεις τὸν ὅσιόν σου ἰδεῖν διαφθοράν, which is cited by Luke in the very next verse (13:35). So Bruce says that the rabbinical principle of *gezerah shawah*, in which the sense of two texts is linked to their sharing of a common term, is here being applied.[22] Conzelmann thinks Luke might have already found this verse combined with Ps 15:10 LXX.[23] This may well be; but if one thinks of God as the speaker of all prophecy, then words and phrases can be taken from anywhere and combined to form one message.

Luke's Paul cites Isa 55:3 as an indication that God would raise his Son (referred to *via* Ps 2 in 13:33) from the dead, and then he quotes LXX Ps 15:10 as evidence that he would not let him see corruption. But how does Isa 55:3 refer to a resurrection? Usually, this question is answered by linking the Isaiah words with those from Ps 2. So Bock, "Looking back to Ps 2:7, the connection goes like this: the promise of the Son has come (Ps 2:7), for God has raised him (Jesus) from the dead no longer to return to corruption (v. 34a). Thus Isaiah says that the sure mercies of David will be given to all of you."[24] This is possible. There's another possibility, however, and that is that Luke wants to maintain the David link, hence the Isa 55:3d quote. But anyone knowing the Isaiah passage would know that 55:3d is preceded by 55:3b, which says, ζήσεται ἐν ἀγαθοῖς ἡ ψυχὴ ὑμῶν. In other words, the "holy and sure blessings of David" include that his ψυχή will live. Read this way, Isa 55:3 refers to Jesus' resurrection, and Ps 15:10 LXX to his incorruptible state.

4. Acts 13:47

Here again, the context is one of dispute between Paul and other Jews over the interpretation of the Scriptures. Here too, Isaiah is cited against those Jews who reviled and opposed Paul and Barnabas and their interpretation of the word of God (13:44-45). The debate has moved out of the synagogue, where Paul has given a brief history of Israel and Jesus' place within it. He claims that the leaders and people of Jerusalem did not recognise Jesus "nor

---

22. Bruce, *Acts*, 260.
23. Conzelmann, *Acts*, 104.
24. Bock, *Proclamation*, 252.

understand the voices (τὰς φωνάς) of the prophets which are read every sabbath" (13:27). The point of conflict is the understanding and interpretation of the prophets, with the Christians claiming that the prophets speak against their opponents. The episode ends with a warning from Hab 1:5 (13:41-43). On the next Sabbath, *"almost the whole city* gathered together to hear the word of the Lord" (13:44), thus allowing for gentiles to be involved. The Jews, however, are "filled with jealousy" and contradict Paul, who in turn says that he is now turning to the gentiles because he has the command of the Lord, a command that is found in Isa 49:6.

> οὕτως γὰρ ἐντέταλται ἡμῖν ὁ κύριος, Τέθεικά σε εἰς φῶς ἐθνῶν τοῦ εἶναί σε εἰς σωτηρίαν ἕως ἐσχάτου τῆς γῆς. (Acts 13:47)

> καὶ εἶπέν μοι Μέγα σοί ἐστιν τοῦ κληθῆναί σε παῖδά μου τοῦ στῆσαι τὰς φυλὰς Ιακωβ καὶ τὴν διασπορὰν τοῦ Ισραηλ ἐπιστρέψαι· ἰδοὺ τέθεικά σε εἰς διαθήκην γένους εἰς φῶς ἐθνῶν τοῦ εἶναί σε εἰς σωτηρίαν ἕως ἐσχάτου τῆς γῆς. (Isa 49:6)

The MT text reads:

וַיֹּאמֶר נָקֵל מִהְיוֹתְךָ לִי עֶבֶד לְהָקִים אֶת־שִׁבְטֵי יַעֲקֹב וּנְצִירֵי יִשְׂרָאֵל לְהָשִׁיב וּנְתַתִּיךָ לְאוֹר

גּוֹיִם לִהְיוֹת יְשׁוּעָתִי עַד־קְצֵה הָאָרֶץ

Some Observations

The LXX has the additional attention marker ἰδού (it is also used in Codex D of Acts). This suggests that Acts is closer to the MT than to the LXX. On the other hand, Luke has used the adverb in the previous sentence (13:46), and this might be intentional, as I note below.

Note the absence of LXX's εἰς διαθήκην γένους from Acts. This might also suggest that the Acts text is more in agreement with the MT than with the LXX; on the other hand, Luke elsewhere (13:34) has excised "covenant" talk from an Isaiah passage. Justin also omits the phrase in his citing of the Isaiah passage (*Dial.* 121.30). It does not necessarily mean that Luke "used a more faithful LXX version than that which we have."[25] The excision of covenant talk from the prophetic text is a sign of Luke's authority as an interpreter.

---

25. Barrett, *Acts*, 1:657.

The introductory formula used by Luke is οὕτος γὰρ ἐντέλαται ἡμῖν ὁ κύριος. The Lord here is Jesus. In Isaiah LXX, it is the Lord (κύριος) who "formed me in the womb to be his servant," and who said (εἶπεν) this to the prophet (49:5). It is probably no accident that Luke omits what precedes the Isaiah quote, since it speaks of the servant raising up the tribes of Jacob and returning (ἐπιστρέψαι) the exiles of Israel (Isa 49:6a–b). Instead, Paul says, "behold, we turn (στρεφόμεθα) to the gentiles" (13:46). Luke omits "behold" (ἰδού) which very often implies a surprising, unexpected action) when he introduces the direct Isaianic words. Instead, he uses it in Paul's statement, "we are turning to the gentiles." Paul is addressing "the exiles of Israel," since they are in Pisidian Antioch, but they generally do not hear, so he picks up on the second part of Isaiah's hope, and turns to the gentiles. The surprising action, expressed by ἰδού, is that Paul is leaving *even the exiles of Israel* and going to the gentiles.

The word of the Lord to the prophet is seen as a command to Paul. For Luke, Paul and Isaiah are complementary—both are servants of Yahweh, both have the command of the Lord, through both, the holy Spirit speaks (cf. Acts 28:25). This is consistent with the notion that the Christians know the true interpretation of the prophets. If they know the true interpretations, it is reasonable to replace the historical prophet with the contemporary one; a word addressed to Isaiah is seen as a word addressed to Paul. This is similar to how the Qumran texts interpret the prophets as referring to their Teacher/s of Righteousness.

In the Acts passage, there is no explicit reference to Isaiah as the source for the scripture cited in Acts. I doubt this is incidental. Rather, by ignoring Isaiah as the source, Luke can make the original words be words of the Lord directed to Paul and Barnabas (οὕτως γὰρ ἐντέταλται ἡμῖν ὁ κύριος). They are true prophets—Paul is listed, as Saul, along with Barnabas among the prophets at Antioch (13:1), both met and opposed successfully the false prophet, bar Jesus (13:6–12), and Paul in the immediate context here, is invited to speak after the reading from "the law and the prophets" (13:15). Once again, the link between prophet and teacher (= interpreter and expounder of scripture) is close.

It is not simply a matter that the Scripture has foretold that Paul and Barnabas go to the gentiles (*pace* Steyn[26]), but rather that the Lord [Jesus] has commanded it, and to support that, Isaiah is cited. In other words, it is not prediction but "interpretation," almost pesher-style. Words from the text can be taken into a new context and seen as direct commands from Jesus. By identifying Jesus as "Lord" in Acts, Luke is being provocative to

---

26. Steyn, *Septuagint Quotations*, 200.

those Jews who rejected the Christian claims about Jesus. It is also a term used some 380 times in Isaiah.

Isa 49:6 is used also in Luke 2:32, where Simeon uses it to speak of Jesus.

5. Acts 28:25-27

The last direct quotation of Isaiah in Acts is found in Paul's final words in Rome. Once again, the prophet Isaiah is cited in the context of exposition—discussions "from morning till evening"—and of differences with other Jews over "the law of Moses and the prophets" (28:23). Note the importance of teaching (= interpretation) in this context (28:23, 31). It is similar to the importance given to it in the Targum on Isa 6:8, the very verse before this cited passage, "And I heard the voice of the Memra of the Lord which said, "Whom shall I send to prophesy, and who will go to teach?""

The session ends with the audience divided between those who were convinced and those who disbelieved. Paul then makes "one statement" (ῥῆμα ἕν) in which he quotes Isaiah directly, explicitly indicating that "Isaiah the prophet" is his source. He cites the words of Isaiah as the reason why "this salvation of God has been sent to the gentiles" (28:28).

Acts 28:26-27 reads:

Πορεύθητι πρὸς τὸν λαὸν τοῦτον καὶ εἰπόν, Ἀκοῇ ἀκούσετε καὶ οὐ μὴ συνῆτε καὶ βλέποντες βλέψετε καὶ οὐ μὴ ἴδητε· ἐπαχύνθη γὰρ ἡ καρδία τοῦ λαοῦ τούτου καὶ τοῖς ὠσὶν βαρέως ἤκουσαν καὶ τοὺς ὀφθαλμοὺς αὐτῶν ἐκάμμυσαν· μήποτε ἴδωσιν τοῖς ὀφθαλμοῖς καὶ τοῖς ὠσὶν ἀκούσωσιν καὶ τῇ καρδίᾳ συνῶσιν καὶ ἐπιστρέψωσιν, καὶ ἰάσομαι αὐτούς.

LXX Is 6:9-10 reads:

καὶ εἶπεν Πορεύθητι καὶ εἰπὸν τῷ λαῷ τούτῳ Ἀκοῇ ἀκούσετε καὶ οὐ μὴ συνῆτε καὶ βλέποντες βλέψετε καὶ οὐ μὴ ἴδητε· ἐπαχύνθη γὰρ ἡ καρδία τοῦ λαοῦ τούτου, καὶ τοῖς ὠσὶν αὐτῶν βαρέως ἤκουσαν καὶ τοὺς ὀφθαλμοὺς αὐτῶν ἐκάμμυσαν, μήποτε ἴδωσιν τοῖς ὀφθαλμοῖς καὶ τοῖς ὠσὶν ἀκούσωσιν καὶ τῇ καρδίᾳ συνῶσιν καὶ ἐπιστρέψωσιν καὶ ἰάσομαι αὐτούς.

The MT text reads:

וַיֹּאמֶר לֵךְ וְאָמַרְתָּ לָעָם הַזֶּה שִׁמְעוּ שָׁמוֹעַ וְאַל־תָּבִינוּ וּרְאוּ רָאוֹ וְאַל־תֵּדָעוּ

הַשְׁמֵן לֵב־הָעָם הַזֶּה וְאָזְנָיו הַכְבֵּד וְעֵינָיו הָשַׁע פֶּן־יִרְאֶה בְעֵינָיו וּבְאָזְנָיו
יִשְׁמָע וּלְבָבוֹ יָבִין

וָשָׁב וְרָפָא לוֹ

Some Observations

Acts 28:26–27 is lacking in Codex D.

There do not appear to be any significant variations between Acts and the LXX. There are variations in the opening line, with the LXX saying, εἰπὸν τῷ λαῷ τούτῳ while Acts says: Πορεύθητι πρὸς τὸν λαὸν τοῦτον καὶ εἰπόν. The MT is more in line with LXX than with Acts. Isa LXX also includes αὐτῶν—not found in Acts (or in the Matthean version), although some manuscripts do include it.

As Steyn notes, four MT imperatives are replaced with future active (ἀκούσετε and βλέψετε) and aorist active (ἤκουσαν ... ἐκάμμυσαν) indicative forms, and one with an aorist passive (ἐπαχύνθη). The MT's Qal futures are subjunctives in Greek (οὐ μὴ συνῆτε ... οὐ μὴ ἴδητε). The LXX inserts γάρ (ἐπαχύνθη γὰρ ἡ καρδία). The word "heart" is the object of the verb in MT, but it is the subject in LXX.[27] Steyn also says that the LXX puts the blame more on the people; the severe picture of God in the MT is toned down; and the judgment is changed a little in the LXX with the possibilities of repentance still open.[28]

The passage is also cited in Matt 13:15: ἐπαχύνθη γὰρ ἡ καρδία τοῦ λαοῦ τούτου, καὶ τοῖς ὠσὶν βαρέως ἤκουσαν καὶ τοὺς ὀφθαλμοὺς αὐτῶν ἐκάμμυσαν, μήποτε ἴδωσιν τοῖς ὀφθαλμοῖς καὶ τοῖς ὠσὶν ἀκούσωσιν καὶ τῇ καρδίᾳ συνῶσιν καὶ ἐπιστρέψωσιν καὶ ἰάσομαι αὐτούς.

This is exactly the same as Acts, except that Matthew picks up Isaiah at a different point. Scholars have noted that Matthew does not normally follow the LXX wording, so his doing so here might suggest that the passage was commonly known in this Greek form. The Isaiah passage is also used in Mark 4:12; Luke 8:10; John 12:40; Rom 11:8.

Luke, in Acts, introduces the Isaiah passage with ὅτι Καλῶς τὸ πνεῦμα τὸ ἅγιον ἐλάλησεν διὰ Ἠσαΐου τοῦ προφήτου πρὸς τοὺς πατέρας ὑμῶν. This is the only occasion in Acts in which the Spirit is said to have spoken through a prophet. The concentration, then, is on what the Holy Spirit says through the prophet rather than on Isaiah himself. The prophetic word is a means

---

27. Steyn, *Septuagint Quotations*, 223.
28. Steyn, *Septuagint Quotations*, 228.

whereby the Holy Spirit addresses the contemporary audience of Luke. This may not be to "plainly" express divine inspiration,[29] so much as to show that those who reject the Christian interpretation are in fact rejecting not merely the prophet, but the Spirit (compare Stephen, who says "your fathers" resisted the Spirit; Paul here also refers to "your fathers" [28:25]). It would seem that here Luke uses Isaiah polemically, as result of the failure of some Jews to agree with Paul on his interpretation of Scripture (28:23). The Holy Spirit is now on the side of Paul's understanding of the prophets, and not of those who are stiff necked and resist the Holy Spirit. Paul, like Isaiah, addresses the whole of Israel.

Steyn thinks that this passage "merely supplies scriptural support" to justify the move away from Jews to gentiles.[30] The way Luke expresses it suggests that it is not only, or even mostly, scriptural support that is being claimed so much as Spirit support. The Spirit is the one who gifts people with insight, wisdom and revelation; and so it is the Spirit who gives the gift of interpretation. In addition, the Spirit who spoke through the prophets is now speaking again through the prophets and teachers of the new Israel, and that might include Luke himself.

The holy Spirit speaking through the prophets is how the Targum of Isaiah also thinks: "Who established the holy spirit in the mouths of all the prophets, is it not the Lord?" says Targ. Isa 40:13. "Behold, my servant . . . I will put my holy spirit upon him, he will reveal my judgments to the peoples" (Targ. Isa. 42:1). The Spirit, generally, is also often associated with prophecy. So the Targum on Isa 61:1 reads, "The prophet said, A spirit of prophecy before the Lord God is upon me."

This is another example of how Luke portrays Isaiah and Paul as complementary witnesses.

In this same context, Paul announces to the disbelieving Jews of Rome that "this salvation of God (τὸ σωτήριον τοῦ θεοῦ) has been sent to the gentiles" (28:28). The Greek phrase certainly echoes Isa 40:5, ὄψεται πᾶσα σὰρξ τὸ σωτήριον τοῦ θεοῦ, and suggests again Luke's LXX language, since the expression is absent in the Hebrew texts (cf. Isa 60:6), and it is used in LXX almost exclusively in the prophetic texts.

Finally, it might be noted that Acts ends along similar lines to Isaiah, even though there are little to no similarities in vocabulary. Isaiah ends with Yahweh's promise that he will "gather the nations," that he will send those who have been saved to the gentiles, and of some of them, "I will make priests and levites" (Isa 66:18-19, 21), with the result that "all mankind will

---

29. Barrett, *Acts*, 2:1244.
30. Steyn, *Septuagint Quotations*, 226.

come to bow down in my presence," but they will also see "the corpses of men who have rebelled against me" (Isa 66:24).

Conflations of Isaiah with Other Scriptures in Acts

1. Acts 3:13

This is an example of the conflation of texts or word strings from the Old Testament—reflecting a common Lukan stylistic feature. The passage reads: ὁ θεὸς Ἀβραὰμ καὶ [ὁ θεὸς] Ἰσαὰκ καὶ [ὁ θεὸς] Ἰακώβ, ὁ θεὸς τῶν πατέρων ἡμῶν, ἐδόξασεν τὸν παῖδα αὐτοῦ Ἰησοῦν ὃν ὑμεῖς μὲν παρεδώκατε καὶ ἠρνήσασθε κατὰ πρόσωπον Πιλάτου, κρίναντος ἐκείνου ἀπολύειν.

Peter is explaining his healing of the cripple. It is to be expected that he used biblical language. Acts 3:13a is clearly not from Isaiah, who never talks of God in these terms. It finds closer resonance with Exod 4:5: κύριος ὁ θεὸς τῶν πατέρων αὐτῶν, θεὸς Αβρααμ καὶ θεὸς Ισαακ καὶ θεὸς Ιακωβ. And Exod 3:6: Ἐγώ εἰμι ὁ θεὸς τοῦ πατρός σου, θεὸς Αβρααμ καὶ θεὸς Ισαακ καὶ θεὸς Ιακωβ. But the phrase ἐδόξασεν τὸν παῖδα αὐτοῦ possibly alludes to Isa 52:13: Ἰδοὺ συνήσει ὁ παῖς μου καὶ ὑψωθήσεται καὶ δοξασθήσεται σφόδρα.

The idea of the servant (παῖς) of God being glorified is quite common in Isaiah (41:8–9; 42:1; 43:10; 44:1, 2, 21; etc.), as is the linking of exaltation and glorification (5:16; 6:1; 10:15; 33:10; etc.).

"The God of our fathers" is the God of promise, and that promise has been kept in his servant/son, Jesus. Peter's address to the crowds in Jerusalem after healing the cripple, echoes these foundational motifs found in "Moses and the prophets." In proclamation, Luke often uses LXX words and phrases without identifying their source. It is much more in confrontation and dialogue that Luke will identify his biblical sources, and usually, he does so pointedly.

2. Acts 8:22–23

μετανόησον οὖν ἀπὸ τῆς κακίας σου ταύτης καὶ δεήθητι τοῦ κυρίου, εἰ ἄρα ἀφεθήσεταί σοι ἡ ἐπίνοια τῆς καρδίας σου, εἰς γὰρ χολὴν πικρίας καὶ σύνδεσμον ἀδικίας ὁρῶ σε ὄντα.

The context of this passage is that Peter is condemning Simon; and it appears he does so in biblical language. It is not unexpected that a leader such as Peter would pronounce a curse on someone like Simon in biblical words to emphasise its severity.

The phrase συνδέσμον ἀδικίας here in Acts 8:23 is found in Isa 58:6, where the context is one of Isaiah's rebuke of Israel for her injustice despite fastings and ritual observances. I doubt that the Isaianic context is significant, although Simon's offer does appear to be a ritual one (8:18).

Jeremiah laments that no one "repents of their wickedness" (μετανοῶν ἀπὸ τῆς κακίας αὐτοῦ) (8:6). And the phrase εἰς χολὴν πικρίας is found in Deut 29:17 LXX (cf. Lam 3:15). It is possible that δεήθητι τοῦ κυρίου echoes 1 Kgs 13:6 (δεήθητι τοῦ προσώπου κυρίου τοῦ θεοῦ σου). The verb form ἀφεθήσεται is used repeatedly in Leviticus almost as a technical term. On the performance of certain atonement sacrifices, "he shall be forgiven" (Lev 4:20, 26, 31; etc.).

So it appears that Luke uses a string of biblical phrases in Peter's rebuke of Simon. One of those phrases derives from Isaiah.

3. Acts 13:22

The sources of the biblical passages used here are not identified. Again, the implication is that Luke is not interested in citing texts, but in claiming the authority of God. It is God, who raised David up as king, "to whom he testified and said" (ᾧ καὶ εἶπεν μαρτυρήσας), Εὗρον Δαυὶδ τὸν τοῦ Ἰεσσαί, ἄνδρα κατὰ τὴν καρδίαν μου, ὃς ποιήσει πάντα τὰ θελήματά μου.

Paul is in the synagogue, where there has been a reading "of the law and the prophets," and he is asked to speak a word of exhortation (λόγος παρακλήσεως) on the basis of that word. This allows Paul to get quickly to David, who is the direct link to Jesus. One might even expect a conflation of, or at least a reference to, biblical phrases in such an address. Acts 13:22 appears to be a conflation of Ps 88:21 LXX, εὗρον Δαυὶδ τὸν δοῦλόν μου; 1 Sam 13:14 LXX: ζητήσει κύριος ἑαυτῷ ἄνθρωπον κατὰ τὴν καρδίαν αὐτοῦ; Isa 44:28 LXX: ὁ λέγων Κύρῳ φρονεῖν, καὶ Πάντα τὰ θελήματά μου ποιήσει· ὁ λέγων Ιερουσαλημ Οἰκοδομηθήσῃ, καὶ τὸν οἶκον τὸν ἅγιόν μου θεμελιώσω.

Clearly, the last clause in Isaiah refers to Cyrus, and that, when combined with the reference to David, reinforces the messianic claims Luke makes about Jesus in this passage. Clement of Rome also links Ps 88:21 LXX with 1 Sam 13:14 (1 Clem 18:1).

Word Strings in Common

There are passages in which is it difficult to claim direct reference to Isaiah by Luke. In most cases, the common word strings and phrases may be explained other than by claiming allusion to Isaiah. Once again, I have arranged these in the order in which they appear in Acts

1. Acts 1:8

Acts 1:8 speaks of the holy spirit coming upon the disciples, enabling them to witness to the ends of the earth: ἀλλὰ λήμψεσθε δύναμιν ἐπελθόντος τοῦ ἁγίου πνεύματος ἐφ᾽ ὑμᾶς καὶ ἔσεσθέ μου μάρτυρες ἔν τε Ἰερουσαλὴμ καὶ [ἐν] πάσῃ τῇ Ἰουδαίᾳ καὶ Σαμαρείᾳ καὶ ἕως ἐσχάτου τῆς γῆς.

This echoes some Isaianic language, especially in LXX Isa 32:15: ὡς ἂν ἐπέλθῃ ἐφ᾽ ὑμᾶς πνεῦμα ἀφ᾽ ὑψηλοῦ. καὶ ἔσται ἔρημος ὁ Χερμελ, καὶ ὁ Χερμελ εἰς δρυμὸν λογισθήσεται.

And when the phrase ἕως ἐσχάτου τῆς γῆς is used in Isaiah, it nearly always is in the context of God's salvific, boundary-stretching action. So, in Isa 48:20: γενέσθω τοῦτο, ἀπαγγείλατε ἕως ἐσχάτου τῆς γῆς. In 49:6: ἰδοὺ τέθεικά σε εἰς διαθήκην γένους εἰς φῶς ἐθνῶν τοῦ εἶναί σε εἰς σωτηρίαν ἕως ἐσχάτου τῆς γῆς. And in 62:11: ἰδοὺ γὰρ κύριος ἐποίησεν ἀκουστὸν ἕως ἐσχάτου τῆς γῆς.

The term "holy spirit," so commonly used in Acts, is very rarely found in the canonical OT. However, Isaiah does use the term twice, and in consecutive verses. In 63:10: αὐτοὶ δὲ ἠπείθησαν καὶ παρώξυναν τὸ πνεῦμα τὸ ἅγιον αὐτοῦ. And then Isaiah asks, "Where is he who placed his holy spirit (τὸ πνεῦμα τὸ ἅγιον) among them [Israel]?" (63:11).

In both verses, the Targ. Isaiah interprets the "holy spirit" as "the Memra of his holy prophets." This despite the fact that the Isaiah Targum tends to use "holy spirit" where MT reads "spirit" (e.g., 42:1; 44:3).

2. Acts 2:39

Acts 2:39 reads: ὑμῖν γάρ ἐστιν ἡ ἐπαγγελία καὶ τοῖς τέκνοις ὑμῶν καὶ πᾶσιν τοῖς εἰς μακράν, ὅσους ἂν προσκαλέσηται κύριος ὁ θεὸς ἡμῶν.

The phrase τοῖς εἰς μακράν might allude to Isa 57:18–19: καὶ ἔδωκα αὐτῷ παράκλησιν ἀληθινήν, εἰρήνην ἐπ᾽ εἰρήνην τοῖς μακρὰν καὶ τοῖς ἐγγὺς οὖσιν·.

Possibly, Luke uses ἐπαγγελία (a word far more common in Luke and in Paul than in the LXX) as a summary of the Isaianic healing, comfort and peace expressed in the latter's passage.

3. Acts 10:38

It is well known that Luke, in his Gospel (4:18), uses Isa 61 as paradigmatic for the ministry of Jesus. That passage seems to be echoed in Acts 10:38 where Jesus is described as one anointed (ἔχρισεν) by God with the holy spirit and with power.

Acts 10:38 goes on to speak of Jesus as going about "doing good and healing those oppressed by the devil," activity closely related to that described in Isa 61:1: ἔχρισέν με εὐαγγελίσασθαι πτωχοῖς ἀπέσταλκέν με, ἰάσασθαι τοὺς συντετριμμένους τῇ καρδίᾳ, κηρύξαι αἰχμαλώτοις ἄφεσιν καὶ τυφλοῖς ἀνάβλεψιν.

It is a little surprising that there are no healings of the blind or deaf in Acts (apart from Paul himself). It would seem that those conditions are used only in reference to "spiritual" blindness and deafness (Acts 26:18; 28:27), as they commonly are also in Isaiah (6:10; 32:3; 35:5; 43:9).

In addition, in that same Acts passage, Peter describes the ministry of Jesus (and of early apostles) in Judaea: [ὑμεῖς οἴδατε] τὸν λόγον [ὃν] ἀπέστειλεν τοῖς υἱοῖς Ἰσραὴλ εὐαγγελιζόμενος εἰρήνην διὰ Ἰησοῦ Χριστοῦ, οὗτός ἐστιν πάντων κύριος (Acts 10:36). This bears some resemblance to Isa 52:7: ὡς ὥρα ἐπὶ τῶν ὀρέων, ὡς πόδες εὐαγγελιζομένου ἀκοὴν εἰρήνης, ὡς εὐαγγελιζόμενος ἀγαθά, ὅτι ἀκουστὴν ποιήσω τὴν σωτηρίαν σου λέγων Σιων Βασιλεύσει σου ὁ θεός·

Luke appears to draw on the activity of the one anointed by the Spirit, according to Isa 61:1–2, as a way of summarizing the activity of Jesus and his apostles.

4. Acts 13:10

The notions that Israel is to walk in straight paths, and that the time will come when the crooked will be made straight, are Isaianic. So Isa 40:3: φωνὴ βοῶντος ἐν τῇ ἐρήμῳ Ἑτοιμάσατε τὴν ὁδὸν κυρίου, εὐθείας ποιεῖτε τὰς τρίβους τοῦ θεοῦ ἡμῶν. And also Isa 45:13: ἐγὼ ἤγειρα αὐτὸν μετὰ δικαιοσύνης βασιλέα, καὶ πᾶσαι αἱ ὁδοὶ αὐτοῦ εὐθεῖαι.

It is an idea that Luke picks up. As is well known, Luke knows the Christians at Damascus as "The Way." I doubt it is co-incidental that Ananias lives in the street/district called "straight" (9:11) and that Paul ends up in his house and is baptised there. In addition, in Paul's confrontation with Bar Jesus over the interpretation of righteousness, the false prophet is accused of perverting "the straight paths of the Lord": Ὦ πλήρης παντὸς δόλου καὶ πάσης ῥᾳδιουργίας, υἱὲ διαβόλου, ἐχθρὲ πάσης δικαιοσύνης, οὐ παύσῃ διαστρέφων τὰς ὁδοὺς [τοῦ] κυρίου τὰς εὐθείας (13:10).

This condemnation of Bar Jesus is part of Luke's claim that Paul is the "straight" interpreter of the ways of the Lord, and those who oppose him are perverters of the path. According to Isaiah, the ideal person is one who πορευόμενος ἐν δικαιοσύνῃ λαλῶν εὐθεῖαν ὁδόν (33:15). Bar Jesus, on the contrary, is a prophet who is full of deceit (δόλος). In the true servant of Yahweh, there is no deceit (Isa 53:9). Righteousness (δικαιοσύνη) is walking in the straight paths of the Lord, and is a common and important motif in Isaiah. As the Isaianic Lord says, ἐγὼ γάρ εἰμι κύριος ὁ ἀγαπῶν (61:8), and the hope is that ὄψονται ἔθνη τὴν δικαιοσύνην σου καὶ βασιλεῖς τὴν δόξαν σου (62:2).

The links in Acts between Paul and Isaiah as prophets of the Lord are quite strong. They both speak the same language.

5. Acts 18:9–10

Μὴ φοβοῦ, ἀλλὰ λάλει καὶ μὴ σιωπήσῃς, διότι ἐγώ εἰμι μετὰ σοῦ καὶ οὐδεὶς ἐπιθήσεταί σοι τοῦ κακῶσαί σε.

This echoes Isa 43:5, μὴ φοβοῦ, ὅτι μετὰ σοῦ εἰμι· ἀπὸ ἀνατολῶν ἄξω τὸ σπέρμα σου καὶ ἀπὸ δυσμῶν συνάξω σε. So also 58:11: καὶ ἔσται ὁ θεός σου μετὰ σοῦ διὰ παντός. And 41:10: μὴ φοβοῦ, μετὰ σοῦ γάρ εἰμι· μὴ πλανῶ, ἐγὼ γάρ εἰμι ὁ θεός σου ὁ ἐνισχύσας σε καὶ ἐβοήθησά σοι καὶ ἠσφαλισάμην σε τῇ δεξιᾷ τῇ δικαίᾳ μου.

Of course, the idea that God is "with" his servant is common (e.g., Gen 26:24; Jer 26:28). On the other hand, again noting the links Luke makes between the servants of God (Jesus, Peter, Paul) and the servant songs of Isaiah, one might be justified in saying Luke here is referring to the promises of Yahweh made in Isaiah.

Following this theme of God protecting his servants, I would draw attention to Isa 37:28: νῦν δὲ τὴν ἀνάπαυσίν σου καὶ τὴν ἔξοδόν σου καὶ τὴν εἴσοδόν σου ἐγὼ ἐπίσταμαι. The expression "going out and coming in" is used in the Pentateuch especially of Israel's leaders, and of their military leaders (almost as a technical term for their military exploits; Num 27:17; Deut 28:6; 31:2). It is also used to describe the whole life of a person, most well-known in Psa 120:7–8 LXX, κύριος φυλάξει σε ἀπὸ παντὸς κακοῦ, φυλάξει τὴν ψυχήν σου. κύριος φυλάξει τὴν εἴσοδόν σου καὶ τὴν ἔξοδόν σου.

I do not have the space or time to develop this idea here, but it is interesting to note that Luke uses the phrase in reference to Jesus in Acts 1:21 (ἐν παντὶ χρόνῳ ᾧ εἰσῆλθεν καὶ ἐξῆλθεν ἐφ᾽ ἡμᾶς ὁ κύριος) where it seems to refer to his leadership—the preposition ἐπί might imply this). And while the exact phrase is not used, the two verbs (εἰσῆλθεν and ἐξῆλθεν) are commonly used in tandem with both Peter and Paul, and sometimes in a clear context of God's protection. This is best illustrated in Acts 14:19–20. Paul is stoned, left for dead, but (miraculously) gets up and goes in and then goes out as if nothing had happened (Ἐπῆλθαν δὲ ἀπὸ Ἀντιοχείας καὶ Ἰκονίου Ἰουδαῖοι καὶ πείσαντες τοὺς ὄχλους καὶ λιθάσαντες τὸν Παῦλον ἔσυρον ἔξω τῆς πόλεως νομίζοντες αὐτὸν τεθνηκέναι. κυκλωσάντων δὲ τῶν μαθητῶν αὐτὸν ἀναστὰς εἰσῆλθεν εἰς τὴν πόλιν. καὶ τῇ ἐπαύριον ἐξῆλθεν σὺν τῷ Βαρναβᾷ εἰς Δέρβην). The Lord preserved his going out and coming in; or, to use the words of Isaiah, the Lord could say to Paul, καὶ τὴν ἔξοδόν σου καὶ τὴν εἴσοδόν σου ἐγὼ ἐπίσταμαι.

Along these lines, the title of David Pao's book, *Acts and the Isaianic New Exodus*, suggests that Pao finds "exodus" language and themes in both writings. That is not really surprising, since prophets very often call Israel back to her roots in God's mythological acts of creation and salvation. It might be worth comparing the use of ἐκ/ἐξ and their compound words in Isaiah and Acts. I know that in Acts 12, for example, the escape of Peter is told with the use of many such words. A very quick count reveals that Isaiah uses the preposition about 120 times and Acts about 85 times, and that the former uses ἐκ/ἐξ compound verb forms at least 150 times, while Acts uses them about 100 times.

6. Signs and Wonders

Signs and wonders (σημεῖα καὶ τέρατα) is a phrase commonly used in Acts (2:43; 4:30; 5:12; 6:8; 7:36; 14:3; 15:12). It is a phrase also found in Isa 8:18; 20:3; but probably more significant is Isa 11:12, where God says that "on that day," he will raise σημεῖον εἰς τὰ ἔθνη. This is possibly picked up by Luke in Acts 15:12, when the council at Jerusalem is glad to hear Paul's report that ἐποίησεν ὁ θεὸς σημεῖα καὶ τέρατα ἐν τοῖς ἔθνεσιν δι' αὐτῶν.

7. Paul's Temple Commission

I have noted already that the call and mission of Paul and that of Isaiah resonate with each other. Both receive their commission in the Temple (Isa 6; Acts 22). While verbal similarities between those two narratives are almost non-existent, there are some faint resonances elsewhere. For example, in Isa 66:19: καὶ καταλείψω ἐπ' αὐτῶν σημεῖα καὶ ἐξαποστελῶ ἐξ αὐτῶν σεσῳσμένους εἰς τὰ ἔθνη, εἰς Θαρσις καὶ Φουδ καὶ Λουδ καὶ Μοσοχ καὶ Θοβελ καὶ εἰς τὴν Ἑλλάδα καὶ εἰς τὰς νήσους τὰς πόρρω, οἳ οὐκ ἀκηκόασίν μου τὸ ὄνομα οὐδὲ ἑωράκασιν τὴν δόξαν μου, καὶ ἀναγγελοῦσίν μου τὴν δόξαν ἐν τοῖς ἔθνεσιν.

In Acts 22:21, in Paul's Temple commission, the Lord says to him, Πορεύου, ὅτι ἐγὼ εἰς ἔθνη μακρὰν ἐξαποστελῶ σε.

8. Some Common Depictions of God

There are a number of theological phrases used in Acts that also are found in Isaiah. Nearly all of these are certainly found elsewhere in Jewish literature, and I certainly would not wish to claim direct or explicit reference to Isaiah when Luke uses them in Acts. For example, both can refer to God as "the living God." So, in Isa 37:4 (cf. 37:17), the king of Assyria is accused of insulting "the living God" (θεὸν ζῶντα). And in Acts 14:15, Paul addresses the Lystrans and calls them to turn to "the living God" (ἐπιστρέφειν ἐπὶ θεὸν ζῶντα). What these passages have in common is that speakers use the phrase when addressing pagans.

A widely used circumlocution (and description) in Jewish literature is to refer to God as the Most High. So Isa 57:15: Τάδε λέγει κύριος ὁ ὕψιστος ὁ ἐν ὑψηλοῖς κατοικῶν τὸν αἰῶνα, ἅγιος ἐν ἁγίοις ὄνομα αὐτῷ. It is an expression used by Stephen also in the context of where God lives, οὐχ ὁ ὕψιστος ἐν χειροποιήτοις κατοικεῖ (Acts 7:48). Given that Stephen in the same verse cites Isa 66:1-2, it is possible that Stephen is using LXX Isaianic language when he refers to God as "the Most High."

Another term used to describe the activity of God that Isaiah and Acts have in common is the "uplifted arm." Isaiah says, κύριε, ὑψηλός σου ὁ βραχίων (26:11), where it appears God's arm is lifted to act decisively. Isaiah also knows that the holy arm of God acts to offer salvation to the gentiles (καὶ ἀποκαλύψει κύριος τὸν βραχίονα αὐτοῦ τὸν ἅγιον ἐνώπιον πάντων τῶν ἐθνῶν, καὶ ὄψονται πάντα τὰ ἄκρα τῆς γῆς τὴν σωτηρίαν τὴν παρὰ τοῦ θεοῦ) (52:10). According to Acts 13:17, God liberated Israel from Egypt μετὰ βραχίονος ὑψηλοῦ. The phrase is more common in the Pentateuch, and it is more likely that Luke is recalling that literature rather than Isaiah, who only uses the phrase once.

9. Salvation of the Gentiles

Another hint of Isaiah being used in Acts is found in the idea of gentiles, in particular, turning to the Lord and being saved. A classic statement of this hope is found in Isa 45:22: ἐπιστράφητε πρός με καὶ σωθήσεσθε, οἱ ἀπ' ἐσχάτου τῆς γῆς· ἐγώ εἰμι ὁ θεός, καὶ οὐκ ἔστιν ἄλλος. While there are few direct verbal parallels linking "turning" and "being saved," the concept is certainly present in Acts. The best example is probably that of the jailer at Philippi, to whom Paul says, Πίστευσον ἐπὶ τὸν κύριον Ἰησοῦν καὶ σωθήσῃ σὺ καὶ ὁ οἶκός σου (Acts 16:31).

The concept of salvation and of God as savior is common to Isaiah and to Luke in Acts. That this salvation is offered to gentiles is also a clear Isaianic expectation (ἰδοὺ τέθεικά σε εἰς διαθήκην γένους εἰς φῶς ἐθνῶν τοῦ εἶναί σε εἰς σωτηρίαν ἕως ἐσχάτου τῆς γῆς [49:6]; καὶ ἀποκαλύψει κύριος τὸν βραχίονα αὐτοῦ τὸν ἅγιον ἐνώπιον πάντων τῶν ἐθνῶν, καὶ ὄψονται πάντα τὰ ἄκρα τῆς γῆς τὴν σωτηρίαν τὴν παρὰ τοῦ θεοῦ [52:10]).

10. Acts 26:18

Paul here recounts his conversion/call experience in which the Lord says that he sends Paul to the gentiles, to "open their eyes, that they may turn from darkness to light":

ἀνοῖξαι ὀφθαλμοὺς αὐτῶν, τοῦ ἐπιστρέψαι ἀπὸ σκότους εἰς φῶς καὶ τῆς ἐξουσίας τοῦ Σατανᾶ ἐπὶ τὸν θεόν, τοῦ λαβεῖν αὐτοὺς ἄφεσιν ἁμαρτιῶν καὶ κλῆρον ἐν τοῖς ἡγιασμένοις πίστει τῇ εἰς ἐμέ.

Again, there are phrases in this verse that can be found in the OT. Isaiah says that Yahweh calls and creates his servant "to open the eyes of the blind" and to lead out of prison those "sitting in darkness" (ἀνοῖξαι ὀφθαλμοὺς τυφλῶν, ἐξαγαγεῖν ἐκ δεσμῶν δεδεμένους καὶ ἐξ οἴκου φυλακῆς καθημένους ἐν σκότει) (Isa 42:7). Later, in the same chapter, Yahweh promises to turn darkness into light for the blind (ποιήσω αὐτοῖς τὸ σκότος εἰς φῶς) (42:16). That God will provide a servant who will be φῶς ἐθνῶν is common to both Isaiah (49:6) and Acts (13:47), as we have already seen.

Given that Luke uses this language for the call of Paul, and given that Isaiah uses similar language in his servant songs, it is likely that Luke has the Isaiah passages in mind. It might be noted at this point that Betz has made a case for understanding Paul's vision in the temple in Acts 22, told in relation to his call, as drawing on Isaiah's temple vision and call. In other words, Luke seems to link Paul's call with Isaiah.

We have already seen that Luke can take a word spoken to Isaiah as a word spoken by the Lord to Paul (13:47). And at the very end of Acts, Paul and Isaiah seem to be portrayed as complementary witnesses, and Paul takes a word of Isaiah and uses it as his own ἓν ῥῆμα (28:25-27).

While the noun κλῆρος used in this verse is not very common in Isaiah, its cognates certainly are, with over twenty uses of them. Here, the gentiles are promised a κλῆρος among the sanctified ones; this possibly resonates with Isa 54:3, where Yahweh promises Israel, τὸ σπέρμα σου ἔθνη κληρονομήσει, and with Isa 63:17, which refers to τὰς φυλὰς τῆς κληρονομίας σου.

The idea of turning from Satan to God, while not used of gentiles in Isaiah, does reflect Isaianic language, since the prophet speaks of day when the remnant of Israel ἔσονται πεποιθότες ἐπὶ τὸν θεὸν τὸν ἅγιον τοῦ Ισραηλ τῇ ἀληθείᾳ (10:20).

Conclusion

It is well known that Luke in his double work draws quite heavily on Isaiah, not only in direct, explicit citation, but as the framework for understanding and interpreting the activity of Jesus and of his apostles and, importantly, as the framework for communicating that interpretation to Theophilus.

In this paper, I have drawn attention to the explicit quotations, but am conscious that many others have already done more detailed work on some of these passages. I have wanted to highlight the indirect references and the Isaianic "air" that Luke appears to have breathed. I realise that this area too has not been fully explored. For example, comparing the understanding of God, of Israel, of eschatology in both Isaiah and Acts might prove valuable. I have also suggested that the role of Luke himself as teacher and interpreter needs to be taken seriously. And I have wanted to emphasise that the interpretation of Isaiah appears to have been at the center of Jewish-Christian dialogues and debates in the first century, at least, of the Christian communities.

Bibliography

Address to Diognetus. In *The Apostolic Fathers: An American Translation*, edited by Edgar J. Goodspeed, 273–84. London: Independent, 1950.
Aesonius. "Mosella." In vol. 1 of *Aesonius*, translated by Hugh G. Evelyn-White. LCL 96. Cambridge, MA: Harvard University Press, 1919.
Amphilochius. *Amphilochii Iconiensis Opera: orationes, pluraque alia quae supersunt, nonnulla etiam spuria: quorum editionem curavit Cornelis Datema*. Corpus Christianorum Series Graeca 3. Turnhout, Brepols; Leuven: University Press, 1978.
Anderson, Graham. *Sage, Saint, and Sophist: Holy Men and Their Associates in the Early Roman Empire*. London; New York: Routledge, 1994.
Anderson, J. G. C. "Exploration in Galatia Cis Halym: Part II." *Journal of Hellenic Studies* 19 (1899) 280–318.
Aulus Gellius. *Attic Nights*. Vol. 3. Translated by J. C. Rolfe. LCL 212. Cambridge, MA: Harvard University Press, 1927.
Appian. *The Civil Wars*. Vol. 3 of *Roman History*. Translated by Horace White. LCL 4. Cambridge, MA: Harvard University Press, 1913.
Apuleius. *Apologia. Florida. De Deo Socratis*. Edited and translated by Christopher P. Jones. LCL 534. Cambridge, MA: Harvard University Press, 2017.
———. *Metamorphoses*. Vol. 2. Edited and translated by J. Arthur Hanson. LCL 453. Cambridge, MA: Harvard University Press, 1989.
Apollonius Rhodius. *Argonautica*. Edited and translated by William H. Race. LCL 1. Cambridge, MA: Harvard University Press, 2009.
———. *The Argonautika*. Translated, with introduction, commentary, and glossary by Peter Green. Berkeley: University of California Press, 1997.
Aristotle. *Meteorologica*. Translated by H. D. P. Lee. LCL 397. London: Heinemann, 1952.
———. *Problems*. Translated by W. S. Hett. LCL 316–17. London: Heinemann, 1965.
Arndt, William F., and F. Wilbur Gingrich, eds. *A Greek-English Lexicon of the New Testament and Other Early Christian Literature*. 2nd ed. Chicago: University of Chicago Press, 1979.
Augustine. *Expositions on the Book of Psalms*. 6 vols. Translated, with notes and indices, by John Henry Parker and F. and J. Rivington. Oxford, 1847.
Aune, David. *Prophecy in Early Christianity*. Grand Rapids: Eerdmans, 1983.
The Babylonian Talmud. 10 vols. Translated by Michael L. Rodkinson. Boston: New Talmud, 1918.
Balz, Horst, and Gerhard Schneider, eds. *Exegetical Dictionary of the New Testament*. 3 vols. Grand Rapids: Eerdmans, 1990–1993.
Bardy, Gustave. *La question des langues dans l'Église ancienne*. Vol 1. Paris: Beauchesne, 1948.

Barrett, Charles Kingsley. "Attitudes to the Temple in Acts." In *Templum Amicitiae: Essays on the Second Temple presented to Ernst Bammel*, edited by William Horbury, 345-67. Sheffield: JSOT, 1991.

———. *A Critical and Exegetical Commentary on the Acts of the Apostles*. 2 vols. Edinburgh: T. & T. Clark, 1994.

———. *The New Testament Background: Selected Documents*. London: SPCK, 1956.

———. "Review: Septuagint Quotations in the Context of the Petrine and Pauline Speeches of the Acta Apostolorum. Contributions to Biblical Exegesis and Theology 12, by Gert J. Steyn." *JTS* 48 (1997) 194-96.

Barton, John, ed. *The Biblical World*. 2 vols. London; New York: Routledge, 2002.

———. *Oracles of God: Perceptions of Ancient Prophecy in Israel After the Exile*. London: Darton Longman & Todd, 1986.

Bauer, Walter, ed. *Griechisch-Deutsches Wörterbuch zu den Schriften des Neuen Testaments und der frühchristlichenLiteratur*. 6th ed. Edited by K. & B. Aland. Berlin; New York: de Gruyter, 1988.

Bauernfeind, Otto. *Kommentar und Studien zur Apostelgeschichte*. Mohr/Siebeck: Tübingen, 1980.

———. "τρέχω ktl." *TDNT* 8:231.

Behm, J. "ἀποφθέγγομαι." *TDNT* 1:447.

Beker, J. Christiaan. *Heirs of Paul: Paul's Legacy in the New Testament and in the Church Today*. Minneapolis: Fortress, 1991.

Bergler, Siegfried. "Jesus, Bar Kochba und das messianische Laubhüttenfest." *JSJ* 29 (1998) 143-91.

Betz, Otto. "φωνή, et al." *TDNT* 9:293.

Bieler, L. ΘΕΙΟΣ ANHP: *Das Bild des göttlichen Menschen in Spätantike und Frühchristentum*. Darmstadt: Wissenschaftliche Buchgesellschaft, 1967.

Black, Matthew. *An Aramaic Approach to the Gospels and Acts*. 3rd ed. Oxford: Clarendon, 1967.

Blass, Friedrich, et al. *A Greek Grammar of the New Testament and Other Early Christian Literature*. Chicago: University of Chicago Press, 1961.

Bock, Darrell L. *Proclamation from Prophecy and Pattern: Lucan Old Testament Christology*. Sheffield: JSOT, 1987.

Boyce, Bret. *The Language of the Freedmen in Petronius's Cena Trimalchionis*. Leiden: Brill, 1991.

Brock, Sebastian. *From Ephrem to Romanos: Interactions between Syriac and Greek in Late Antiquity*. Brookfield, VT: Ashgate, 1999.

Brockelmann, Carl. *Lexicon Syriacum*. Hildesheim: Georg Olms, 1966.

Brockington, Leonard H. "LXX and Targum." *ZAW* 66 (1954) 80-86.

Brown, Francis, et al. *A Hebrew and English Lexicon of the Old Testament*. Oxford: Clarendon, 1907.

Brown, Raymond E. *An Introduction to the New Testament*. New York: Doubleday, 1997.

Bruce, Frederick F. *The Acts of the Apostles: The Greek Text with Introduction and Commentary*. London: Tyndale, 1951.

———. *The Book of Acts*. Rev. ed. Grand Rapids: Eerdmans, 1988.

———. *Commentary on the Book of Acts: The English Text with Introduction, Exposition, and Notes*. London: Marshall Morgan & Scott, 1977.

Buck, Carl D. *The Greek Dialects: Grammar, Selected Inscriptions, Glossary*. Chicago: University of Chicago, 1955.

Cadbury, Henry J. "Lucius of Cyrene." *BegChr* 5:489–95.
Calvin, John. *Commentary on Acts*. Grand Rapids: Baker, 1984.
Chrysostom, John. *Homilies on the Acts of the Apostles*. Translated by J. Walker, et al. Revised by George B. Stevens. Nicene and Post-Nicene Fathers Series 1, 11. Buffalo, NY: Christian Literature, 1889.
———. *Homilies on the Gospel of John*. Translated by Charles Marriott. Nicene and Post-Nicene Fathers, Series 1, 14. Buffalo, NY: Christian Literature, 1889.
———. "Homily XXXV." In *The Homilies of S. John Chrysostom on the First Epistle of St. Paul the Apostle to the Corinthians*, edited by Hubert Kestell Cornish and John Medley, 487–503. Library of Fathers of the Holy Catholic Church 4. Oxford: J. H. Parker, 1839.
Clarke, W. K. L. "The Use of the Septuagint in Acts." *BegChr* 2 (1922) 66–105.
Clement of Alexandria. *The Stromata*. Translated by William Wilson. In vol. 2 of *Ante-Nicene Fathers*, edited by Alexander Roberts et al., 299–368. Buffalo, NY: Christian Literature, 1885.
Collange, J. F. *Énigmes de la deuxième épître de Paul aux Corinthiens: étude exégétique de 2 Cor 2:14–7:4*. Cambridge: Cambridge University Press, 1972.
Conzelmann, Hans. *Die Apostelgeschichte*. Mohr: Tübingen, 1963.
Cumont, Franz. *The Oriental Religions in Roman Paganism*. Chicago: Open Court, 1911.
Daniélou, Jean. *Platonisme et théologie mystique, doctrine spirituelle de Saint Grégoire de Nysee*. Paris: Aubier, 1944.
Danker, Frederick W., et al. *Greek-English Lexicon of the New Testament and Other Early Christian Literature*. 3rd ed. Chicago: University of Chicago Press, 2000.
Deissmann, Adolf. *Light from the Ancient East: The New Testament Illustrated by Recently Discovered Texts of the Graeco-Roman World*. Grand Rapids: Baker, 1965.
Denis, A-M. *Concordance grecque des pseudepigraphes d'Ancien Testament: concordance corpus des textes indices*. Avec collaboration d'Yvonne Janssens. Louvain-la-Neuve: Université Catholique de Louvain, Institut Orientaliste, 1987.
Dibelius, Martin. *From Tradition to Gospel*. London: James Clark, 1971.
Dio Chrysostom. *Discourses 12–30*. Translated by J. W. Cohoon. LCL 339. Cambridge, MA: Harvard University Press, 1939.
Diodorus of Sicily. *Library of History*. Translated by C. H. Oldfather, et al. LCL 279. London: Heinemann, 1933–67.
Diogenes Laertius. *Lives of Eminent Philosophers*. Vol. 2. Translated by R. D. Hick. LCL 185. Cambridge, MA: Harvard University Press, 1925.
Dionysius of Halicarnassus. *Roman Antiquities*. 7 vols. Translated by Earnest Cary. LCL 319. Cambridge, MA: Harvard University Press, 1937–1950.
Dodds, E. R. *The Greeks and the Irrational*. Berkeley: University of California Press, 1951.
Dölger, Franz Josef. "ΘΕΟΥ ΦΩΝΗ: Die 'Gottes-Stimme bei Ignatius von Antiochen, Kelsos und Origines." *Antike und Christentum: Kulture-und religionschichtliche Studien* 5.2 (1936) 218–23.
Dunn, James G. D. *The Acts of the Apostles*. Valley Forge, PA: Trinity, 1996.
———. *Jesus and the Spirit. A Study of the Religious and Charismatic Experience of Jesus and the First Christians as Reflected in the New Testament*. Grand Rapids: Eerdmans, 1975.

Ehrman, Bart. *The New Testament: A Historical Introduction to the Early Christian Writings*. Oxford: Oxford University Press, 2000.
Eitrem, Samson. "Dreams and Divination in Magical Ritual." In *Magika Hiera, Ancient Greek Magic and Religion*, edited by Christopher A. Faraone and Dirk Obbin, 175–87. Oxford: Oxford University Press, 1991.
Eliade, Mirce. *Shamanism: Archaic Techniques of Ecstasy*. London: Routledge & Kegan Paul, 1964.
Epp, Eldon J. *The Theological Tendency of Codex Bezae Cantabrigiensis in Acts*. Cambridge: Cambridge University Press, 1966.
Esler, Philip F., ed. *The Early Christian World*. 2 vols. London; New York: Routledge, 2000.
Eunapius. *Lives of Philosophers and Sophists*. Translated by Wilbur C. Wright. LCL 134. Cambridge, MA: Harvard University Press, 1921.
Eusebius. *The Theophania*. Translated by Samuel Lee. Cambridge: Cambridge University Press, 1843.
Evans, Craig A., and Stanley E. Porter, eds. *The Dictionary of the New Testament Background*. Leicester: InterVarsity, 2000.
Fine, Steven. *Art and Judaism in the Graeco-Roman World: Towards a New Jewish Archaeology*. Cambridge: Cambridge University Press, 2005.
Fisher, E. W. "Let Us Look Upon the Blood of Christ (1 Clement 7:4)." *VigChr* 34 (1980) 218–36.
Fitzmyer, Joseph A. *The Acts of the Apostles: A New Translation with Introduction and Commentary*. New York: Doubleday, 1998.
Forbes, Christopher. *Prophecy and Inspired Speech in Early Christianity and its Hellenistic Environment*. WUNT 2.75. Tübingen: Mohr/Siebeck, 1995.
Frisk, H. *Griechisches etymologisches Wörterbuch*. Vol. 1. Heidelberg: Carl Winter Universitätsverlag, 1973.
Galen. *On the Doctrines of Hippocrates and Plato*. Translation and commentary by Phillip De Lacy. Berlin: Akademie-Verlag, 1981.
Garrett, Susan. *The Demise of the Devil: Magic and the Demonic in Luke's Writings*. Minneapolis: Fortress, 1989.
Gaventa, Beverly Roberts. *The Acts of the Apostles*. Abingdon New Testament Commentaries. Nashville: Abingdon, 2003.
Gertner, Meir. "Terms of Scriptural Interpretation: A Study in Hebrew Semantics." *BSOAS* 25 (1962) 1–27.
Ginzberg, Louis. *The Legends of the Jews*. Philadelphia: Jewish Publications, 1937.
Goodman, Felicitas. *Ecstasy, Ritual, and Alternate Reality: Religion in a Pluralistic World*. Bloomington: Indiana University Press, 1988.
———. *Speaking in Tongues: A Cross-Cultural Study of Glossolalia*. Chicago: University of Chicago Press, 1972.
Goodspeed, Edgar, ed. *The Apostolic Fathers: An American Translation*. London: Independent, 1950.
———. *Die ältesten Apologeten: Texte mit kurzen Einleitungen*. Göttingen: Vandenhoek and Ruprecht, 1984.
Gorgias. *Encomium of Helen*. Translated by Malcolm D. McDowell. Bristol: Bristol Classical, 1982.
Gow, A. S., and D. L. Page. *The Greek Anthology: The Garland of Philip*. Cambridge: Cambridge University Press, 1968.

Graves, Robert. *The Greek Myths.* Vol. 1. Middlesex: Penguin, 1960.
Green, H. B. "Matthew, Clement, and Luke: Their Sequence and Relationship." *JTS* 40 (1989) 1–25.
Green, Peter, trans. *The Argonautika, by Apollonios Rhodios.* Translated with introduction, commentary, and glossary. Berkeley: University of California, 1997.
Gregory Nyssa. *Traité de la virginité.* Introduction, translation, and commentary by Michel Aubineau. Sources chrétiennes 119. Paris: Editions du Cerf, 1966.
Guthrie, W. K. *The Greeks and Their Gods.* London: Methuen, 1950.
Haar, Stephen. *Simon Magus: The First Gnostic?* Berlin; New York: Brill, 2003.
Haenchen, Ernst. *The Acts of the Apostles.* Oxford: Blackwell, 1971.
Hagner, Donald A. *The Use of the Old and New Testaments in Clement of Rome.* Leiden: Brill, 1973.
Hamm, Dennis. "Acts 3:1–10: The Healing of the Temple Beggar as Lucan Theology." *Bib* 67 (1986) 305–19.
Harnack, Adolf von. *The Mission and Expansion of Christianity in the First Three Centuries.* London: Williams and Norgate; New York: Putnam's Sons, 1908.
Heliodorus. *Aethiopica.* Translated by Thomas Underdowne. Revised by F. A. Wright. London: Routledge, 1923.
Hemer, Colin J. *The Book of Acts in the Setting of Hellenistic History.* Tübingen: Mohr/Siebeck, 1989.
Hengel, Martin. *Judaism and Hellenism: Studies in their Encounter in Palestine During the Early Hellenistic Period.* 2 vols. London: SCM, 1974.
———. "Luke the Historian and the Geography of Palestine in the Acts of the Apostles." In *Between Jesus and Paul: Studies in the Earliest History of Christianity*, by Martin Hengel, 97–128. Philadelphia: Fortress, 1983.
Hennecke, Edgar. *New Testament Apocrypha.* 2 vols. Edited by W. Schneemelcher. Translated by R. McL. Wilson et al. London: SCM, 1973, 1975.
Hippocrates. *Epidemics 2, 4–7.* Edited and translated by Wesley D. Smith. LCL 477. Cambridge, MA: Harvard University Press, 1994.
———. *Prognostic. Regimen in Acute Diseases. The Sacred Disease. The Art. Breaths. Law. Decorum. Physician (Ch. 1). Dentition.* Translated by W. H. S. Jones. LCL 148. Cambridge, MA: Harvard University Press, 1923.
Hippolytus. *Refutatio omnium haeresium.* Edited by P. Wendland. Hildesheim; New York: Olms, 1977.
Hobart, W. K. *The Medical Language of St. Luke.* Dublin: Hodges, Figgis; London: Longmans, Green, 1882.
Holladay, Carl. *Theios Aner in Hellenistic Judaism: A Critique of the Use of This Category in New Testament Christology.* SBLDS 40. Missoula: Scholars, 1977.
Holladay, William L. *Jeremiah: A Commentary on the Book of the Prophet Jeremiah.* Philadelphia: Fortress, 1986.
Homer. *Iliad.* Vol. 1. Translated by A. T. Murray. Revised by William F. Wyatt. LCL 170. Cambridge, MA: Harvard University Press, 1924.
———. *Odyssey.* Vol. 2. Translated by A. T. Murray. Revised by George E. Dimock. LCL 105. Cambridge, MA: Harvard University Press, 1919.
Horace. *Satires. Epistles. The Art of Poetry.* Translated by H. Rushton Fairclough. LCL 194. Cambridge, MA: Harvard University Press, 1926.
Horsley, Greg H. R., ed. *New Documents Illustrating Early Christianity.* Vol. 5. Sydney: Macquarie University, 1989.

Hull, John M. *Hellenistic Magic and the Synoptic Tradition*. London: SCM, 1974.
Huskinson, Janet, ed. *Experiencing Rome: Culture, Identity, and Power in the Roman Empire*. London: Routledge, 2000.
Iordanes. *The Origin and Deeds of the Goths*. Translated by Charles Christopher Mierow. Princeton: Princeton University Press; London: Humphrey Milford; Oxford: Oxford University Press, 1915.
Irenaeus. *Against Heresies*. Translated by Alexander Roberts and William Rambaut. In vol. 1 of *Ante-Nicene Fathers*, edited by Alexander Roberts, et al., 309–567. Buffalo, NY: Christian Literature, 1885.
Jerome. "Preface to the Epistle to the Galatians: Book II." In *St. Jerome: Commentary on Galatians*, translated by Andrew Cain, 129–34. The Fathers of the Church: A New Translation. Washington, DC: Catholic University of America, 2010.
Jervell, Jacob. *Die Apostelgeschichte*. Göttingen: Vandenhoeck & Ruprecht, 1998.
———. *Luke and the People of God: A New Look at Luke-Acts*. Minneapolis: Augsburg, 1972.
John Damascene. *Barlaam and Ioasaph*. Translated by G. H. Woodward and H. Mattingley. Cambridge, MA: Harvard University Press.
Johnson, Luke Timothy. *The Acts of the Apostles*. Collegeville, MN: Liturgical, 1992.
———. *Luke*. Sacra Pagina. Collegeville, MN: Liturgical, 1991.
Jones, A. H. M. *The Greek City: From Alexander to Justinian*. Oxford: Clarendon, 1940.
Josephus. *Josephus*. Translated by H. St. J. Thackeray. London: Heinemann, 1926–1965.
———. *The Works of Josephus*. New updated edition. Translated by William Whiston. Peabody, MA: Hendrickson, 1987.
Justin. *Dialogue with Trypho*. Translated by Marcus Dods and George Reith. In vol. 1 of *Ante-Nicene Fathers*, edited by Alexander Roberts, et al., 194–270. Buffalo, NY: Christian Literature, 1885.
———. *Die ältesten Apologeten: Texte mit kurzen Einleitungen*. Edited by Edgar Goodspeed. Göttingen: Vandenhoeck and Ruprecht, 1984.
Juvenal. "Satires." In *Juvenal and Persius*, translated by G. G. Ramsay, 128–505. Cambridge, MA: Harvard University Press, 1940.
Kahl, Werner. *New Testament Miracle Stories in the Religious-Historical Setting: A Religiongeschichtliche Comparison from a Structural Perspective*. Göttingen: Vandenhoeck & Ruprecht, 1994.
Kaimio, Jorm. *The Romans and the Greek Language*. Helsinki: Societas Scientiarum Fennica, 1979.
Keel, Othmar. *Song of Songs*. Minneapolis: Augsburg Fortress, 1994.
Kittel, Gerhard, and Friedrich Gerhard, eds. *Theological Dictionary of the New Testament*. Translated by Geoffrey W. Bromiley. 10 vols. Grand Rapids: Eerdmans, 1964–1976.
Klauck, Hans-Josef. *Magic and Paganism in Early Christianity. The World of the Acts of the Apostles*. Translated by Brian McNeil. Edinburgh: T. & T. Clark, 2000.
———. *Magie und Heidentum in der Apostelgeschichte des Lukas*. SBS 167. Stuttgart: Katholisches Bibelwerk, 1996.
Knoch, Otto. *Eigenart und Bedeutung der Eschatologie im theologischen Aufriss des ersten Clemensbriefes*. Bonn: Peter Hanstein Verlag, 1964.
Knopf, Rudolf. *Die Lehre der Zwölf Apostel; Die zwei Clemensbriefe*. Tübingen: Mohr/Siebeck, 1920.

Knowling, R. J. *The Acts of the Apostles: The Expositor's Greek Testament*. London: Hodder and Stoughton, 1912.
Koester, Helmut. *History, Culture, and Religion of the Hellenistic Age*. Vol. 1 of *Introduction to the New Testament*. Philadelphia: Fortress; Berlin; New York: de Gruyter, 1982.
Kolenkow, Anitra B. "Relationships between Miracle and Prophecy in the Greco-Roman World and Early Christianity." In *ANRW* 2.23.2, edited by Wolfgang Haase, 1470–1506. Berlin/New York: de Gruyter, 1980.
Lake, Kirsop, and F. J. Foakes-Jackson. *The Beginnings of Christianity: The Acts of the Apostles*. 5 vols. Grand Rapids: Baker, 1979.
Leary, T. J. "The 'Aprons' of St Paul—Acts 19:12." *JTS* 41 (1990) 527–29.
Levison, John R. "Did the Spirit Withdraw from Israel? An Evaluation of the Earliest Jewish Data." *NTS* 43 (1997) 35–57.
Liddell, Henry George, et al. *A Greek-English Lexicon*. 9th ed. with revised supplement. Oxford: Clarendon, 1996.
Lindblom, Johannes. *Prophecy in Ancient Israel*. Philadelphia: Muhlenberg, 1963.
Lindemann, Andreas. *Die Clemensbriefe*. HzNT 17. Tübingen: Mohr/Siebeck, 1992.
Lipsius, R. A., and M. Bonnet, eds. *Acta Apostolorum Apocrypha*. Darmstadt: Wissenschaftliche Buchgesellschaft, 1959.
Lucan. *Bellum Civile. The Civil War (Pharsalia)*. Translated by J. D. Duff. LCL 220. Cambridge, MA: Harvard University Press, 1928.
Lucian. *Anacharsis or Athletics. Menippus or the Descent into Hades. On Funerals. A Professor of Public Speaking. Alexander the False Prophet. Essays in Portraiture. Essays in Portraiture Defended. The Goddesse of Surrye*. Translated by A. M. Harmon. LCL 162. Cambridge, MA: Harvard University Press, 1925.

———. *The Dead Come to Life or the Fisherman. The Double Indictment or Trials by Jury. On Sacrifices. The Ignorant Book Collector. The Dream or Lucian's Career. The Parasite. The Lover of Lies. The Judgement of the Goddesses. On Salaried Posts in Great Houses*. Translated by A. M. Harmon. LCL 130. Cambridge, MA: Harvard University Press, 1921.

———. *The Downward Journey or the Tyrant. Zeus Catechized. Zeus Rants. The Dream or the Cock. Prometheus. Icaromenippus or the Sky-man. Timon or the Misanthrope. Charon or the Inspectors. Philosophies for Sale*. Translated by A. M. Harmon. LCL 54. Cambridge, MA: Harvard University Press, 1915.

———. *How to Write History. The Dipsads. Saturnalia. Herodotus or Aetion. Zeuxis or Antiochus. A Slip of the Tongue in Greeting. Apology for the "Salaried Posts in Great Houses." Harmonides. A Conversation with Hesiod. The Scythian or the Consul. Hermotimus or Concerning the Sects. To One Who Said "You're a Prometheus in Words." The Ship or the Wishes*. Translated by K. Kilburn. LCL 430. Cambridge, MA: Harvard University Press, 1959.

Lüdemann, Gerd. *Early Christianity According to Traditions in Acts: A Commentary*. Minneapolis: Fortress, 1989.
Malina, Bruce. "Assessing the Historicity of Jesus' Walking on the Sea: Insights from Cross-Cultural Social Psychology." In *Authenticating the Activities of Jesus*, edited by Bruce Chilton and Craig Evans, 351–72. Leiden: Brill, 1999.
Marshall, I. Howard. *The Acts of the Apostles: An Introduction and Commentary*. Leicester: InterVarsity, 1980.

———. *Luke: Historian and Theologian*. Grand Rapids: Eerdmans, 1978.

Martial. *Epigrams.* Vols. 1–2. Edited and translated by D. R. Shackleton Bailey. LCL 94–95. Cambridge, MA: Harvard University Press, 1993.

Martin, Louise. "Gazelle (Gazella spp.) Behavioural Ecology: Predicting Animal Behaviour for Prehistoric Environments in South-West Asia." *Journal of Zoology* 250 (2000) 13–30.

Martin, Luther H. "Gods or Ambassadors? Barnabas and Paul in Lystra." *NTS* 41 (1995) 152–56.

Martin, Ralph P. *Second Corinthians.* Word Biblical Commentary 40. Waco, TX: Thomas Nelson, 1986.

McClure, M. L., and Charles L. Feltoe, eds. *The Pilgrimage of Etheria.* London: SPCK, 1919.

Meyer, Marvin W., ed. *The "Mithras Liturgy."* Translated by Marvin W. Meyer. Missoula, MT: Scholars, 1976.

Migne, Jacques-Paul, ed. *Patrologiae cursus completes.* Series Graeca. Turnhout, Belgium: Brepols, 1959–1996.

Miller, Merrill P. "Targum, Midrash, and the Use of the Old Testament in the New Testament." *JSJ* 2 (1971) 29–82.

Momigliano, Arnoldo. *Alien Wisdom: The Limits of Hellenization.* Cambridge: Cambridge University, 1975.

Morgenstern, Julian. "The Gates of Righteousness." *HUCA* 6 (1929) 1–37.

Morpurgo Davies, Anna. "The Greek Notion of Dialect." In *Greeks and Barbarians,* edited by T. Harrison, 153–71. Edinburgh: Edinburgh University, 2002.

Moulton, J. H. "Characteristics of New Testament Greek, III." Sixth Series. *Expositor* 9 (1904) 313–14.

———. "New Testament Greek in the Light of Modern Discovery." In *The Language of the New Testament: Classic Essays,* edited by Stanley E. Porter, 60–97. Sheffield: JSOT, 1991.

Mowinckel, Sigmund. *The Psalms in Israel's Worship.* Oxford: Blackwell, 1982.

Munck, Johannes. *The Acts of the Apostles.* Anchor Bible 31. Garden City, NY: Anchor Bible, 1973.

Mussies, Gerard. "Identification and Self-Identification of Gods." In *Knowledge of God in the Graeco-Roman World,* edited by R. van den Broek et al., 1–18. Leiden: Brill, 1988.

Najjar, M., and F. Sa'id. "A New Umayyad Church At Khilda-Amman." *Liber Annuus* 44 (1994) 547–60.

Neusner, Jacob. "Rabbi and Magus in Third-Century Sasanian Babylonia." *History of Religions* 6 (1967) 169–78.

———. *Song of Songs Rabbah: An Analytical Translation.* Atlanta: Scholars, 1990.

Origen. *Contra Celsum.* Translated by Frederick Crombie. In vol. 4. of *Ante-Nicene Fathers,* edited by Alexander Roberts, et al., 395–698. New York: Christian Literature, 1885.

Ovid. *Tristia. Ex Ponto.* Translated by A. L. Wheeler. Revised by G. P. Goold. LCL 151. Cambridge, MA: Harvard University Press, 1924.

———. *Metamorphoses.* Vol. 1. Translated by Frank Justus Miller. Revised by G. P. Goold. LCL 42. Cambridge, MA: Harvard University Press, 1916.

Palmer, Leonard R. *The Greek Language.* Atlantic Highlands, NJ: Humanities, 1980.

Pao, David. *Acts and the Isaianic New Exodus.* Grand Rapids: Baker Academic, 2002.

Pausanias. *Description of Greece.* Translated by W. H. S. Jones, et al. LCL 188. Cambridge, MA: Harvard University Press, 1918–1935.
Payne Smith, J. A. *Compendious Syriac Dictionary.* Oxford: Oxford University Press, 1903.
Pervo, Richard I. *Profit with Delight: The Literary Genre of the Acts of the Apostles.* Philadelphia: Fortress, 1987.
Pesch, Rudolf. *Die Apostelgeschichte.* 2 vols. Zürich: Benziger, 1986.
Petronius. *Seneca. Satyricon. Apocolocyntosis.* Translated by Michael Heseltine, W. H. D. Rouse. Revised by E. H. Warmington. LCL 15. Cambridge, MA: Harvard University Press, 1913.
Philo. *Philo.* Translated by F. H. Colson, et al. London: Heinemann, 1929–1962.
The Works of Philo. New updated edition. Translated by C. D. Yonge. Peabody, MA: Hendrickson, 1993.
Philostratus. *Eunapius: Lives of the Philosophers and Sophists.* Translated by Wilmer C. Wright. LCL 134. Cambridge, MA: Harvard University Press, 1921.
Pilch, John J. "The Transfiguration of Jesus: An Experience of Alternate Reality." In *Modelling Early Christianity: Social-Scientific Studies of the New Testament in its Context*, edited by Philip Esler, 47–64. London; New York: Routledge, 1995.
Plato. *Republic.* Vol. 2. Edited and translated by Christopher Emlyn-Jones and William Preddy. LCL 276. Cambridge, MA: Harvard University Press, 2013.
Pliny. *Natural History.* 10 vols. Translated by H. Rackham et al. LCL 330–419. Cambridge, MA: Harvard University Press, 1938–1962.
Plotinus. *Plotinus.* Translated by A. H. Armstrong. London: Heinemann; Cambridge, MA: Harvard University Press, 1966.
Plutarch. *Lives.* Vols. 2–3. Translated by Bernadotte Perrin. LCL 47, 65. Cambridge, MA: Harvard University Press, 1914–1916.
———. *Moralia.* Translated by F. C. Babbitt et al. London: Heinemann, 1927–2004.
Polybius. *The Histories.* Translated by W. R. Paton. London: Heinemann; Cambridge, MA: Harvard University Press, 1922–1927.
Porter, Stanley E., ed. *The Language of the New Testament: Classic Essays.* Sheffield: JSOT, 1991.
Preisigke, Friedrich. "Die Gotteskraft der frühchristlichen Zeit." In *Der Wunderbegriff im Neuen Testament*, edited by A Suhl, 210–47. Darmstadt: Wissenschaftliche Buchgesellschaft, 1980.
Quintilian. *Institutio Oratoria.* Translated by H. E. Butler. LCL 124. Cambridge, MA: Harvard University Press, 1920.
Rackham, Richard B. *The Acts of the Apostles: An Exposition.* 7th ed. London: Methuen, 1912.
Rahlfs, Alfred, ed. *Septuaginta, id est Vetus Testamentum Graece iuxta LXX interpretes.* 2 vols. Stuttgart: Württembergische Bibelanstalt, 1935.
Ramsay, William M. *Cities and Bishoprics of Phrygia: Being an Essay of the Local History of Phrygia from the Earliest Times to the Turkish Conquest.* Oxford: Oxford University, 1895–1897.
———. *St. Paul the Traveller and the Roman Citizen.* London: Hodder and Stoughton, 1935.
Richter Reimer, I. *Women in the Acts of the Apostles: A Feminist Liberation Perspective.* Minneapolis: Fortress, 1995.

Roberts, Alexander, and James Donaldson, eds. *The Ante-Nicene Fathers.* 10 vols. New York: Scribner's Sons, 1885–1887.

Robertson, J. C. *Sketches of Church History: From AD 33 to the Reformation.* London: SPCK; New York: Edwin S. Gorham, 1904.

Rubenstein, Jeffery L. "The Symbolism of the Sukkah." *Judaism: A Quarterly Journal of Jewish Life and Thought* 43 (1994) 371–87.

Russell, D. S. *The Jews from Alexander to Herod.* Oxford: Oxford University Press, 1982.

Safrai, Shmuel. "Religion in Everyday Life." In *The Jewish People in the First Century: Historical Geography, Political History, Social, Cultural, and Religious Life and Institutions.* Edited by S. Safrai et al., 793–833. CRINT. Assen: Van Gorcum, 1974–1976.

———. "The Temple." In *The Jewish People in the First Century: Historical Geography, Political History, Social, Cultural, and Religious Life and Institutions.* Edited by S. Safrai et al., 865–907. CRINT. Assen: Van Gorcum, 1974–1976.

Sanders, Jack T. *The Jews in Luke-Acts.* Philadelphia: Fortress, 1987.

Sanders, James. "Isaiah in Luke." In *Luke and Scripture: The Function of Sacred Tradition in Luke-Acts*, edited by Craig Evans and James A. Sanders, 14–25. Minneapolis: Fortress, 1993.

Sbordone, F., ed. *Physiologus.* Hildesheim: Georg Olms, 1991.

Schille, Gottfried. *Die Apostelgeschichte des Lukas.* THKNT V. Berlin: Evangelische Verlagsanstalt, 1983.

Schleusner, Johann Fr., ed. *Novus Thesaurus philologico-criticus sive Lexicon in LXX et reliquos interpretes Graecos ac scriptores apocryphos Veteris Testamenti.* London: A. and J. M. Duncan, 1829.

Schmidt, W. H. "דבר." *TDOT* 3:111.

Schmiedel, P. W. "Barjesus." In *Encyclopedia Biblica: A Dictionary of the Bible*, edited by Thomas Kelly Cheyne and J. Sutherland Black, 478–83. London: Macmillan, 1899.

Schneider, Gerhard. *Die Apostelgeschichte.* I. Teil. Einleitung. Kommentar zu Kap. 1, 1–8, 40. Feiburg. Basel/Wien: Herder, 1980.

———. *Clemens von Rom: Epistola ad Corinthios. Brief an die Korinther.* Fontes Christiani 15. Freiburg: Herder, 1994.

Schneider, J. "ἀναβαίνω." *TDNT* 1:519.

Schoedel, William R. *Ignatius of Antioch: A Commentary on the Letters of Ignatius of Antioch.* Philadelphia: Fortress, 1985.

Schubart, Wilhelm, and Diedrich Schäfer, eds. *Spätptolemäische Papyri aus amtlichen Büros des Herakleopolites.* Ägyptische Urkunden aus den Staatlichen Museen Berlin. Griechische Urkunden 8. Milano: Cisalpino-Goliardica, 1972.

Schwartz, Seth. "Language, Power, and Identity in Ancient Palestine." *Past and Present* 148 (1995) 3–27.

Scott, Walter, ed. *Hermetica: The Ancient Greek and Latin Writings Which Contain Religious or Philosophic Teachings Ascribed to Hermes Trismegistus.* Translated with notes by Walter Scott. 4 vols. Oxford: Clarendon, 1924–1936.

Selwyn, E. C. "The Christian Prophets at Philippi." *The Expositor* 4 (1901) 29–38.

Sextus Empiricus. *Against the Professors.* Translation by R. G. Bury. LCL 382. Cambridge, MA: Harvard University Press, 1949.

———. *Outlines of Pyrrhonism.* Translation by R. G. Bury. LCL 273. London: Heinemann, 1933–1949.

Silius Italicus. *Punica*. Vol. 1. Translated by J. D. Duff. LCL 277. Cambridge, MA: Harvard University Press, 1934.
Sleeman, J. H., and G. Pollet, eds. *Lexicon Plotinianum*. Leiden: Brill; Leuven: Leuven University Press, 1980.
Smith, C. W. F. "Tabernacles in the Fourth Gospel and in Mark." *NTS* 9 (1963) 130-46.
Socrates. *Church History*. Translated by A. C. Zenos. In vol. 2 of *Nicene and Post-Nicene Fathers*, Second Series, edited by Philip Schaff and Henry Wace, 19-325. Buffalo, NY: Christian Literature, 1890.
Spencer, F. Scott. *Acts*. Sheffield: Sheffield Academic, 1997.
Speyer, Wolfgang. "Die Vision der wunderbaren Höhle." In *Frühes Christentum im antiken Strahlungsfeld: Ausgewählte Aufsätze*, 322-31. Tübingen: Mohr/Siebeck, 1989.
―――. "Mittag und Mitternacht als heilige Zeiten in Antike und Christentum." In *Frühes Christentum im antiken Strahlungsfeld: Ausgewählte Aufsätze*, 340-52. Tübingen: Mohr/Siebeck, 1989.
Spicq, Ceslas. "ἀτενίζω." In vol. 1 of *Theological Lexicon of the New Testament*, edited by James D. Ernest, 227. Peabody, MA: Hendrickson, 1994.
Stählin, Gustav. *Die Apostelgeschichte*. NTD 5. Göttingen: Vandenhoeck & Ruprecht, 1975.
―――. "ξένος κτλ." *TDNT* 5:2-3.
Stephanus, Henricus. *Thesaurus Graecae Linguae*. Graz: Akademische Druck-u. Verlagsanstalt, 1954.
Steyn, Gert. *Septuagint Quotations in the Context of the Petrine and Pauline Speeches of the Acta Apostolorum*. Kampen: Pharos, 1995.
Strabo. *Geography*. Vol. 1. Translated by Horace Leonard Jones. LCL 49. Cambridge, MA: Harvard University Press, 1917.
Strelan, Richard. *Paul, Artemis, and the Jews in Ephesus*. Berlin: de Gruyter, 1996.
Strelan, Rick. *Strange Acts*. Berlin: de Gruyter, 2004.
―――. "Strange Stares: Atenizein in Acts." *Novum Testamentum* 41.3 (1999) 235-55.
Suetonius. *Lives of the Caesars*. Vols. 1-2. Translated by J. C. Rolfe. Introduction by K. R. Bradley. LCL 31, 38. Cambridge, MA: Harvard University Press, 1914.
Swain, Simon. *Hellenism and Empire: Language, Classicism, and Power in the Greek World AD 50-250*. Oxford: Clarendon, 1996.
Tacitus. *Annals: Books 4-6, 11-12*. Translated by John Jackson. LCL 312. Cambridge, MA: Harvard University Press, 1937.
Tannehill, Robert C. *Luke*. Abingdon New Testament Commentaries. Nashville: Abingdon, 1996.
Themistius. *Themistii orationes quae supersunt*. Edited by H. Schenkl. Lipsiae: in aedibus Teubneri, 1965-1974.
Theissen, Gerd. *The Miracle Stories of the Early Christian Tradition*. Translated by F. McDonagh. Edited by J. Riches. Edinburgh: T. & T. Clark, 1983.
Theodoret. *Church History*. Translated by Blomfield Jackson. In vol. 3. of *Nicene and Post-Nicene Fathers*, Second Series, edited by Philip Schaff and Henry Wace, 52-327. Buffalo, NY: Christian Literature, 1892.
Thomson, George D. *The Greek Language*. Cambridge: Heffer, 1960.
Thornton, T. G. C. "Stephen's Use of Is. LXVI.1." *JTS* 25 (1974) 432-34.
Tischendorf, K. von. *Apocalypses Apocryphae*. Hildesheim: Georg Olms, 1966.

Torrey, Charles C. *The Composition and Date of Acts*. Cambridge, MA: Harvard University Press, 1916.

Valerius Maximus. *Memorable Doings and Sayings*. Vol. 1. Edited and translated by D. R. Shackleton Bailey. LCL 492. Cambridge, MA: Harvard University Press, 2000.

van der Horst, Pieter W. "Peter's Shadow." *NTS* 23 (1974) 204–12.

van der Kooij, Arie. "'The Old Greek of Isaiah in Relation to the Qumran Texts of Isaiah: Some General Comments.'" In *Septuagint, Scrolls, and Cognate Writings*, edited by G. Brooke and B. Lindars, 195–213. Atlanta: Scholars, 1990.

van Unnik, W. C. "Der Befehl an Philippus." *ZNW* 47 (1956) 181–91.

Vermes, Geza. *The Dead Sea Scrolls in English*. 4th ed. London: Penguin, 1991.

Vernant, Jean-Pierre. "Mortals and Immortals: The Body of the Divine." In *Mortals and Immortals: Collected Essays of J.-P. Verman*, edited by F. Zeitlin, 27–49. Princeton, NJ: Princeton University Press, 1991.

Versnel, Henk S. "Beyond Cursing: The Appeal to Justice in Judicial Prayers." In *Magika Hiera: Ancient Greek Magic and Religion*, edited by C. A. Faraone and D. Obbink, 60–91. Oxford: Oxford University Press, 1991.

Virgil. *Eclogues. Georgics. Aeneid: Books 1–6*. Translated by H. Rushton Fairclough. Revised by G. P. Goold. LCL 63. Cambridge, MA: Harvard University Press, 1916.

———. *Aeneid: Books 7–12. Appendix Vergiliana*. Translated by H. Rushton Fairclough. Revised by G. P. Goold. LCL 64. Cambridge, MA: Harvard University Press, 1918.

Wallace, Daniel B. *Greek Grammar Beyond the Basics*. Grand Rapids: Zondervan, 1996.

Walker, Peter. *Jesus and The Holy City: New Testament Perspectives on Jerusalem*. Grand Rapids: Eerdmans, 1996.

Walther, Fritz, et al. *Gazelles and Their Relatives: A Study in Territorial Behaviour*. Park Ridge, NJ: Noyes, 1983.

Weitzman, Steven. "From Feasts Into Mourning: The Violence of Early Jewish Festivals." *JRel* 79 (1999) 545–59.

Wikenhauser, Alfred. *Die Apostelgeschichte, übersetzt und erklärt*. Regensburg: Friedrich Pustet, 1961.

Williams, Margaret. "Palestinian Jewish Personal Names in Acts." In *The Book of Acts in its Palestinian Setting*, edited by Richard Bauckham, 79–114. The Book of Acts in its First Century Setting 4. Grand Rapids: Eerdmans, 1995.

Windisch, Hans. *Der zweite Korintherbrief*. Göttingen: Vandenhoeck & Ruprecht, 1924.

Yaure, L. "Elymas-Nehelemite-Pethor." *JBL* 79 (1960) 297–314.

Ziegler, Joseph. "Die Vorlage der Isaias–Septuaginta (LXX) und die erste Isaias-Rolle von Qumran (1QIsa)." *JBL* 78 (1959) 34–59.

Author Index

Anderson, Graham, 12n32
Aune, David

Bardy, Gustave, 2
Barrett, Charles Kingsley, 28n18, 28n22,
    29, 32, 35-6, 56, 70n21,
    75, 80, 81, 84, 85, 90, 91, 95, 108, 110,
    11, 113, 119, 120n30, 147, 155,
    164, 165, 167n25, 171n29
Barton, John, 1n3, 38n7
Bauernfeind, Otto, 56n9, 57n20, 109,
    133, 147
Behm, J., 39n9
Beker, J. Christiaan, 43
Bergler, Siegfried, 28n20
Betz, Otto, 119, 124, 125n39, 179
Bieler, L., 53n41
Black, Matthew, 155n6
Bock, Darrell L., 166n24
Brock, Sebastian, 2n7, 90
Brockelmann, Carl, 88n31
Brockington, Leonard H., 154
Brown, Raymond E., 1
Bruce, Frederik Fyfe, 29, 43, 56, 61n9,
    77n30, 80, 89, 95, 108, 109, 110,
    111, 112, 113, 129, 135, 147,
    150, 164n20, 166
Buck, Carl D., 6

Cadbury, Henry J., 95, 109, 111, 147,
    157n13
Calvin, John, 109, 112
Clarke, W. K. L., 154
Collange, J. F., 106

Conzelmann, Hans, 56, 147, 162,
    164n20, 166
Cumont, Franz, 14

Deissmann, Adolf, 5
Dibelius, Martin, 117
Dodds, E. R., 126
Dölger, Franz Josef, 119n23, 119n29
Dunn, James G. D., 27, 32, 43, 43n20,
    43n22, 51, 55, 56, 61n8, 78n3,
    88n32, 90, 94n4, 95, 112, 119,
    148, 151

Ehrman, Bart, 1
Eitrem, Samson, 44
Eliade, Mirce, 126
Epp, Eldon J., 108n80
Esler, Philip F., 1n3
Evans, Craig A., 1n3

Feltoe, Charles L., 20n42
Fine, Steven, 65n15
Fisher, E.W., 96n12, 105, 105n65,
    106n68
Fitzmyer, Joseph A., 61n2, 61n4, 78, 81,
    88n32
Forbes, Christopher, 121n33

Gaventa, Beverly Roberts, 73
Garrett, Susan, 78n4, 80
Gertner, Meir, 157n10, 158n15
Ginzberg, Louis, 30, 56n12
Goodman, Felicitas, 126
Graves, Robert, 46n28

Green, H. B., 105n61
Green, Peter, 141n5
Guthrie, W. K., 121

Haar, Stephen, 78n1
Holladay, Carl, 53n41, 58n24
Haenchen, Ernst, 22, 22n2, 29, 37, 57, 78, 81, 90n42, 91, 96n11, 108, 109, 110, 111, 112, 113, 119, 150
Hagner, Donald A., 105
Hamm, Dennis, 24, 25,26n15, 35
von Harnack, Adolf, 14, 106n69
Hemer, Colin J., 16n39, 89n35
Hengel, Martin, 22n1, 22n2, 23, 48
Hobart, W. K., 95n7
Holladay, Carl, 53n41
Holladay, William L., 58n24
Horsley, Greg., 1, 48n34
Hull, John M., 126
Huskinson, Janet, 71n24

Jervell, Jacob, 27n17, 32, 55, 57, 61n2, 61n7, 79n5, 81, 84n22, 86, 89, 137n6
Johnson, Luke Timothy, 74, 95n5, 147n18, 151
Jones, A. H. M., 3

Kahl, Werner, 45, 128
Kaimio, Jorm, 3, 4n14
Keel, Othmar, 67
Klauck, Hans-Josef, 84, 89n35, 116n15
Knoch, Otto, 106
Knopf, Rudolf, 106
Knowling, R.J., 57n20
Koester, Helmut, 1n1, 2
Kolenkow, Anitra B., 114n6, 118n21

Lake, Kirsop, 90
Leary, T. J., 129, 131
Levison, John R., 81n18
Lindblom, Johannes, 57
Lindemann, Andreas, 106n68
Lüdemann, Gerd, 22n2
Malina, Bruce, 117n17
Marshall, I. Howard, 147, 148, 150, 157n12
Martin, Louise, 63

Martin, Luther H., 114, 115n9
Martin, Ralph P., 106, 107n73
McClure, M. L., 20n42
Miller, Merrill P., 156n11
Momigliano, Arnoldo, 3n12
Morgenstern, Julian, 22n1, 23n3, 23n5, 31n33
Moulton, J.H., 2, 7
Morpurgo Davies, Anna, 6, 8n25
Mowinckel, Sigmund, 23
Munck, Johannes, 55, 111
Mussies, Gerard, 114n8, 116, 119n22

Najjar, M., 65n16
Neusner, Jacob, 59n27, 79n7

Palmer, Leonard R., 9n26
Pao, David, 177
Pervo, Richard I., 150
Pesch, Rudolf, 41, 43n18, 56, 61n10, 81, 110n98, 119n26
Pilch, John J., 117n17
Porter, Stanley, E. 2n6
Preisigke, Friedric, 131n5

Rackham, Richard B., 55, 57, 133
Ramsay, William M., 12n31, 95
Richter Reimer, I.61n10
Robertson, J. C., 21n44
Rubenstein, Jeffery L., 28n21
Russell, D. S., 5

Safrai, Shmuel, 29n29, 30, 33
Sa'id, F., 65n16
Sanders, Jack T., 80
Sanders, James, 157
Schille, Gottfried, 40n13, 47n33, 81, 89, 96n11, 110n97, 11, 112n108,116, 119
Schmidt, W. H., 40n11
Schmiedel, P. W., 87, 89n36, 91
Schneider, Gerhard, 85n24, 89n35, 95n5, 105, 110, 112n110
Schneider, J., 26n12
Schoedel, William R., 126
Schwartz, Seth, 1n4
Selwyn, E. C., 155
Smith, C. W. F., 28n20

Spencer, F. Scott, 73n26
Speyer, Wolfgang, 141, 142
Spicq, Ceslas, 94, 96n17, 105n65
Stählin, Gustav, 81n14, 109, 115, 119, 120, 128
Steyn, Gert, 155, 168, 170, 171
Strelan, Rick, 48n34, 73n25, 117n16, 132n6
Swain, Simon, 9

Tannehill, Robert C., 107
Theissen, Gerd, 46n30, 118, 122n35
Thomson, George D., 5
Thornton, T. G. C., 160
Torrey, Charles C., 155

van der Horst, Pieter, W., 142n7

van der Kooij, Arie, 154n4
van Unnik, W. C., 147
Vernant, Jean-Pierre, 114
Versnel, Henk S., 43n21, 44n26

Wallace, Daniel B., 4
Walker, Peter, 25n11
Walther, Fritz, 63n13
Weitzman, Steven, 35
Wikenhauser, Alfred, 110, 119
Williams, Margaret, 61n6
Windisch, Hans, 107

Yaure, L., 89n35

Ziegler, Joseph, 154n4

www.ingramcontent.com/pod-product-compliance
Lightning Source LLC
Chambersburg PA
CBHW070329230426
43663CB00011B/2257